UNDERSTANDING
CLASSICAL SOCIOLOGY

UNDERSTANDING CLASSICAL SOCIOLOGY

Marx, Weber, Durkheim

John A. Hughes, Peter J. Martin
and W.W. Sharrock

SAGE Publications
London • Thousand Oaks • New Delhi

First published 1995. Reprinted in 1995, 1996, 1997

SAGE Publications Ltd
6 Bonhill Street
London EC2A 4PU

SAGE Publications Inc
2455 Teller Road
Thousand Oaks, California 91320

SAGE Publications India Pvt Ltd
32, M-Block Market
Greater Kailash – 1
New Delhi 110 048

British Library Cataloguing in Publication data

A catalogue record for this book is available from the British Library

ISBN 0 8039 8635 1
ISBN 0 8039 8636 X (pbk)

Library of Congress catalog card number 95–067898

Typeset by Photoprint, Torquay, Devon
Printed in Great Britain by The Cromwell Press Ltd,
Broughton Gifford, Melksham, Wiltshire

Contents

Preface

This book has taken longer than we envisaged and immediate thanks are to the publisher for forbearance and patience. One of the major reasons for the delay is that what seemed like a good idea at the time proved to be a much more formidable challenge than we envisaged. Trying to state complex ideas as clearly as we could, making sure that we had reasonably covered all the various interpretations and debates surrounding the works which are presented here, even if erudite scholarship is not the intention, were considerable tasks. Another major reason was trying to weave the writing into all the other things that are now the academic's lot. None the less, we hope that students will find this a useful resource for their study of sociology.

What originally prompted the idea for a book of this kind was a growing frustration that we felt in our teaching in the different universities in which we are placed that many of our students seemed to know insufficient about the classic thinkers and, more than this, the tradition of sociology itself. There are many reasons for this, of course, not least the possibility that we ourselves belong to an older generation which is now no longer at the 'cutting edge' of the discipline. Sociology has moved on and we have been left behind. Although there may be an element of truth in this we would, not unnaturally, dispute the main substance of the claim. Sociology has indeed moved on, but whether or not this amounts to progress in the discipline is an arguable point, and it is the argumentative nature of the discipline that we wish to emphasise. Sociology is, among other things, a discipline which has to be profoundly concerned with argument and debate, and this therefore necessitates being clear about these, and trying as best one can to prove ideas through them. There are no settled principles for the discipline, no theories that all would espouse and no methods of approach which receive universal assent. What there is, instead, is a tradition of ideas which try to formulate the idea of the social as a topic of inquiry, and, despite well over a hundred years of sociology, this attempt continues.

Another reason for the seeming neglect of the classic thinkers in sociology teaching is that, in recent years, the vague boundaries of the discipline have been blurred even further by its close association with efforts to reconfigure disciplines into more appealing interdisciplinary packages. We do not have objections to such efforts but do note the extent to which there is a danger of the sociological tradition becoming lost, to the detriment of what such reconfigurations are intended to achieve. There is, too, the influence of 'postmodernism', which seeks to decry the achievements of thinkers such as Marx, Durkheim and Weber as no longer relevant to a postmodern era. Whatever the merits or otherwise of this point of view, the important point to bear in mind is that it is but one set of arguments within sociology and, moreover, a set of arguments which, ironically, has a close affinity with the concerns which motivated these classic thinkers.

Finally, one of the things that the book tries to convey is that sociology is a great deal harder than it is often made out to be. As our exposition will try to make clear, Marx, Weber and Durkheim each spent much of their lives trying to articulate ways in which the social could be the subject of a disciplined inquiry. That they did not succeed in settling this once and for all is, we suggest, not evidence of their vaulting ambition nor of their intellectual inadequacies, but, rather, a demonstration of just how difficult a task it is.

Inevitably there are a number of people to thank for their generous help and advice during the progress of this book. Colin Hay and Lou Armour both carefully read various drafts of the chapters and made invaluable contributions. Maeve Conolly also shouldered many of the burdens of administering the department of one of the authors; Cath Fletcher, Karen Gammon and Diane Faichney are the best secretarial support team in the business. Thanks, too, are due to Jason Khan, Kjeld Schmidt, Tom Rodden, Mark Rouncefield, Jon O'Brien, Jenny Ball, John Bell, Barry Sanderson, Caroline Schwaller, Betty Hewitt and, finally, to our colleagues.

1

Introduction

It may seem strange to be offering an exposition of the ideas of Marx, Weber and Durkheim in an era when, so it is argued by some in the discipline, the 'grand narratives' of thought, as Lyotard (1984) terms over-arching theoretical schemes, have lost their validity. New identities, new forms of knowledge, new patterns of social relationships, new sources of division, and more, are all forcing a break, it is claimed, with a past shaped by modes of thought originating over three hundred years ago during the Enlightenment. Marx, Weber and Durkheim are Victorian scholars and it is perhaps hard to grasp that they have anything of relevance to say to a world which has dramatically changed since their time.

Of course, there has always been a prominent strand in sociological thought which is sensitive to the idea that the world or the discipline, most often both, is in an impending state of crisis. Indeed, a strong case can be made that such a sense was critical in the very formation of the discipline in the early nineteenth century as industrialism began to effect major changes in patterns of life throughout Europe. Later in that century, a young French philosophy teacher was particularly concerned with what he saw as the growing instability of social life. Long-established values and ways of life seemed to be breaking down as industrialisation and urbanisation transformed the society of his day. Where once the authority of church and monarchy had gone unquestioned, there now seemed to be no authority which could hold society together. Employers and workers confronted each other with undisguised hostility, rates of crime were rising and individuals tended to see each other simply as means to achieve their own selfish ends. Suicides, too, were increasing as the old links to family and community grew weaker. The young Frenchman, says one commentator, was 'haunted by the thought that modern society . . . was a fragile affair, a potentially unstable mix of elements that was always on the verge of dissolving into chaos'. His writings were an effort to try to understand how this state of affairs had arisen so that it could be put right, stressing the 'urgency of this task, as though he saw himself in a race against time with the gathering forces of anarchy' (Parkin, 1992: 59). The worried young thinker was Émile Durkheim, who addressed these problems in his first major work, *On the Division of Labour in Society*, published in 1893.

In Durkheim, we see not only a motivation for sociological thinking drawn from a sense of impending crisis, but also a formulation of what is, with strong justification, the central question of sociology itself, namely: how is social order possible? Although, and as we shall see, there are many different ways of formulating this question, as well as different answers, it is perhaps to Marx, Weber and Durkheim that we owe the greatest debt for the most systematic attempts to set out just how the question might be addressed; ideas which are of enduring concern and relevance. When post-structuralists tell us, for example, that 'authors' are not really free, autonomous and creative spirits, but people whose words and thoughts bear the imprint of the social context in which they live, they are reviving a theme which was fundamental in Durkheim's work. When the postmodernists insist that we must abandon 'meta-narratives', that is, the great theoretical schemes which attempt to comprehend vast tracts of reality, we are hearing echoes of Weber's contention that such schemes are, indeed, unsustainable and that all knowledge is limited, provisional and generated only from a particular point of view. Examples could, we believe, be multiplied. The point, however, is that the issues confronted by these classic sociological theorists, and the ideas they developed from them, are of continuing relevance for the discipline and the world which it tries to understand.

Despite the often bewildering succession of theoretical fashions which sociology seems heir to, the ideas of these thinkers continue to exert a powerful if often unacknowledged influence in the discipline. But what seems to have been lost, especially on the part of students, is an adequate sense of what these thinkers were trying to say and, equally important, what sociological problems they were trying to address. So much so that there is a danger of losing sight of what current debates within the discipline are about, where they arose and what continuities and divergences they represent within the sociological tradition.

It would be quite wrong, of course, to imply that the voices of Marx, Durkheim and Weber have been silenced. On the contrary. If anything the respect accorded to the three of them has increased over the years since they first wrote. It was not until 1937, with the publication of Talcott Parsons', *The Structure of Social Action*, that Durkheim and Weber became firmly established among scholars in the English-speaking world. Interest in their thought gathered momentum with the expansion of academic sociology in the 1950s and 1960s. Moreover, during the 1960s and 1970s there was an intense and widespread renewal of interest in Marx's thought.

Marx, Durkheim and Weber are widely, if unfortunately, regarded as the 'founding fathers' of modern sociology. Indeed, it would be hard to underestimate the influence of Marx in fields such as social stratification and mobility, education, economic development, the state, culture and media, among others. Even non-Marxist sociologists have adopted concepts and ideas, such as those of class and class structure, class consciousness and alienation, in ways that are clearly derived from Marx's writings. The influence of Durkheim, too, has been pervasive, though more indirect. Functionalism, for example, in both sociology and social anthropology reflects fundamentally Durkheimian assumptions about the nature of sociology and social life. As we shall see, the whole tradition of structuralist thought in the twentieth century owes much to Durkheim's later work. Furthermore, it was Durkheim who also pioneered the use of quantitative analysis, using statistical methods, in the investigation of society, driven by his ambition to develop sociology as a rigorous science in place of the speculative and impressionistic approaches of most social thinkers before him. Weber was no less committed to the development of a social science but, coming from a different intellectual tradition, expressed doubts about the validity of viewing societies as structures, as wholes which had properties independent of the elements which composed them. He also inaugurated a tradition of 'interpretative' sociology which takes human individuals, their ideas and their actions, as the starting point for socio-logical analysis. Weber's rather pessimistic conclusions about the future of industrialised, rationalised modern societies have echoed throughout the years, notably in the work of the Frankfurt School of critical theorists, such as Adorno, Marcuse, Horkheimer and others, and, more recently, in the thought of Habermas, widely regarded as their intellectual heir.

For all these reasons, and more, the sheer extent of the influence exerted by these three thinkers makes them essential reading for anyone seeking to understand the nature of modern sociology as a body of thought in which particular problems, theories and perspectives are established. It is, however, important to bear in mind, as we have already hinted, that it is not altogether satisfactory to regard the three as the 'founding fathers' of sociology. Important as their contribution has turned out to be for sociology, this should not, even unintentionally, obscure the importance of other scholars. Figures such as Vilfredo Pareto (1848–1923) and Herbert Spencer (1820–1903) were influential in their day even if uncelebrated now. By contrast, Georg Simmel (1858–1918) and George Herbert Mead (1863–1931) are beginning to attract greater attention than they ever did in their lifetimes or at any time since. Yet each of them played a crucial part in the development of modern sociological thought. We resist, then, the idea that Marx, Durkheim and Weber are to be regarded as the trinity who created modern sociology. Nevertheless, because of their influence, and because of the ways in which the sociological agenda reflects many of their concerns, we believe that a presentation of their ideas is a potent way of understanding the nature of sociological thought. Each, in his own way, exhibits the difficult analytic problems which arise from the fundamental insight that human beings are essentially social creatures. It is not individuals who create forms of society, Durkheim argued, but forms of society that create individuals. The point is developed in a variety of ways, in all styles of sociological thinking, from the great generalities of structural Marxism to the detailed investigation of interpersonal interaction. Even Weber, who clearly saw the danger of reducing people to mere puppets whose strings were pulled by invisible social forces, and who wished to preserve the idea of the autonomous individual, none the less insisted that the actions and beliefs of such individuals could only be understood by taking into account the specific cultural characteristics of their social context. Indeed, one of the fundamental theoretical tasks of sociological thought has been to try to reconcile the individual and the social, the personal and the cultural, individual action and social structures. The issues involved are displayed clearly, and forcefully, in the works of all three of these thinkers as are a host of problems surrounding the debates about the nature and form of sociological inquiry.

Of course, we acknowledge the criticism that we should not let the assumptions and preoccupations of Dead White European Males, or DWEMs, govern our thinking about contemporary society and social life. Each of them, from what we know of their biographies, exhibited the patriarchal attitudes and assumptions which were dominant in their time. It is also evident that none of them, not even Marx, could pass contemporary tests of 'political correctness'. We take the view, however, that this does not in itself invalidate their sociological ideas. These need to be judged in terms of sociological criteria, and should stand or fall by these. However, there are in their works various ideas which have relevance to contemporary critical social thought, including the feminist critique of patriarchal society. Marx and Engels, for example, on the way in which capitalism depends on the unpaid but essential domestic work done by women, or their reduction to the status of property in the context of bourgeois family life, are cases in point. Similarly, Weber's insistence that not all forms of exploitation are economic, as well as his recognition of the importance of status in social life, is useful in attempting to understand the nature and the persistence of gendered inequalities.

The works of these classic theorists, then, provides us with a way of coming to understand fundamental theoretical and methodological issues within sociology as well as with a means of appreciating the intellectual concerns which give sociology coherence as a discipline. This point is worth emphasising at a time when several forces are combining to place this coherence under some strain. The impact of postmodernism, for example, and the rise of cultural studies has been to fragment sociology so that a clear sight of its central preoccupations is in danger of being lost. As we have already noted, one paradoxical consequence of the recent revival of interest in general social theory has been a tendency to marginalise the classic authors as 'writers about modernity' rather than about the post-modern world which, it is argued, we currently inhabit. However, and as we suggested earlier, many of the issues and problems engaged with by recent theorists were, in fact, originally confronted by Marx, Durkheim and Weber, often with a greater degree of clarity than has been customary of late. Further, in asserting the importance of their ideas we wish also to reassert the validity of the sociological tradition that they did so much to establish. As we have already seen, it is a persistent, and persuasive, claim of postmodern theorists that the era of the 'grand narrative' which provides an account of all history is over and that all knowledge is provisional and partial. Such a view was shared by Weber. His response, however, was not to withdraw into relativism, speculation or navel-gazing, but to begin the elaboration of a programme which would allow for the systematic analysis of the social world, in all its richness and complexity: a task, incidentally, which 'postmodernist' writers would regard as futile. To do this, he reasoned, it is necessary to develop a coherent perspective to guide our investigations, and sociology itself is such a perspective, the distinctiveness of which owes much to the works of Marx, Durkheim and Weber.

For now, we want to prepare for the more detailed discussion which follows in subsequent chapters by outlining some general themes which constitute sociology's distinctiveness.

Sociology's intellectual character

Recognisably sociological ideas have been part of the Western intellectual tradition for centuries, certainly since the time of the first Greek philosophers. However, it is not our purpose here to review the complete history of social thought. What we are about is setting the scene by briefly summarising some aspects of the European thought to which Marx, Durkheim and Weber responded. In this respect, our starting point is the reorientation of European intellectual life in the eighteenth century: the Enlightenment. The authority of tradition, of religion, of custom, were all subjected to examination by 'Reason' and found wanting as so much superstition and mystification. Received wisdom was to be replaced by scientific knowledge obtained through careful and systematically organised inquiry and experimentation, rather than by means of mere speculation or the unquestioned acceptance of customary beliefs. The result was the growth of science and technology from the seventeenth century onwards, which provided the capacity to control and exploit the environment and the forces of nature in unprecedented ways. Indeed, it is this spirit of rational inquiry which, it is argued, typifies the modern world.

Inevitably, it was not long before this new faith in reason and science was seen as relevant to the organisation of human affairs. Thinkers increasingly came to regard society and its arrangements not as matters which were preordained and inevitable, but as things which could be changed for the better in the interests of the general welfare. For the radical theorists of the French Enlightenment, it was existing social institutions, notably the church and the state, which constituted the major obstacle to the liberation of humanity. 'Man is born free', wrote Jean-Jacques Rousseau (1712–78), 'but is everywhere in chains'. Meanwhile in Scotland, a remarkable generation of intellectuals, including Adam Smith (1723–90), John Millar (1735–1801) and Adam Ferguson (1723–1816), applied their formidable powers to the analysis of human societies. Ferguson, for example, wrote that society had a definite structure and the relation of its parts to the whole was the 'principal object' of a social science. Clearly, the development of this social science would have just as corrosive an effect on established beliefs and ideas as natural science had on beliefs about the natural world; perhaps more so since the implications of the new social theorists' ideas were to challenge the foundations of the social and political order. The idea of God as the supreme being was opened to doubt, the rights of monarchs to rule put to question, and the accepted hierarchies of the traditional social order increasingly challenged.

Of course, throughout history there have been challenges by the dispossessed against the holders of power and privilege. These were rarely conceived, however, as attempts to alter the shape of society itself, a shape which was typically considered to have been divinely ordained or beyond human capacity to alter. Such challenges were often directed at reasserting traditional rights rather than arguing for the major restructuring of society itself. By contrast, what the eighteenth century generated was a group of thinkers who argued that social arrangements themselves, rather than wickedness, ill luck or divine retribution, could be the source of human misery and inequality. For some, as we have suggested, the conclusion to be drawn was that society itself required radically restructuring. But how was this to be brought about? By what principles should the new order be organised? In order to change society it was first of all necessary to understand it. For Auguste Comte (1798–1857), who coined the name for the discipline, sociology was to be the science by which an understanding of society could be achieved and, thus, provide the basis for its reconstruction. In this respect, with his emphasis on emancipating social thought from theological and metaphysical speculation and establishing it anew on rational, scientific principles, Comte was heir to the Enlightenment tradition – but with an important difference. He was critical of his French compatriots who, like Rousseau, had seen social institutions as corrupting and inimical of the true freedom of the individual. Decomposing society into an aggregate of individuals would, Comte argued, result in social breakdown, anarchy and chaos rather than human liberation. For Comte, some form of coherent social organisation, a more or less integrated system of institutions, was a precondition for human life, and was the reason why he so firmly resisted the revolutionary idealism of the earlier French thinkers, emphasising instead the importance of order and social control.

The details of Comte's elaborate account of society and of sociology need not concern us. What is essential to note is his insight that society cannot be explained in terms of the characteristics of its individual members. In his *Course of Positivist Philosophy* (1854) he was insistent that 'the scientific spirit forbids us to regard society as composed of individuals'. In making this point, Comte did not intend to deny the existence of real human individuals. What he had in mind was the important notion that if there is to be a scientific sociology which is concerned with the distinctive and particular characteristics of social life, then it must be concerned above all with the relationships among individuals, with the patterns of social organisation which link individuals together and bind them into some unity. It must be concerned, too, with the ways in which individuals are, in fundamental and inescapable ways, products of society rather than the other way around. It is in this sense that sociology may be regarded as a critique of the individualism which permeated Enlightenment thought, and which has persisted in many branches of the human sciences to this day.

Sociology as a critique of individualism

While it is always dangerous to characterise a complex body of ideas in terms of a single theme, it is not too much of a distortion to describe the rise of sociology as part of a reaction against the individualism so prominently displayed in the thought of the Enlightenment during the seventeenth and eighteenth centuries. Underlying much of this theorising about human beings and their relation to society is the insistence that it is the individual who is of ultimate value, and who must not be sacrificed to the claims either of the state or of society. This was an age in which many thinkers, perhaps too optimistically, saw the progressive forces of their world as freeing individuals from the ancient and constraining bonds of feudal obligation and, through this, releasing the mind from its enslavement to traditionally accepted ideas. Central to this was the belief in the reasoning individual. For the philosopher René Descartes (1596–1650), truth was to be sought by means of natural reason which is possessed by each individual. Indeed, it is this, he argued, which is the essential characteristic of the human being: 'I think, therefore I am' was the conclusion of his philosophical ruminations into the source of knowledge. For Thomas Hobbes (1588–1679), the original 'state of nature' was one in which aggressively competitive individuals would simply lead to a constant 'war of all against all' in which life would be 'solitary, poor, nasty, brutish, and short'. Civilisation, social order and progress, Hobbes argued, could only occur when thinking individuals realised the benefits to be gained from accepting the authority of a monarch, the Leviathan, who would have the power to enforce the rule of law. As we shall see, this theory of the social contract, as it came to be known, has been enormously influential in social and political thought. Here we only wish to emphasise the idea that, for all their differences, both Descartes and Hobbes took the idea of the reasoning individual as the basis for their thinking about the human condition.

The period also saw the beginning of what we now refer to as the discipline of psychology; for many the quintessential subject concerned with inquiry into the reasoning capacity of the individual. John Locke (1632–1704), for example, proposed that knowledge is acquired as a result of the pictures of the world that we form on the basis of the simple sensations that each of us has. This theory of the empirical basis of knowledge, in contrast to the rationalist theory of Descartes, once again placed the reasoning individual as the principal object of philosophical inquiry, with society regarded as a secondary product of individual reasoning.

The ideas of Descartes, Hobbes and Locke had a momentous effect on the course of social thought in the Western world and have their direct descendants today. The classical economists represented human nature in terms of *homo economicus*, an individual whose acts are governed by the rational calculation of self-interest. Political theorists, as we have seen, thought of the origins of the state and social order as a consequence of an agreement reached by reasoning individuals. Philosophers, particularly in the nineteenth century, saw human action as the result of a 'utilitarian' calculation in which individuals decided what to do on the basis of seeking pleasure and avoiding pain. It followed that morality, and politics, could be reduced to the pursuit of the 'greatest happiness of the greatest number', as Jeremy Bentham (1748–1832) summarised it. In later years, the rise of scientific psychology was to give further boost to the belief that the social world can be understood in terms of the characteristics of individuals.

Examples of the influence of individualistic thought could be multiplied. Indeed, it is part of the common sense of the modern Western world that each of us is, or ought to be, a unique, autonomous person, possessing free will and certain inalienable rights. Yet, even with its rise to some pre-eminence, both the theory and the practice of individualism came under attack. By the first quarter of the nineteenth century, the tide of individualism had begun to turn. Adam Smith's belief, expressed in *The Wealth of Nations* (1776), that the pursuit of individual self-interest, the efficiencies of human effort produced by the division of labour, and the consequent increase in commercial and industrial activity would lead to a general improvement in the welfare of all was beginning to look more like a pious hope than a realistic prediction. It seemed to many contemporary observers that a general improvement in the welfare of all was not evident in the newly industrialising cities, where they watched, with some alarm, the growth of a huge working class existing in conditions of abject deprivation and who knew no loyalty to either sacred or secular authority. Similarly, the transformation of property under capitalism into impersonal share-holding created, in the minds of many, an image of an atomised and fragmented society populated only by the selfish individuals of Hobbes' nightmare 'state of nature'.

Such concerns provoked a new wave of thought about the nature of society and the social order. Although there is a danger of painting too simple a picture of what were elaborate currents of thought, what became more distinctive in nineteenth-century thought was a reaction against individualism. This took many forms. The art and the music of the Romantic movement, for example, has often been interpreted in terms of a sense of loss, a quest for a genuine community which had all but disappeared, and a search for a feeling of belonging in a new social order. Similarly, the reaction was polarised between conservative thinkers, on the one hand, who sought to restore the stability and the certainties of the old order, and radicals, on the other, who urged a programme of fundamental social reconstruction and produced a series of utopian visions which had powerful political resonances. What united conservatives and radicals was a distaste for the industrial order of the time; a loathing for the factory system which had subordinated, sometimes enslaved, the worker to the dictates of the machine, abolishing craft and skill, decrying the need for intelligence, destroying family life, separating the town from the country and the rich from the poor.

For present purposes, the essential point about these intellectual reflections, be they 'conservative' or 'radical', is that in trying to comprehend the consequences of industrialism they began to identify forces and processes which were not encompassed by the individualistic presuppositions of Enlightenment thought. The release of the individual from the yoke of conformity to traditional institutions and beliefs, as recommended in their rather different ways by figures such as Rousseau and Adam Smith, seemed to be producing not a new age of human freedom, but, rather, new constraints for old – submission to the yoke of 'market forces', for example, or bondage to grinding poverty which was the lot of a large proportion of citizens. Moreover, the excesses of capitalist industrialism did not seem to be explicable in terms of the individual failings of the bad kings and wicked barons of medieval folklore, but were, rather, consequences of impersonal forces over which no one had control. From this perspective, the industrial revolution and its aftermath appeared as a decisive demonstration of the failure of Enlightenment individualism to generate a sustainable theory of society and social change.

It is in the context of the critique of individualism that we can detect the emergence and the development of many of the concepts and ideas which are now central to modern sociological thought. As we suggested above, at the heart of the sociological enterprise is the notion that individuals cannot be the starting point for the analysis of society since all individuals are shaped, influenced and constrained by the social order in which they live. It cannot be the case that organised society and its values are the outcome of isolated, antagonistic, self-interested individuals getting together to accept the authority of social institutions. Such an idea, as Durkheim was to argue, presupposes just those things, namely a social order and shared values, that it is supposed to explain. Accordingly, some social and political thinkers in the nineteenth century began to articulate and develop the idea of the 'social' and elaborate a set of concepts which stood in stark contrast to those of individualism: society, community, nation, group, social class, social solidarity, social structure, culture and more, all expressing aspects of the collective rather than the individual character of human experience.

Thus, Marx takes issue with the classical economists in his claim that it is not acquisitive and competitive individuals who produce capitalist society. On the contrary, it is capitalist society that produces competitive and acquisitive individuals. The central theme running through Durkheim's work is, as he put it, the priority of society over the individual. Like Marx and Durkheim, Weber insisted that the concepts of economic thought assume, but barely recognise, fundamentally sociological presuppositions.

Of course, individualism did not go away and remains entrenched in many areas of the human sciences as well as in much of the 'common sense' of modern life. Accordingly, in challenging individualistic assumptions, sociology has developed ideas which are, in some sense, counter-intuitive to ordinary habits of thought, and often hard to express clearly and precisely. However, the sociological task was not so much to eliminate the individual as a focus of intellectual attention as to find a way of understanding the relationship between the individual and society, to see human beings, always and inevitably, as part of a wider set of organised relationships; a domain that, hitherto, had been much speculated about but little studied. The question of how this new domain could be studied brings us to our next theme, that is, the nature of sociological knowledge.

Sociology as science

Introductory courses and textbooks often describe sociology as the 'science of society', a term which is particularly unilluminating. There are no universally accepted definitions of either 'society' or 'science' and, for some very good reasons, there has been a great deal of debate about both concepts at every stage in the development of sociology.

As we have seen, the idea of a science of society was conceived by Comte as an essential element in his scheme for the total reform of society and its reconstruction on rational principles. Comte's early inspiration was the French socialist thinker Henri Saint-Simon (1760–1825) and, though be broke with Saint-Simon in later years, Comte remained committed to the idea of social life as essentially collective, and of society as an organic whole rather than a simple aggregate of individuals. Although Comte's elaborate system of ideas is now largely forgotten, his distinctive contribution was to insist that society could be understood through the methods of science, that is, observation, experiment and calculation, and, by these means, the universal laws which govern society and its workings could be uncovered. In this way, 'positive' knowledge of both the natural and the social worlds could be used to free humanity from the theological fantasies and metaphysical speculations that had dominated thought prior to the rise of science and 'Reason'. It is largely due to Comte that the term 'positivism' has come to be applied, within sociology, to the claim that objective knowledge of the social world may be obtained by using the same procedures as those of the natural sciences.

Today, of course, Comte's ambitious plan for social reconstruction is regarded as unrealistic and as naïve as the metaphysical speculations he himself so derided. Yet his conviction that a scientific understanding of society is essential to its renewal was shared, albeit in very different ways, by both Marx and Durkheim. Marx is well known for his commitment to the idea that social transformation would be brought about by political, indeed revolutionary, means. He was equally convinced that such political action would have to be informed not by pious hopes and utopian dreams but by a thoroughly scientific understanding and critique of capitalist society. Like Comte, Marx looked forward to the time when the natural and the social sciences would be unified and when all the laws of social development would finally be discovered. Uncovering such laws required lifting the veil of mystical and religious beliefs which, in all past societies, had prevented people from realising the truth about their situation and the sources of their exploitation. Understanding the forces that shape society requires, first, a 'demystification' which restores human beings and the material conditions of their lives as the principal focus of scientific concern and, second, research and analysis to reveal the real underlying causes of social change. At his graveside, Marx's friend and collaborator, Friedrich Engels, described Marx's greatest achievement as the identification of the laws of motion of human society.

For Durkheim, as we have seen, the social problems created by the development of capitalist industrial societies were sufficiently acute as to demand urgent correction. To be effective, however, such remedies had to be based on a scientifically grounded understanding of the ways in which societies worked. Here the influence of Comte on Durkheim is quite clear, particularly in his rejection of individualistic explanations, his conception of society as a reality *sui generis* existing over and above its individual members, and his conception of sociology as a science concerned with 'social facts'. Moreover, Durkheim developed the notion of society as an organic whole with its various institutions, as component parts of a system, contributing to the state of the whole, just as a human body may be analysed as a system of interrelated parts, each of which contributes to the functioning of the whole organism. Such a mode of thought was greatly extended by functionalist theorists in both sociology and social anthropology. However, the point we want to emphasise here is that Durkheim saw sociological research as analogous to medical science. Just as medical knowledge allows doctors to distinguish normal from the pathological conditions of the body, so, Durkheim reasoned, the sociologist should be able to diagnose the nature of society's ills and suggest appropriate treatment.

Whereas Marx saw the solution to social problems in terms of direct political action, Durkheim took a more 'clinician-*cum*-managerialist' view by emphasising the effective treatment of the pathological conditions which can afflict society through the deliberate reorganisation of its institutions. Both, however, believed that their task was to discover the laws which governed the organisation of the social order and drew parallels with the ways in which the natural sciences had revealed the laws of nature. Both also believed that scientifically based knowledge of society could be used to improve the condition of humanity. In this respect, despite their rejection of individualism, both were heirs to the intellectual tradition of the Enlightenment. Weber, on the other hand, was more sceptical about the possibilities for a social science and its role in human affairs. He could not accept that there were general laws governing social processes. On the contrary, he emphasised the importance of contingency and chance in human affairs. He also denied that the actions of human beings could be explained in terms of the cause-and-effect sequences of positivist science, arguing instead that an understanding of action requires a process of interpretation through which we can relate an act to the values and subjective meanings which influence the actor. These ideas have stimulated a whole tradition of interpretivist sociology which rejects positivist precepts in favour of an understanding of the role of meanings in the formulation of action. That is, and for example, what makes 'buying a car' a social action is the whole complex set of meanings and understandings which makes this a transaction which is institutional for societies with a particular type of economic system. For Weber, this centrality of meaning to social inquiry did not imply an abandonment of scientific ambitions. Any explanation of human conduct which does not take account of the actor's own meanings is spurious and unscientific. A properly scientific sociology must develop its own appropriate methodology, irrespective of whether this accords with accepted practice in the natural sciences. Weber denied that the nature of their subject-matter inevitably made the social sciences 'softer' or less objective than the natural sciences. All human knowledge, he argued, is generated from a particular point of view and depends on the ideas and concepts available.

Nevertheless, Weber insisted that the sociologist must always aim to separate the facts of the matter from the values which make them interesting in the first place. Sociology is no less rigorous than the natural sciences in its efforts to arrive at valid explanations. It is, however, a much more modest enterprise than the grand science of social reconstruction envisaged by Comte, by Durkheim and by Marx. For while science may decide on matters of fact, it cannot judge between different values. The gap between 'is' and 'ought', between matters of fact and matters of moral duty, cannot be bridged. It is in the realm of politics, not sociology, that questions of value must be debated and decided. The dream of a new social order organised on rational principles was, for Weber, just as much a fantasy as the religious ideologies that the Enlightenment thinkers so abhorred. Indeed, he argued that rationality, unquestioningly accepted as the fundamental liberating principle of the Enlightenment, was itself a value and, as such, a mixed blessing. It is true that rational inquiry has led to an unprecedented progress in science and technology but, Weber worried, the increasing tendency towards the rational organisation of social life was leading to a soulless, planned, bureaucratised world where spontaneity, creativity, freedom of thought and expression were being eliminated in favour of routine efficiency. Rather than offering the hope of social reconstruction, Weber's bleak vision is that of the 'iron cage' of rationality.

The nature of society

Each of the three authors accepted that, despite all the evident difficulties and complexities it would encounter, there could be a science which took the social world as its subject-matter. But what exactly is this subject-matter? The notion that human life is social, in the sense that human life involves relationships with others, is not a discovery of sociology. What is distinctive about the treatment of this idea during the formative period of modern sociology is the strong intimation that the 'social' can be the subject of disciplined reflection. In such a context the 'social' becomes a theoretical construct designed to draw attention to those features of ordinary social life which sociologists consider important. Terms such as 'social order', 'social organisation', 'society' and so forth become central to its vocabulary.

However, though essential to the sociological project, such terms become problematic precisely because of their centrality. For one thing, and as pointed out earlier, they seem to fly in the face of common sense. How, to put it simply, can we conceive of something involved in the course of human life which is not a characteristic of the real, breathing individuals who live that life? A 'something', moreover, that has a major effect even if individuals are unaware of it. We have already noted the strong resistance to sociological ideas in a culture permeated by individualistic presuppositions. Yet, in another way, the essentially social nature of human life is readily apparent. The language we speak, to take but one example, is a system of practices which we learn by virtue of growing up within a particular society. Language is not innate; we can learn different languages, and in learning language we not only learn how to communicate but also how to think and experience in similar ways to others. In the process our individual characters are deeply imbued with an attachment to conventions, ways of understanding, ways of expressing ourselves, which reflect the sociality of much of our lives.

A major problem is determining how social phenomena are to be conceived of and described. Even Adam Smith's *Wealth of Nations*, widely regarded as a celebration of individualism, pointed to the importance of what we would now call 'social organisation' in furthering individual self-interest. He produced a famous description of pin-making as a simple task which, when distributed among a number of people through a division of labour, could be made much more productive than it would when carried out by a single individual. Similarly, economic activities can be effectively co-ordinated through markets which link producers and consumers to the benefit of all. But how do such patterns of organisation come about? Smith himself used the metaphor of the 'invisible hand' which guided such activities and shaped them into orderly patterns; patterns which are the unanticipated consequences of individuals pursuing their own interests. Though Smith intended this only as a metaphor, from a sociological point of view it is deficient. It suggests social organisation, but it fails to explain it. As we have seen, theorists such as Comte and Durkheim rejected the individualistic assumptions upon which such a model was based and argued, instead, that the relentless pursuit of self-interest would not produce social harmony but, on the contrary, a 'war of all against all'. Socialist thinkers, too, along with other critics of industrialisation, argued that the result of unrestrained capitalist competition was not a free and fair society, but one in which there was a small class of rich and powerful people and a great mass who lived in miserable poverty.

Smith's work illustrates some of the difficulties encountered in attempting to provide an account of 'the social'. Reacting against this kind of individualism in seeking to characterise the nature of social phenomena, Durkheim moved, on some interpretations, to the opposite extreme, seeing society as something that existed independently of individuals, a reality *'sui generis'*, as he put it. Like many nineteenth-century thinkers, and as we mentioned earlier, Durkheim made use of the analogy with a biological organism, seeing society as a system of interrelated parts with the activities of individuals generated by the properties and processes of the system as a whole. Marx's view is similarly 'holistic'. Society is seen as a coherent totality, though one which is full of contradictions. Commentators differ, however, as we shall see in the exposition of Marx's thought, on the extent to which it is to be regarded as an objective reality independent of the individuals who comprise it. 'Structural' Marxists, for example, see the 'social formation' as the structural framework which determines the course of society. Others, however, emphasise the view that the distinction between the individual and society is a false one. Similar difficulties attach to the interpretations of Durkheim.

Weber insisted that it is wrong to regard society, or any other collectivity, as a real entity with an existence independent of the living individuals who constitute it. Such an error, he argued, has the effect of reifying the concept of society by treating it as if it were a real thing with the capacity to act as if it were a person. Only individuals can act; they do not respond or simply react passively to forces, social or otherwise, which may be thought to determine their behaviour. For Weber, patterns of social organisation are rooted in the subjectivities of individuals. He does not mean by this that their actions can be explained in terms of individual psychology. On the contrary, Weber emphasises that all actions and interactions occur within specific cultural contexts and that in formulating courses of actions individuals not only have to take account of established conventions and meanings, but actually think in concepts and categories which have their origin within the culture. From such considerations, as we shall see, there has emerged a tradition of sociological work which rejects the view of society as some kind of structure or system which exists independently of real people, but which concentrates instead on the ways in which patterns of social organisation are constantly being created and sustained through the routines of everyday life.

The relevance of history

The last theme we want to address by way of introduction is that of history, and by this we mean the temporal course of actual human affairs. All three of the thinkers who are our concern had an acute sense of human history as well as a strong realisation that sociology would need to say something about it. Not only were all of them vitally interested in social change, but they understood this in terms which are familiar to us as the historical passage of events and people in calendric time. The changes which brought about industrialism began in a particular period, in particular places and involved real people living real lives. They all made use of the kind of materials historians make use of in their studies: reports, statistics, biographies, records of various kinds and so on. Indeed, as far as Marx and Weber are concerned, it is difficult to disentangle their sociological from their historical interests. For Marx, his inquiries were very much about explaining why actual human affairs had taken the course they had, trying to show that this was not some happenstance but the working through of a mighty engine that drives human history. Weber, on the other hand, saw history as a matter of contingency not determination, but, none the less, argued for the importance of sociology in enabling us to understand at least some of history's immense complexity. Indeed, Weber largely saw sociology as the servant of historical understanding rather than, as Comte did, the master science of human life. Even Durkheim, who is commonly presented as an ahistorical sociologist, developed his theories, in part, to account for social change, including its 'pathologies'.

There is, however, an uneasy tension here between the generalising possibilities of sociology and the particularities of history. It was perhaps Weber of the three who saw this most clearly. The generalisations which sociologists produced, he argued, were causal, just like those of natural science, except they could never attain the status of laws of nature. Instead, their role was to underpin our understanding of the contingent and the particular course of historical change. For Marx, by contrast, history was nothing less than the expression of the 'invisible' laws of social development which, with the abolition of capitalism, would cease to operate and history itself come to an end. This, as we shall see, has a strong Hegelian flavour which Marx retained throughout much of his life despite his philosophical rejection of Hegel's idealism. Despite their differences, however, all three of these thinkers attached especial importance to the relationship between sociology and the history of human life. For them it would be unthinkable for sociology to regard itself as a discipline with nothing to say about human history.

Conclusion

It is perhaps hard to appreciate the respective achievements of these three scholars since so many of their ideas are now part of the standard wisdom of the discipline, albeit often in a much diluted and unattributed form. The sheer difficulty of attempting to develop a systematic intellectual apparatus to address issues about the nature of society meant that they spent the great proportion of their adult lives writing and thinking about the problems. And while they were not entirely successful, the enduring character of their attempts, though in significant respects this is a consequence of hindsight, is a measure of the tremendous quality of their efforts. Although, to repeat a point we made earlier, Marx, Weber and Durkheim are not the 'only begetters' of the discipline, they did much to show just how difficult it is to formulate and address the questions of sociology. It is to them that we owe much of the contemporary character of sociology with its attention to society as a whole, to social change, its epochal sweep and its moral and political sensitivities. This is not, we hasten to add, the whole of sociology. There are sociologies, symbolic interactionism and ethno-methodology being perhaps the more prominent of these, which pay very different attentions to the social. Nevertheless, it is the tradition to which these scholars belong which is the predominant one.

In what follows we have attempted to provide a thorough exposition of the main ideas of each of these scholars. In this respect our aims are modest. We are not presenting an extensive, scholarly and weighted analysis of each of them. There are many books which do just this and we have, in developing our own expositions, made full use of many of these. Our objective is to make their main ideas and arguments as accessible as we can to students of sociology and, in so doing, indicate how and in what ways these ideas have contemporary relevance. These are not, in other words, efforts to present the latest scholarly interpretations of the thought of Marx, Weber and Durkheim. Instead, our aim has been to present, as clearly as we can, the lineaments of their sociological ideas and, at the same time, bring out, again as clearly as we can, the contours of their respective sociological projects.

Select bibliography and further reading

There are many good accounts of social thought since the Enlightenment. Robert A. Nisbet's *The Sociological Tradition* (Heinemann, 1966), though written some time ago is still worth reading. Jonathan Turner's *The Structure of Sociological Theory*, (Dorsey Press, 1974) is a more up-to-date source. Thomson's small edited collection of essays *Political Ideas* (Penguin, 1990) is a useful introduction to a range of thinkers of relevance to the development of sociological thought including Hobbes, Locke, Rousseau and Hegel among others. Anthony Giddens' *Social Theory and Modern Sociology* (Polity Press, 1987), E.C. Cuff, W.W. Sharrock and D. Francis' *Perspectives on Sociology* (Unwin Hyman, 3rd edition, 1990) and R. Anderson, J.A. Hughes and W.W Sharrock (eds), *Classic Disputes in Sociology* (Allen and Unwin, 1986) are in different ways good introductions to sociology.

Talcott Parsons' *The Structure of Social Action* was originally published in 1937. The 1968 Free Press edition is in two volumes. Volume 1 deals with Marshall, Pareto and Durkheim and Volume 2 with Weber. Jean-François Lyotard's *The Postmodern Condition: A report on knowledge* (Manchester University Press, 1984) and his *Towards the Postmodern* (Humanities Press, 1993) are the sources of the critiques of the Enlightenment project and their implications for the nature of sociological theory.

2

Karl Marx

Unlike Durkheim and Weber, Marx was not a university professor. He was a revolutionary as well as a notable thinker, his life's work dedicated to the overthrow of the capitalist order, which he saw as responsible for the degradation and the enslavement of the vast mass of its population. He spent most of his productive adult life as a refugee from his native Germany, living for more than thirty years in impoverished exile in London. His radical ideals were pursued at great cost to himself, and to his family, and for long periods he was dependent on gifts from friends, most notably Friedrich Engels, and small earnings from journalism. The whole point of his work was to provide an understanding of the nature of capitalism in order that people could regain control of their lives. 'The philosophers', he wrote in 1845 when still in his twenties, 'have only interpreted the world, in various ways; the point is to change it' (Marx, 1845: 158).

It was in the course of his life-long study of the origins, nature and development of capitalism that Marx formulated some of the ideas which have become fundamental to a sociological understanding of the dynamics of modern societies. 'Class', 'alienation', 'revolution' and 'communism', the 'dialectic', 'mode of production' and many more are ideas which, if not necessarily original to Marx, have become intimately associated with his thought. Similarly, and as we shall see, it would be difficult to exaggerate the influence of his basic proposition that the character of a society's institutions and culture depend on the organisation of its economic life – its 'mode of production', in Marx's terms. Many of the ideas which Marx explored in relation to the economy and society have become conventional wisdom, and some of his expectations concerning the likely development of capitalism have a familiar ring to them when we hear of 'booms' and 'slumps', the global movement of investment capital, the increasing concentration of production and distribution, unemployment due to the introduction of new technologies, and so on.

If we consider that his ideas were formulated one hundred and fifty years ago in a society where capitalist production was small and rudimentary by modern standards, his achievements are impressive. Quite apart from inspiring the major political movements which have borne his name, and which have had, and continue to have, a decisive effect on the history of the twentieth century, Marx has had an unparalleled influence across a wide range of the human sciences, including sociology, economics, history, political theory, philosophy, anthropology, literary criticism, art history and more. The inevitable result is that an enormous literature has been generated, encompassing not only Marx's own life and times, but his ideas and their vast range of applications and interpretations, as well as an ever expanding exegesis of his thought. This presents us with obvious problems of interpretation: it is impossible to offer an introduction to Marx's thought which does justice to all the different versions of Marxist thinking which have emerged. Accordingly, what follows is an account of the ideas which have had a significant influence on *sociological* thought.

Biography and social background

Although Marx's name will forever be identified with the 'workers of the world', his own family circumstances were very different from those of a manual worker or a landless peasant. He was born on 5 May 1818, the son of Heinrich Marx, a highly respected lawyer in the market town of Trier in the Rhineland. Both sides of his family had been steeped in Jewish culture and among his forebears were a succession of rabbis (McLellan, 1980: 28–9). Heinrich Marx, however, had made a decisive break with Judaism before Karl was born, when the Prussian authorities enforced the Rhineland laws which forbade Jews to hold any positions in the state, except by special permission. In order to retain his senior post in the Court of Appeal in Trier, Heinrich Marx was baptised as a Christian. The story conveys something of the repression and intolerance of the time, though it seems that Heinrich's conversion caused him little anguish. His intellectual leanings were away from the Jewish traditions of his background and toward the French Enlightenment, particularly to Voltaire and Rousseau. Such thinkers emphasised the progressive power of Reason rather than faith and it is highly likely that some of these sentiments were formative in Karl's own development. What is more certain is that he was considerably influenced by Baron von Westphalen, a leading figure in Trier society, who, after 1819, lived next door to the Marx family. The Baron took an interest in Karl and spent much time with him as he grew up, giving him a life-long attachment to the works of Homer and Shakespeare, as well as introducing him to the radical political ideas of Saint-Simon. In 1836 Marx became engaged to the Baron's daughter, Jenny, and after their marriage in 1843 they remained together until her death in 1881.

Marx's early years, then, were spent in a comfortable upper-middle-class home in an atmosphere of respect for the great achievements of European culture, especially its progressive thinkers. He was a capable but not outstanding student. During his first year at the University of Bonn, he proved a dismal failure as he spent less and less time working and more and more time duelling, drinking and writing poetry. Before the year was through, and deep in debt, his father removed him from Bonn in order that he could make a fresh start at the University of Berlin. This was to prove a major turning point in his career.

He arrived in Berlin in 1836 to study law, although he was becoming increasingly interested in philosophy and history. At the time, intellectual life in Germany was dominated by the vast and ambitious philosophical system of G.W.F. Hegel (1770–1831) and, after some initial misgivings, Marx immersed himself in this work. Soon he became a member of the 'Doctors' Club', a group of young intellectuals who provided 'hard-drinking and boisterous company' (McLellan, 1980: 50). For the next four years, during part of which he wrote a PhD thesis in the hope of gaining a university post, Marx could be counted among the circle of youthful intellectuals who, inspired by the teachings of Hegel, came to be known as the Young Hegelians.

Following the acceptance of his doctoral thesis in 1841, Marx still had hopes of securing a university position. However, the Prussian authorities were becoming increasingly intolerant of the radical attitudes and activities of the Young Hegelians, and his academic prospects disappeared completely when his friend and mentor, Bruno Bauer, was dismissed from his lectureship in 1842. By this time Marx was already moving into journalism, an activity which provided him with some income for the rest of his life. The Young Hegelians spread their ideas through articles, reviews and pamphlets, so it was natural that, early in 1842, Marx was invited to contribute to the *Rheinische Zeitung*, a newspaper which had started with financial backing from some business interests in the Rhineland with the intention of promoting the development of trade and industry. In representing the interests of the commercial middle class, the paper was drawn into conflict with the entrenched agricultural and aristocratic interests which dominated government and politics. The paper was reforming rather than revolutionary, and even when he became editor, in October 1842, Marx tried to avoid a full-scale confrontation with the Prussian censor.

However, his very success as editor brought the *Rheinische Zeitung* into conflict with the authorities. As circulation rose it became increasingly difficult for them to ignore the paper and they were soon to ban it. None the less, the year he spent as editor had a decisive effect on Marx's life. It led him away from the speculative philosophy of the Young Hegelians and toward a direct confrontation with the practicalities of social and political issues. He became aware at first hand, for example, of the way in which changing patterns of trade had all but destroyed the traditional livelihood of the peasant wine-growers from the Moselle valley around his home town. Their poverty, he concluded, was not their fault but the inevitable outcome of relationships 'which determine both the action of private persons and of individual authorities, and which are as independent of the will as breathing' (quoted in McLellan, 1977: 24). The economic forces which had sustained their way of life had now so altered as to destroy it.

Paris and Brussels

After the suppression of the paper, Marx travelled to Kreuznach, where he married Jenny von Westphalen, and began to devote himself to a detailed study of Hegel's political thought. In October 1843, Marx and his wife left for Paris, where they shared a house with other radically minded intellectuals. At this time, Paris was a magnet for revolutionary thinkers and Marx took full advantage of this favourable atmosphere. Already familiar with the works of the French socialists, Marx flourished in his cosmopolitan surroundings, and began to devote himself to developing ideas which marked a major break from the thought of his German contemporaries. By far the most important results of this period are the series of documents known as *The Economic and Philosophical Manuscripts of 1844* or, simply, the *Paris Manuscripts*. It is in these that Marx began to apply his own philosophical perspective to the analysis of economic life and to elaborate a fundamental critique of orthodox political economy.

Marx finished these manuscripts in August of the following year – though they were not to be published until the 1930s – and, in the same month, in the Café de la Régence, he met Friedrich Engels. Also from the Rhineland, Engels was two years younger than Marx. The pair had met briefly before during 1842 when Engels was still associated with the Young Hegelians. Marx, it seems, had been 'cool towards his future friend and partner' (Hunley, 1991: 15). Since then, however, things had changed. Marx had become increasingly concerned with economic questions and their social consequences, and Engels had been greatly influenced by an early communist, and former colleague of Marx, Moses Hess. As the son of one of the partners in a flourishing textile business based in his home town of Barmen, with a mill in Manchester, Engels' conversion to communism was unusual, to say the least, as he was both an active capitalist and a political radical.

From the end of 1842 until the summer of 1844 Engels had worked as a clerk at Ermen and Engels' cotton mill in Manchester in order to complete his business training. He had become appalled at the extent of the poverty and misery of the mill workers. On his return to Germany he wrote of this in a book which has become one of the great documents of nineteenth-century history, *The Condition of the Working Class in England* (1845). At that time England was the richest and most powerful nation in the world, and yet, as Engels saw it, the English people were being progressively reduced to conditions worse than those of farm animals.

The respective intellectual contributions of Engels and Marx will be discussed later, but it is incontestable that Engels' relationship with Marx was important in many ways, not least in providing financial support for Marx and his family in the years following his flight to London in 1849. Their writings between 1844 and 1848 developed the major ideas which have come to be regarded as the foundations of Marxist thought, although much of this work was not published in their lifetimes. Accordingly, later generations of scholars, including Max Weber, were acquainted with only fragments of Marx's thought. Many of the Marxist ideas which influenced the development of European socialist movements in the latter part of the nineteenth century were, to a considerable extent, made public by Engels, with all the problems that this engendered for the 'correct' interpretation of Marx's thought. While the reduction of any thinker's work to a number of ideas, no matter how fundamental or essential they might seem, is always problematic, such a treatment of Marx is particularly hazardous. We will, of necessity, have to return to the matter of whether there was, or was not, a significant divergence between the approaches of Marx and Engels, as well as to other issues concerning the reading and the interpretation of their works. Many of these were written, over a lengthy period, as criticisms of the ideas of many of their contemporaries and, inevitably, it is possible to find inconsistencies and, some would argue, contradictions in them. It is hardly surprising, therefore, that a whole range of contrasting interpretations of Marx have been developed over the years, all of them claiming the authority of the original texts. Several of these interpretations will be touched upon in the following discussion, but we should emphasise once again that our main concern is not with arguing for or against any of the available versions of Marx's thought, but to highlight the sociological themes that emerged in his, and in Engels', various works.

By the mid-1840s Marx's radical political activities had become well known to the Prussian authorities and even in Paris he and his revolutionary collaborators were kept under surveillance. Eventually, on the urging of the Prussian government, he was expelled and the next three years were spent in Brussels. As a wave of revolutionary agitation spread across Europe, his position became more and more precarious and, in 1848, not long after the *Communist Manifesto* had been published, he was deported once more. Such was the revolutionary clamour that even the Prussian monarchy seemed threatened, and Marx seized the chance to return to Cologne to edit a revived version of the *Rheinische Zeitung*. However, the authorities reasserted control and early in 1849 Marx was prosecuted for incitement to armed rebellion. At his trial he defended himself in a speech which cogently expressed his theoretical perspective:

> Society is not based on the law . . . rather law must be based on society; it must be the expression of society's common interests and needs, as they arise from the various material methods of production. . . . The Code Napoléon, which I have in my hand, did not produce modern bourgeois society. Bourgeois society . . . merely finds its legal expression in the Code. (quoted in McLellan, 1976: 215)

Marx was acquitted, but his fate was already sealed. In May 1849 he was expelled from Prussia. He returned to Paris still optimistic about the prospects for revolution, but by this time reactionary forces were in the ascendant and, in July, his family was expelled. They set sail for England and were to remain in London for the rest of their lives.

Exile in London

There could hardly have been a better place to study the development of modern capitalism than the England of the mid-nineteenth century. It was the world's pre-eminent industrial power. In little more than a lifetime, changes in the nature of the economy had resulted in major social transformations. By 1851, for example, more people lived in towns than in the countryside; over one-third of the population lived in towns of more than 50,000 inhabitants, whereas a century earlier there had been only two such towns, London and Edinburgh. Such a vast and unprecedented social transformation, Marx realised, had been brought about by capitalist industrialisation, and, soon after his arrival, he resumed the study of political economy that he had started during his time in Paris. Despite an acute shortage of money, and living in a shabby and overcrowded apartment in Soho, Marx soon established a working routine which revolved around lengthy visits to the reading room of the British Museum. By late 1850 he had reached the conclusion that 'a commercial and financial crisis would be the inevitable precondition of any revolution' (McLellan, 1976: 281), a view which inspired the economic studies which absorbed him for the rest of his life.

His original plan was to write a lengthy study which would set out his ideas and his critique of orthodox economics, but in 1852 he was forced to resume journalistic work. His enthusiasm was revived in 1857, with the coming of an economic crisis which he had long anticipated, and in a frantic burst of activity during the winter of 1857–8 he produced a full-scale outline of his ideas in a series of notebooks which have come down to us as the *Grundrisse*, literally the 'ground plans'. These were not written for publication and, in fact, did not become widely available until a German edition of 1953 and an English one in 1973; it is now one of his most widely cited works. Most of the *Grundrisse* deals with Marx's economic ideas, often expressed as criticisms of established economic thought. However, the work also displays the enormous scope of Marx's intended project. His plan was for six books, three of which – on the state, foreign trade and the world market – were never written. The material in the three volumes of *Capital* includes much of what Marx intended for the first three books, although only Volume 1 of *Capital* was published in his lifetime, in 1867. The others were edited by Engels for publication in 1885 and 1894 respectively. *Theories of Surplus Value* is an edited version of the voluminous manuscripts produced by Marx in the early 1860s and intended as a critical review of economic ideas. It was published by Karl Kautsky more than twenty years after Marx's death in 1883.

Marx's theorical work was elaborated not for its own sake but as a guide to practical political action. His reflections on the failure of the revolutionary movements of the late 1840s led him to conclude that while incompetent leadership was partly to blame, equally important was the lack of a clear understanding of what he took to be the basic processes of social development, processes which were fundamentally economic. His writings were devoted to providing this understanding, though his great theoretical project, like his political ambitions, was never realised in anything like a finished form.

Early years: the critique of Hegel's idealism

'Karl Marx was a German philosopher.' It is with these words that Kolakowski (1978: 1) begins his three-volume survey of Marx and Marxism, to make the point that to understand Marx's work it is essential to see it as emerging from a particular philosophical tradition and so retaining some of the central concepts and themes of that tradition. Yet, by the time he was 30, in a series of essays and commentaries, Marx had come to question almost every aspect of the orthodox thought of his day and laid the foundations for his own work.

As pointed out earlier, German intellectual life at this time was dominated by the influence of, and reaction against, the 'idealist' philosophy of G.W.F. Hegel. In general, idealists have argued that ultimate reality does not consist of the people, the material objects and physical environment which surround us, but, on the contrary, it is an immaterial force or essence which is present in all things and which has brought them into being. Though a strange sounding idea, and one which flies against our common-sense experience, it is not unlike the more familiar Christian idea of God as an all-powerful, non-material being who is the creator of the world. For Hegel, ultimate reality was to be conceived of as *Geist*, or 'Spirit', a being which had brought the material world into existence and which is expressed in it. 'The central aim of Hegel's philosophy', writes Dallmayr, 'was to demonstrate the role of spirit as the founding agency and animating truth in all reality' (1993: 23–4).

Hegel's idealism and philosophy of history

Hegel's writings and ideas, whether deservedly or not, contributed much to the conception of German philosophy as unnecessarily complex, abstract and obscure, comprising a huge, far-ranging and relentlessly detailed body of work which resists condensation into two or three pages. Nevertheless, it is important to touch on certain aspects of Hegel's work since it was a major influence on Marx's early writings and, perhaps more contentiously, was a lifelong influence on Marx's thought. Above all, it was in opposition to Hegel's idealism that Marx worked out his materialist conception of history. Or, as Marx later put it, having found Hegel standing on his head, he set him the right way up.

The aspect of Hegel's philosophy which is most relevant here is his account of history. Like many thinkers of the eighteenth and nineteenth centuries, Hegel believed that there was more to history than simply a succession of events. He wanted to show that human history conformed to an underlying pattern; a process of development in which the potential of human beings was realised. A seed has the potential to develop into a plant, but this process can only occur over time and through various processes of transformation, including those of destruction. In the process of growth, for example, the seed itself will be destroyed as it realises its potential to develop into a plant. In the same way, Hegel thought, the earliest, the most primitive stages of human life must already have the potential to develop into more advanced ones, but, and as with the plant, the actualising of that potential will involve a long period of growth, that is, history. As far as Hegel was concerned, that process of growth was essentially about the capacity of the human mind to understand itself. The whole of human history was the process through which human beings have increased their rational understanding of the world.

For Hegel, two important conclusions followed. First, the increasing rationality of human thought amounted to equivalent increases in human freedom, since if we understand the nature of the world, we will be able to control it instead of being at the mercy of events. Second, the development of rational thought in humanity was the process by which the real world and the ideal world could be reconciled. In a society organised on rational principles, age-old ideals – of justice, of freedom, of happiness – could become realities. For Hegel, of course, the purpose of history was not so much the emancipation of humanity as the fulfilment of 'Spirit'. He spoke of the 'cunning of reason' in bringing about the transformation of societies through the actions of people who were unaware of their consequences.

As told by Hegel, the story of history is primarily about the ways in which historical changes bring about the advance of the power of reason and the expansion of understanding. From a sociological point of view, it is important to note that when Hegel talks of the development of reason and understanding he does not mean the psychological capacity of particular human beings but, rather, the maturation of the collective resources for understanding. When he writes of the 'spirit of the time', or the 'spirit of a nation', he means something similar to what nowadays we would call a society's culture. When, for example, we speak of the 'mind' of the ancient Greeks, we are referring to characteristic patterns of thought as revealed in the products of their culture, such as their plays, sculpture, architecture, philosophy and so on. It is this that was the focus of Hegel's philosophy, and his view of the development of 'Spirit', 'Mind', 'thought' or 'conscious-ness' – as his own expressions have been variously translated – is an account of the development of religious thought, art, science, the law and, above all, philosophy, for these are the ways in which human beings have sought to express understanding of the world around them. Philosophy, however, was the means by which that ultimate rational understanding would eventually be achieved. Indeed, Hegel seems to have believed that the whole course of human thought had culminated in his own, and final, philosophical system.

As befits an 'idealist' thinker, Hegel's view of history concentrates primarily on the development of human thought. This does not mean that he disregards economic and political affairs; rather, he sees these as sub-servient to the main purpose of the development of thought as expressions of the conflicts and problems that 'Mind' seeks to resolve. As we have suggested, Hegel believed that in pursuing their own interests in their own ways human beings bring about the realisation of Spirit without knowing it.

What is crucial is that they are acting rationally, gaining mastery of the world by using their reason. Thus, each main stage of history is portrayed by Hegel as exhibiting a higher degree of rational control over nature than its predecessor. Nothing is permanent, everything is changed and ultimately transformed by the relentless pressure of rationality. While the culture of each era represents an advance in the progress of humanity, and through that the fulfilment of Spirit, it is in turn corroded from within by rational criticism. Just as the power of the gods and demons was revealed as illusory, so that of kings and emperors has been exposed as arbitrary. When this happens, the social system becomes fatally weakened and a period of decay and disintegration follows, preparing the way for the emergence of the next, higher stage.

As we have said, it is impossible to do justice to Hegel's work in a short summary. However, for the purposes of considering his influence on Marx, it is useful to emphasise three themes: change as a dialectical process, the concept of alienation, and the state and civil society.

Change as a dialectical process   While Hegel viewed human history as progressive, in the sense that it moved from lower to higher stages of development, he did not see this as a steady, unilinear process. As suggested by the analogy with the plant, growth involves transformation and destruction. For Hegel, conflict in human affairs, however unpleasant it may be, is a necessary and productive force. It is through repeated patterns of conflict that human progress is achieved. This idea was also central in Marx's thought and is referred to as a dialectical process of change.

The term 'dialectic' is derived from the Greek word for conversation, and its sense is preserved in the English word 'dialogue'. In philosophy, dialogues have often been debates between two people of opposed views who try to arrive at the truth through a process of logical argument. By retaining what is true from each viewpoint, and discarding what is false, the two opposing points of view can, ideally, be reconciled in a new, superior one which possesses elements of the original viewpoints. It is this kind of pattern which Hegel sees as underlying the process of historical change. At every stage of social development there are contradictions, for example, between actual real conditions and some ideal state of affairs, which lead to conflicts and antagonisms and, through this, to social transformations. An existing state of affairs comes into conflict with an opposed, incompatible one and these are eventually reconciled in a new, higher stage.

Hegel saw this logic of contradiction and transformation as applying not only to the stages through which humanity achieved emancipation through rational understanding, but also to the entire process of the development of Spirit. In order to escape from the state of simply 'being', Spirit has to create something, namely the material world. In the course of human history, the progressive development of rational understanding leads to the reconciliation of the ideal and the real, the immaterial Spirit and the material world. Once the full understanding of this process has been achieved – and Hegel felt that his own work was this achievement – history is at an end. While, as we shall see, there was much in Hegel that Marx rejected, the ideas of contradiction, conflict and transformation played a major part in Marx's account of social change, as did the belief that history was moving toward a final stage in which the emancipation of humanity would be realised.

The concept of alienation We referred above to Hegel's idealist belief that the world has been brought into being by the power of Spirit, much as in Christian belief in which the world has been created by God. But why should Spirit generate the world? Hegel's answer was that while Spirit simply existed, it was incomplete. Its potential was unrealised. In order to actualise its powers, Spirit had to create something other than itself – the material world – which then came to confront Spirit as something separate and different. It is this process of externalising itself, of realising its powers, that Spirit can be said to have alienated itself; that is, created something which is independent and opposed to it, as something alien. For present purposes, the point is that, in Hegel's view, the material world must be understood as alienated Spirit.

The term 'alienation' has been used in various ways, but common to them is the idea that the products of activity may come to be seen as independent and opposed to those who created them. Hegel himself spoke of the condition of alienation in which the products of human thought and actions, such as belief systems and social institutions, come to seem independent of those who ultimately created them. Indeed, Hegel argued against religions which, as he saw them, divided humanity against itself by projecting essentially human qualities onto mythical deities, and then claimed that it was one's duty to worship and obey them. As we shall see, this was an aspect of Hegel's thought which was soon seized on by his critics.

The state and civil society For Hegel, and despite its vicissitudes, the course of human history was progressive. Through the development of human consciousness, the real world of nature and the ideal world of Spirit would eventually be reconciled. Hegel's discussion of political institutions provides some indication of what he means.

The development of human societies, he suggested, through conflict and transformation, has led to increasing freedom for individuals. Like Durkheim long after him, Hegel argued that the earliest societies must have been repressive ones in which their members were forced to conform to tribal conventions and, further, were constantly at the mercy of the forces of nature. The idea of individual freedom is evident in ancient Greece and in Rome, but it is still far from realised since, for one thing, slavery persisted. In modern societies, however, the reconciliation of the idea and reality has come much closer. As Hegel wrote: 'the right of subjective freedom is the pivotal and focal point in the difference between antiquity and the modern age.' According to Hegel, it was Christianity which had brought about this new view of the rights of the individual and established 'the universal and actual principle of a new form of the world' (1991: 151).

The new modern social order in which individuals were free to pursue their own interests Hegel referred to as 'civil society', a notion which anticipates at several points Durkheim's view of modern societies as held together by relations of interdependence between their different parts. And, like Durkheim, Hegel saw that the unrestricted pursuit of interests would soon lead to disorder, inequality and conflict. The authoritative regulation of activities was, therefore, necessary. For Hegel, this could only be provided by the modern state, a state which was not, as in earlier times, founded on coercion or dominated by powerful interests, but embodied universal rational principles. The ideas of justice and the equality of all citizens before the law are such principles and their realisation in the modern state a further example of the ways in which, for Hegel, the real world and the ideal could be reconciled. Moreover, as the consciousness of individuals becomes increasingly rational, the tension between the interests of the individual and those of the collectivity will also be transcended.

> Since the state is objective spirit, it is only through being a member of the state that the individual himself has objectivity, truth, and ethical life. Union as such is itself the true content, and end, and the destiny of individuals is to lead a universal life. (ibid.: 276)

The implication, of course, is that it is the duty of individuals in modern societies to obey the state, a conclusion which has led many to view Hegel's political philosophy as little more than an apology for tyrannical regimes of all kinds. Others argue that this is less than fair. Nevertheless, the belief that Hegel was intent on providing a justification for the authoritarian state can be found in the writings of the Young Hegelians who developed their critical ideas in the years after his death. As we shall see, it is a view which also found expression in the writings of the young Marx.

The Young Hegelians and the critique of Hegelianism

Marx was not in Berlin long before he became increasingly engrossed in Hegel's ideas as one of the Young Hegelians. They, however, were not disciples who rigidly adhered to the teachings of their master. In particular they were sceptical of any claim that the ultimate stage of human liberation had been reached. It was evident to the Young Hegelians that the world in which they lived was not the ideal world of freedom and justice which Hegel had envisaged. Moreover, it also became apparent that a view of human history as the unfolding struggle of mind for fulfilment brought about by the 'cunning of reason' could be used to justify any act, however abhorrent, and any institution, however corrupt. All could be explained away as a necessary stage in the evolution of Mind. The question arose as to whether Hegel's conclusions were entailed by his philosophical methods, or whether the method of theoretical criticism might be used independently of

Hegel's own conservative conclusions. It was the latter view to which the Young Hegelians were drawn.

For Bruno Bauer, a young theology lecturer and a close associate of Marx, history was indeed progressive and driven by the engine of rationality. But it was not yet complete. 'History is determined by the permanent antagonism between what is and what ought to be, the latter being expressed by the spirit in its quest for self-consciousness' (Kolakowski, 1978: 89). Bauer's critical impulses led him to a radical critique of Christianity in which he used one of Hegel's own arguments to show that faith in God did not bring about freedom, but rather its opposite. Whereas Hegel had spoken of a transient phase in which human beings projected their own essence onto God as a mythical representation of Mind, Bauer generalised this conclusion by arguing that the whole idea of God involved individuals in surrendering themselves to the control of a mythical character.

Feuerbach and the critique of religion   Marx was impressed by Bauer's ideas, and by the critique of religion central to a book which was to become the most influential of all the Young Hegelians' work, *The Essence of Christianity*, by Ludwig Feuerbach (1804–72). This appeared in 1841 and challenged the accepted view of religion by its claim that the 'secret of theology is anthropology'. Instead of God (or Mind) being the creator of the world, such conceptions are really the inventions of human beings, ideas that they create as they seek to understand their lives and the world. As such they are representations of human qualities and aspirations. The Christian idea of God, for example, is a personification, in supernatural form, of the ideas of infinite power and goodness. The belief that God created the world is a myth which explains how things come to be the way they are. It is human beings who create God, not vice versa. However, such a myth is a powerful constraint against people coming to understand their true situation and to transform it. If a state of affairs is understood as God's will, and God is believed to be benevolent and omnipotent, then people will fail to realise that it is only by action in the real world that the human condition can be improved.

It is in the notion of the 'real world' that we can begin to see the extent to which Feuerbach's ideas constituted a challenge to Hegel. For Feuerbach, ultimate reality is the world of people and things, not some abstract notion of Mind or Spirit. In this respect, he was a materialist rather than an idealist. Whereas Hegel saw human beings as externalised, or alienated Mind, Feuerbach saw Mind as alienated humanity. Moreover, in creating mythical figures, such as God, people mystified their own true nature and abandoned their capacity to control their own world. If human lives are governed by the belief that we must do 'God's will', and that it is our duty to obey 'Him', they surrender their powers to a wholly imaginary being, one which they themselves have created. It is this process which, for Feuerbach, constitutes the essence of human alienation. In externalising ideas such as that of God, human beings begin to believe that God has a real, independent existence with power over them. Investing powers in God robs human beings of them. It is in this sense that the term 'alienation' has been used since, largely as a result of the use that Marx made of it in his writings during the years following the appearance of Feuerbach's work.

For Feuerbach religion was 'the root of all social evil' (Kolakowski, 1978: 118). He believed that once its true, mystifying nature had been understood, people would be able to regain control over the social world which they had surrendered, and so reorganise society in genuinely humane ways. A major obstacle remained: Hegel's philosophical system. In 1843 Feuerbach published his 'Preliminary Theses for a Reform of Philosophy', which also greatly impressed Marx. This 'reform', Feuerbach argued, would involve the abolition of Hegel's idealist philosophy follow-ing the realisation that 'the true relationship of thought to being is this: being is the subject, thought the predicate. Thought arises from being; being does not arise from thought' (quoted in McLellan, 1980: 107).

The critique of Hegel's view of the state   The appearance of Feuerbach's critique of Hegel was fortuitous for Marx's intellectual development. We have already mentioned how his move into journalism led him away from the speculative philosophy of the Young Hegelians as he began to pay attention to the social and political issues of his day. In his first major article as editor of the *Rheinische Zeitung* he had discussed the problem of timber theft, which had become a significant social issue as the courts became full of such cases. Traditionally, people had been able to collect dead wood from the land, now, however, landlords were enforcing their rights of ownership. For Marx, it seemed that what had once belonged as of right to the people in general had now become legally redefined as the property of the rich. He detected, too, a contradiction in the way that the law, with its strict and narrow definition of property rights, paid no attention to the consequent problems of the poor peasantry and their simple, but vital, need for wood to keep them warm. Instead of the state acting to improve the condition of the people and defend their interests, the law relating to timber produced only profit for the few and suffering for the many.

For Marx the state was acting not as the expression of the general will of the people in Hegel's sense, but as the defender of particular, and powerful, interests. Those who spoke on behalf of the state were motivated not by ideals of truth and justice, but by specific class interests. In another article, Marx contrasted this with the Hegelian ideal. A law relating to the press, he argued, should exist as a guarantee of its freedom in the interests of all rather than seeking to protect the rich and the powerful. It was the press rather than the state which could protect the freedom of the people, and to do this it must be free to criticise the state and its functionaries. Needless to say, the authorities took a different view and the *Rheinische Zeitung* was banned at the end of March 1843.

Marx's response was to write a critical study of Hegel's political thought, and in it to develop some of Feuerbach's ideas but in relation to the nature of the state. Just as Feuerbach had argued that, in Hegel, the real relationship between humanity and religion is reversed, so Marx argued that the state does not embody the general will. On the contrary:

> Hegel starts from the state and makes man into the subjective aspect of the state; democracy starts from man and makes the state into objectified man. Just as religion does not make man, but man makes religion, so the constitution does not make people, but the people make the constitution. (Marx, 1843b: 28).

Whereas Feuerbach had diagnosed the condition of religious alienation, in which people obeyed 'gods' which were nothing but mythical representations, so Marx identified political alienation as the situation in which people become subordinate to a state which, though a human creation, has become independent of them. Far from representing the general interest, or arbitrating among competing social groups, in reality the state acted to defend the rich and the powerful few against the claims of the majority of the people. The idea that the state acts in the general interest, or is a neutral arbiter, is itself ideological; that is, a belief that serves only to give legitimacy to an institution which is, in reality, the instrument of dominant groups. Hegel's view of the state, argued Marx, was *ideological* in the sense that while it claimed to be a true analysis of political institutions, in fact it mystified them to protect dominating interests.

Moreover, whereas Hegel had regarded the state bureaucracy as a corps of officials who acted independently and impartially to regulate the conflicts and competition of civil society in the best interests of all, Marx's frustrating experiences with the Prussian censors demonstrated how the state itself had become a powerful self-interested group which would defend itself and suppress criticism when it could. In lines which anticipate his later analyses, Marx characterised the actions of state officials:

> Bureaucracy holds in its possession the essence of the state, the spiritual essence of society, it is its private property. The general spirit of bureaucracy is secret, mystery, safeguarded inside itself by hierarchy and outside by its nature as closed corporation. Thus public political spirit and also political mentality appear to bureaucracy as a betrayal of its secret. The principle of its knowledge is therefore authority, and its mentality is the idolatry of authority. (ibid.: 31)

Marx goes on to argue that the ethos of bureaucratic officials, far from embodying the general will is, in fact, one of 'passive obedience', conformism and careerism. So, not only does the state operate in defence of powerful interests; it has itself become one.

The critiques of the state and of religion are themes which come together in Marx's works during this period, and illustrate the rapidity with which his writings moved beyond those of the Young Hegelians. One of these was a response to an article of Bauer's, in which he had argued that in order to achieve Jewish emancipation it was necessary for a separation of church and state, and for both Jews and Christians to realise that it was their religious beliefs which enslaved them both. Marx agreed with Bauer but suggested that his analysis did not go far enough. In *On the Jewish Question* (1843a) Marx dismisses the idea that the disestablishment of the church will solve the problem. Relegating the church to the arena of civil society only served to give people the 'freedom' to persist in their subjection to religious mythologies; it does nothing to alter the conditions which create their need for religion and their consequent alienation. The essence of the problem lay in the continuing opposition between the political institutions of the state, on the one hand, and civil society, the arena of everyday, individual interests, on the other. Real human emancipation could only come about when this opposition was transcended and the spheres of public and private life reconciled.

Marx goes on to pour scorn on the ideals of human liberty inscribed in the great revolutionary texts of the late eighteenth century. The rights of man are, for him, only the rights to remain in conditions of subjection to religion, the state and private property. 'Man was therefore not freed from religion; he received freedom of religion. He was not freed from property; he received freedom of property. He was not freed from the egoism of trade; he received freedom to trade' (ibid.: 56). For Marx, the attainment of such 'rights' does not realise the condition of human freedom; on the contrary, it establishes a society of isolated, competitive, alienated individuals which is the very opposite of what human emancipation should achieve. Thus, the overthrow of feudal societies, of the *anciens régimes*, had not brought about the ideal society in which social institutions were at one with human nature. As long as the state is separated from civil society, Marx argued, 'the right of man to freedom ceases to be a right as soon as it enters into conflict with political life' (ibid.: 54). Above all, the philosophers had confused a particular historical form of society with the realisation of human emancipation: for them 'it is not man as citizen but man as bourgeois who is called the real and true man'.

Turning Hegel the right way up   By this stage Marx had come to reject Hegel's philosophical system, although, as we shall see, the concepts and methods of Hegel's work remained an important part of his analytic approach to the understanding of society. To Hegel's idealism he counterposed, like Feuerbach, a materialist understanding of society, beginning with real people and the environment in which they find themselves. Where Hegel had regarded humanity as alienated Spirit, Marx reversed this: human alienation was the process in which the products of people's activities, both mental and physical, come to acquire an apparently independent existence and then, like God or the state, come to dominate the lives of real people. These ideas attacked the two central institutions, the church and the state, of the society in which he lived, and this was more than enough to earn him the reputation of being a dangerous radical. Also, he was moving beyond the critical ideas of Feuerbach, Bauer and other Young Hegelians: religious tolerance still leaves religion intact, and the achievement of political constitutions still presupposes a separation between the state and civil society, in which the former dominates the latter. Those who hold that religious tolerance and political constitutions represent the attainment of human freedom were regarded by Marx as apologists for societies in which people are still fundamentally alienated from a genuinely communal existence in which the opposition between the state and civil society has been overcome.

The attainment, then, of the so-called 'rights of man' was for Marx not enough to overcome religious and political alienation. Religion was not the source of human oppression, but a symptom of it. To overcome the effects of religion it was necessary to remove the human suffering which gave rise to them. In a famous passage, Marx argued that

> Religious suffering is at the same time an expression of real suffering and a protest against real suffering. Religion is the sigh of the oppressed creature, the feeling of a heartless world, and the soul of soulless circumstances. It is the opium of the people . . . the abolition of religion as the illusory happiness of the people is the demand for their real happiness. (Marx, 1844a: 64)

As far as the state was concerned,

> none of the so-called rights of man goes beyond egoistic man, man as he is in civil society, namely an individual withdrawn behind his private interests and whims and separated from the community. Far from the rights of man conceiving of man as a species-being, species-life itself, society appears as a framework exterior to individuals, a limitation of their self-sufficiency. (Marx, 1843a: 54)

Marx not only deplored the separation between state and civil society, but saw the latter as perverting the real essence of humanity by replacing communal values with competitive, individualistic ones. For him, then, the state was neither a neutral arbiter between contending interests, as in the social contract theories of Hobbes and Rousseau, nor an integrated whole, as in Hegel's version of the state as the expression of the General Will. What is at stake here is a contrast between two different modes of conceptualising society and the role of the state within it. From Hegel's point of view society is a more or less integrated totality, greater than the sum of the individual and groups which make it up. In this image the state appears as an institution which serves to control the operation of the system as a whole. For Marx, however, society is the outcome of the struggle of real people, or, more precisely, classes of people, pursuing their interests with the state as one highly effective means by which dominant groups can exercise control over the mass of the people, and is all the more effective for being *perceived* as embodying the interests of society as a whole and acting impartially.

Increasingly, the fundamental idea which emerged in Marx's work at this time is that the root causes of human misery and alienation are not religious or political, but economic. Human emancipation, he began to argue, would not come about through the philosophical critiques of religion and politics. What was needed was a revolution by transformation of the mode of production, and this could only be achieved through direct action. Because of its relative economic and political backwardness compared to Britain and France, Germany would need a dual revolution, the first to bring it to the level of the more politically and economically advanced of the nations, and another to take it to the 'human level that is the immediate future of these peoples'. Marx was optimistic about such prospects, since the country was productive of ideas: 'In politics the Germans have thought what others have done.' What was necessary was a union of theory and practice in which 'theory . . . will become material force as soon as it seizes the masses' (Marx, 1844a: 68–9). The vehicle of revolution would have to be a class of people who were excluded from the benefits of civil society, whose suffering was the direct result of the establishment of civil society, and whose emancipation would be that of all humanity. The limited extent of industrialisation in Germany meant that such a class had as yet barely formed. But in France and Britain, it was made up of 'those who have their origin in society's brutal dissolution and principally the dissolution of the middle class' (ibid.: 73). This class, Marx believed, was the proletariat.

His concern for revolution was a fusion of theorising and practical action. 'As philosophy finds in the proletariat its material weapons, so the proletariat finds in philosophy its intellectual weapons' (ibid.: 73). As Kolakowski points out, the idea that the proletariat, in seeking to liberate itself, is destined to bring about universal human emancipation is a 'philosophical deduction rather than a product of observation' (1978: 130). But by the time Marx had begun to write about the proletariat, he had left Germany and settled in Paris, where he encountered not only revolutionary intellectuals like himself, but also, for the first time, groups of socialist workers who had already developed a body of ideas critical of the existing social order.

The critique of political economy

Paris, as we noted above, was a magnet for radical thinkers, and Marx was already familiar with the French socialist tradition. Indeed, it has been suggested that his use of the term 'proletariat' is derived from his studies of the French Revolution (McLellan, 1980: 156). As we have seen, in the *Economic and Philosophical Manuscripts of 1844*, Marx began to apply his philosophical perspective to the analysis of economic life. In contrast to Hegel's idealism, Marx presented a materialist view in which the point of departure was the conception of real people in a real environment. Religious alienation was not, as Feuerbach supposed, the cause of human misery but its consequence, and it was necessary to extend the critique to the fundamental level of human life, namely, economic activity. 'Religious alienation as such', Marx wrote in the *Paris Manuscripts*, 'occurs only in the realm of consciousness, but economic alienation is that of real life; its transcendence therefore covers both aspects' (1844b: 96). Just as he had poured scorn on the political theorists who had failed to realise that the 'rights of man' could not be attained in civil society, so he became bitterly critical of economic doctrines which confused, he argued, a particular historical situation for the natural, universal condition of humanity.

The elements of political economy

The dominant economic theories of the day were those of Adam Smith (1723–90) and David Ricardo (1772–1823). In *The Wealth of Nations* (1776), Smith had argued that the unrestricted pursuit of commerce was the means by which countries could achieve prosperity, and that the productive capacity of economic activity was increased with the progressive division of labour. Such ideas, familiar enough today, were radical in their time, challenging the 'mercantilist' view which argued for the regulation of trade through the granting of state monopolies or imposing protectionist customs duties. The main object of trade was seen as the accumulation of wealth in the form of precious metals. For Smith, the real source of wealth was not gold and silver but the production of commodities for sale on the market. In place of regulation by tradition or political authority, Smith's view was that the 'invisible hand' of the market should be allowed to determine the conduct of economic affairs. Individuals are motivated to sell commodities on the market as a means of increasing their own wealth, and so will produce what others want. At the same time, the prices they charge will be kept down through the inevitable competition among rival producers and there will be an incentive to improve both products and the production process in order to gain a competitive advantage. Prosperity and social harmony, then, will arise out of the pursuit of individual self-interest in 'civil society', and the less state interference, the more effectively the market will operate.

In his political philosophy, Hegel had made use of Smith's distinction between 'civil society' – the sphere of self-interest – and 'political society' – the sphere of collective interests – arguing that the two could only be reconciled by strong institutions, such as the Prussian monarchy, which were above particular and sectional interests. It is hardly surprising, therefore, that Marx began to develop a thorough critique of the ideas of Smith and the other political economists; thus, his own thinking on economic matters was influenced in important ways by his reading of the political economy of his day. He accepted, for example, the distinction between the 'use value' of a commodity, that is, its practical utility, and its 'exchange value', the price it could command on the market. Clearly, the two are distinct: gold and silver have, for example, a low utility value, but have a high exchange value. This was something of a problem for the political economists, and they sought to discover the ultimate source of the value of commodities in general. Smith's solution, which Marx adopted, was that the exchange value of goods was set by the amount of human labour involved in their production. For Marx, however, the workers whose efforts gave commodities their value ought to be entitled to the full proceeds of the sale of those commodities. Thus, the profits extracted by the capitalist from the sale of commodities was nothing less than exploitation. For the present, the essential point to note is that the political economists, according to Marx, failed to see that human labour was capable of producing 'surplus value', that is, the excess of the value of the product over the value of the wages which are paid to the workers. Marx was critical of Ricardo in particular for failing to see that it was this 'surplus value' which is the source of the capitalists' profits.

The failings of the political economists' theories, Marx argued, arose because they simply took for granted 'the actual fact of capitalist production' rather than seeing it as one particular and historically specific form of production. Thus, they presumed the universal validity of concepts which were, in fact, culturally specific, such as that of 'private property'. Private property, Marx stressed, is not part of the natural human condition. It does not occur in all societies and is only maintained in ours by an elaborate system of laws supported by the power of the state. For the political economists the acquisition of private property motivated people to produce wealth, but for Marx it was precisely this which resulted in the breakdown of genuine social relationships. One person's ownership of an object denies its benefits to another, creates a basic conflict between them and produces a competition over resources. When this property is actually the product of another person's work this is, for Marx, the ultimate condition of human alienation in which those who work create an external world which then appears 'alien' to them and operates so as to dominate them.

In the *Paris Manuscripts* Marx subjects the basic concepts of political economy, such as 'private property', 'wages', 'labour', 'capital', 'land', 'profit', 'rent', 'the division of labour', 'exchange value', 'competition' and so on, to detailed and critical scrutiny. As we have said, his main complaint against the political economists was their presumption of the general validity of what were, in fact, historically specific economic relationships. Moreover, his reading, his experience of life in Paris, and his conversations with radical and socialist thinkers had made him increasingly aware of the social effects of capitalist industrial production as it was developing in Britain and France. Although his fuller analysis of capitalism came later, he anticipates it by noting what, for Marx, is an obvious and inhuman paradox: as capitalist production vastly increases the wealth of society, so the workers themselves are impoverished:

> the worker sinks to the level of a commodity and becomes indeed the most wretched of commodities . . . the wretchedness of the worker is in inverse proportion to the power and magnitude of his production . . . the necessary result of competition is the accumulation of capital in a few hands . . . finally the distinction between capitalist and land-rentier, like that between the tiller of the soil and the factory worker, disappears and . . . the whole of society must fall apart into two classes – the property owners and the propertyless workers. (Marx, 1844b: 64)

In these remarks Marx introduces many of the themes which were to preoccupy him for the remainder of his life. Their original purpose was to indicate the social consequences of 'alienated labour', a condition which reached its most highly developed form within capitalism.

Alienated labour   Marx considers four aspects of alienated labour. The first occurs when the things workers produce become the property of someone else, in this case the capitalist employer, and so contribute to the creation of an 'alien' world: 'the more objects the worker produces, the fewer he can possess and the more he falls under the domination of his product, capital' (ibid.: 66). The end result of the workers' efforts is to enrich and empower those who oppress them, the capitalists, and to impoverish themselves. Marx's second point follows on from this. If the products of labour contribute to the degradation of the producers, then labour itself becomes an activity directed against itself; it is, as Marx puts it, 'self-alienation'. Workers do not enjoy their work or, more important for Marx, confirm their real human nature in it. It is forced drudgery which negates their personal feelings and their objective interests.

It is here that we see the extent to which a materialist perspective has replaced Hegelian idealism in Marx's thought. Alienated labour, argues Marx, not only separates people from the products of their work and from their true selves, it also separates them from the very essence of humanity. People live in a natural world and depend upon its resources for survival, for food, for shelter, for clothing, and so on. All human life depends on this vital relationship. Of course, other species also depend on this natural environment, but what distinguishes human beings from other species is the *way* in which we produce the means of life. Other species must survive on what they can find in their environment or adapt themselves to it, whereas human beings *work* on their environment, transforming it rather than themselves. The range of variation in the physical characteristics of peoples throughout the world is relatively small, yet human beings have created cultures which allow them to live in extremely diverse environments, from the Arctic to the deserts. The history of human civilisation is, thus, a history of human ability to act on the environment to transform it to meet their needs. Hunting, then agriculture, then industrial production, are all human inventions which have increased the human capacity to control the environment and create wealth from it. We no longer shelter in caves but build houses. If we wish to cross the oceans we do not evolve into fish but build boats. If we wish to fly we do not grow wings, we build aircraft. There is, then, in Marx's view, a decisive difference between the ways in which humans and other animal species relate to their environment: 'In creating an objective world by his practical activity, in working-up inorganic nature, man proves himself a conscious species being' (1844b: 71). It follows, according to Marx, that the activity of work has a special significance as the affirmation of our essential nature as human beings. However, under conditions of alienated labour, this is denied:

> The object of labour is . . . the *objectification of man's species life*: for he duplicates himself not only, as in consciousness, intellectually, but also actively,

in reality, and therefore he contemplates himself in a world he has created. In tearing away from man the object of his production, therefore, estranged labour tears from him his *species life*. (ibid.: 72)

So under conditions of alienated labour, work, which should be the ultimate fulfilment of human life, is degraded to a process by which people are enslaved and impoverished. Work, which should be an end, becomes a means.

The final aspect of alienation Marx identifies extends this idea. As well as separating humans from their essential nature, alienated labour separates them from each other, so destroying the possibility of experiencing a genuine community with one's fellow beings. The product of labour becomes the property not of oneself, or the 'gods', but of another person: 'The relationship of the worker to labour engenders the relation of it to the capitalist, or whatever one chooses to call the master of labour' (ibid.: 75–6).

From a sociological perspective this is an argument of considerable importance. What Marx is proposing is an understanding of society in which a fundamental *economic* relationship, that between labour and capital, brings about a definite pattern of *social* relationships. Alienated labour not only destroys the possibility of a genuine human community based on co-operation and fellow-feeling, but also creates social arrangements which are conflictual. There is an inherent clash of interests between workers and capitalists. There is also, as we shall see, antagonism between workers who must compete with each other for jobs, and hostility between capitalists who have to compete for profit in the market. Alienated labour in the context of capitalist production had brought about the replacement of human co-operation by conflict as the basic organising principle of society, and gave rise to a fundamental social antagonism between the majority of the people who work to produce wealth and the minority who are able to appropriate this wealth as private property.

In direct contrast to the political economists, Marx argued that the acquisition of private property could not be the original impulse motivating people to engage in productive activity; rather, it is the consequence of alienated labour 'just as the gods in *the beginning* are not the cause but the effect of man's intellectual confusion'. More generally, the theorists of political economy had not created a science of economic life propounding universally valid principles, they had merely 'formulated the laws of estranged labour' (ibid.: 76). From this point of view, economics was not a science at all but had to be understood as an ideology, as Marx was soon to call it; that is, a set of ideas which, though claiming to express general truths, in fact only expresses the ideas which legitimate the dominance of a class. Just as Hegel's philosophy came to be seen as an expression of alienation, and needed to be turned upside down in order to restore human beings to their proper place at the centre of things, so Marx had come to view political economy in the same way. The proper purpose of economic activity was not the production of profits for a few, and the consequent impoverishment of the many, but the satisfaction of human needs and the production of general well-being. In political economy God had been replaced by Capital: an apparently independent entity which dominated people's lives. And just as Hegel's philosophy had been the subject of a sustained and necessary critique, so Marx embarked on a critique of political economy and an elaboration of an alternative, non-alienated account of economic life.

However, as always with Marx, there was a direct link between this academic critique of political economy and his practical political commitments. The conclusion that it was private property that was ultimately responsible for the degradation of the workers implied that by freeing themselves from their enslavement to private property they could bring about a general emancipation of humanity from its alienated condition:

> the emancipation of society from private property . . . from servitude, is expressed in the *political* form of the *emancipation* of the *workers* . . . because the whole of human servitude is involved in the relation of the worker to production, and every relation of servitude, is but a modification and consequence of this relation. ((ibid.: 77)

Marx could never be included among those like the Young Hegelians whose critique of society remained theoretical and academic. For him, the intellectual task of demystifying orthodox political economy was a counterpart to his practical political activities in support of workers' movements. This commitment, in its turn, was sustained by the theoretical conclusion that by freeing themselves the workers could liberate humanity from its alienation.

The idea that a working-class movement could produce a revolutionary transformation of society as a prelude to universal human liberation is only one of the themes which Marx develops in the *Paris Manuscripts*. The emphasis on labour and economic activity as the fundamental way in which human beings produce the conditions of life and the basis for the organisation of other relationships has already been discussed. Important, too, is the idea of the opposition between the producers of wealth and those who expropriate the products of this labour: the fundamental conflict which gives rise to particular patterns of social organisation. Of major consequence also is the conception of political economy as an ideological representation which serves the interests of the dominant class, rather than being a neutral scientific analysis of economic activities. And, above all, there is the belief in the fundamentally alienated nature of human existence under capitalism. People become dominated by Capital both in its legal form as private property and in its symbolic form as money. The goal of the system is the creation of capital rather than the satisfaction of human needs. The ambition of individuals is to accumulate money rather than achieve well-being. Thus the doctrines of political economy turn means into ends: 'Self-denial, the denial of life and of all human needs, is its cardinal doctrine. . . The less you *are*, the more you *have*; the less you express your own life, the greater is your *alienated* life – the greater is the store of your estranged being' (ibid.: 110).

The partnership with Engels

In August 1844, as we mentioned above, Marx met Friedrich Engels. Both had come to break with their earlier attachment to Hegel's idealist philosophy and stressed, instead, the importance of material factors. Later, Engels was to write that 'while I was in Manchester it was tangibly brought home to me that economic facts, which have so far played no role or only a contemptible one in the writing of history, are, in the modern world at least, a decisive historical fact' (quoted in Rigby, 1992: 39).

It was during his first period in Manchester that Engels wrote the *Outlines of a Critique of Political Economy*, which evidently made a deep impression on Marx; he acknowledged his debt to the book in the *Paris Manuscripts*. In his essay, Engels developed many of the themes which were to play a major role in the thinking of both men. Political economy is portrayed as the ideology of the advocates of free trade as they sought to destroy the old mercantilist system and its monopolies. The success of the free traders, however, only brought about the greatest monopoly of all, namely private property. For Engels, trade carried out 'under the domination of private property' is no more than 'a developed system of licensed fraud' (Engels, 1844: 166, 161) in which people are motivated only by self-interest and inevitably placed in antagonistic relations with others. The result is the destruction of established social institutions. Nationalities are dissolved as humanity is transformed into a 'horde of ravenous beasts (for what else are competitors?)'. The factory system of work tears families apart and turns familial bonds into economic transactions. However, what the political economist did not realise was that 'by his dissolution of all sectional interests he merely paves the way for the great transformation to which the century is moving – the reconciliation of mankind with nature and with itself' (ibid.: 168).

In the course of his denunciation of political economy, Engels indicates at various points that modern capitalism is doomed. The domination of humanity by private property is the final stage before the 'great transform-ation' which will restore a genuine community of human beings – a clear echo of Hegelian thought. However, this final, transcendental state of affairs will only come as a result of material economic activity which will transform ideas. Intense and incessant competition among capitalists will lead to trade crises, cycles of booms and slumps with each increasingly severe crisis eliminating the weaker competitors. As time goes by capitalist production will become concentrated in fewer and fewer large firms. The social structure is also transformed: 'The middle classes must increasingly disappear until the world is divided into millionaires and paupers, into large landowners and poor farm labourers' (ibid.: 188).

The similarities between the analyses of Marx and Engels are clear enough. What is less clear, however, is the precise nature of the intellectual partnership between the two, who were to remain firm friends and collaborators up to Marx's death in 1883. As Engels himself saw it, he was very much the junior partner and, as a result, has been held responsible for the simplified versions of Marx's ideas which became prominent after the latter's death. In particular, in contrast to Marx, Engels was accused of holding a deterministic view of history in which social and political change could be explained in terms of general laws, as well as a radically materialist view of the world in which everything could be understood as 'matter in motion', thus denying the possibility of mind and consciousness. He has been blamed, too, for the 'vulgar Marxism' which, it is claimed, influenced the European socialist movements toward the end of the nineteenth century, and the version which became the official doctrine of the Communist Party in the Soviet Union during the twentieth. Therefore some commentators have argued that there were very considerable differences between the positions of Marx and Engels. 'Engels' doctrines owed little or nothing to Marx', writes one, and his version of Marxism 'had an improperly scientist aspect that is at variance with what we can now identify as Marx's approach, method and subject matter' (Thomas, 1991: 41).

Other authors, however, have sought to restore Engels' reputation and contribution. Collins (1985: 56–62), for example, argues that Engels was a 'thinker of considerable originality and breadth: in some respects more so than Marx' and often provided the leads which Marx then followed; he was much the more sociologically aware of the two. Two recent biographers of Engels have tried to steer a middle course. Hunley (1991: 114) argues that Marx and Engels were 'in fundamental agreement' on all important matters, but since both were inconsistent in their views either of them could be interpreted in various ways. Similarly, Rigby concludes that it is 'pointless to counterpoise Marx against Engels when the individual works of each of the two men are so internally contradictory' (1992: 236). This debate as to the relative merits and contributions of each to Marxist thought is far from concluded (see Carver, 1983).

Whatever the details of his intellectual contribution, Engels' relationship with Marx was an extremely important one. The two friends, after their meeting in Paris, individually and jointly produced a series of works in which they developed the fundamental themes of Marxist thought. Characteristically, they did so by subjecting the ideas of others, particularly their former Young Hegelian friends, to rigorous and often withering criticism as the basis for the formulation of their own alternative ideas. Thus, in *The Holy Family* (1845) their target is the lingering Hegelianism of Bruno Bauer and, in the same year, in his *Theses on Feuerbach* Marx crystallises his differences with Feuerbach. Feuerbach is also the first target of *The German Ideology*, written in late 1846 and early 1847. In this work Marx and Engels present what was the fullest exposition of their own

' at that time, an approach which has come to be known, largely
 ᶜᵉls, as the materialist conception of history.

The materialist conception of history

Marx's next work was an attack on the French socialist Proudhon, who had
published a book called *The System of Economic Contradictions: The
Philosophy of Poverty*. In his vehement riposte of 1843 entitled *The
Poverty of Philosophy*, Marx criticised the Hegelian elements in Proudhon's
work, and denounced the political economists as 'the scientific represen-
tatives of bourgeois production'. But, most importantly, he produced a
statement which he himself saw as the first systematic presentation of the
link between patterns of economic production and the forms of social
organisation which they generate. Finally in this period, Marx and Engels
collaborated on writing a policy statement for the Communist League, a
workers' party with which they had become involved. This eventually
appeared in 1848 as *The Communist Manifesto*, a document widely
accepted as the clearest and most concise statement of their position, and
probably the most influential political manifesto of all time.

The works produced by Marx and Engels during the period 1845 to 1848
amount to a comprehensive and coherent analysis of history and human
society, and one which has had an enormous effect on the ways in which
these matters are now thought about. In a famous passage, written a
decade later, Marx summarised the major ideas they had developed:

> In the social production of their life men enter into definite relations that are
> indispensable and independent of their will, relations of production which
> correspond to a definite stage of development of their material productive
> forces. The sum total of these relations of production constitutes the economic
> structure of society, the real foundation on which rises a legal and political
> superstructure and to which correspond definite forms of social consciousness.
> The mode of production of material life conditions the social, political, and
> intellectual life process in general. It is not the consciousness of men that
> determines their being, but, on the contrary, their social being that determines
> their consciousness. At a certain stage of their development, the material
> productive forces of society come into conflict with the existing relations of
> production or – what is but a legal expression for the same thing – with the
> property relations within which they have been at work hitherto. From forms of
> development of the productive forces these relations turn into their fetters. Then
> begins an epoch of social revolution. With the change of the economic
> foundations the entire immense superstructure is more or less rapidly trans-
> formed. (Marx, 1859: 38)

As a guide to Marx and Engels' fundamental ideas, it is useful to consider,
in turn, the various claims encapsulated in this passage.

The priority of society

> *In the social production of their life, men enter into definite relations that
> are indispensable and independent of their will . . .*

Human beings are essentially *producers* who must work in and on their natural environment in order to survive. Production is not a solitary activity: it is carried out in the context of an organised human group. People are *social* animals and societies cannot be understood simply as aggregates of individuals. Membership in a society means that individuals' characters are shaped and moulded by its culture or, as we would say now, they are socialised into the ways of society. Thus, Marx emphasises the historical priority of society. As he put it: 'The more deeply we go back into history, the more does the individual, and hence also the producing individual, appear as dependent, as belonging to a greater whole . . . an animal which can individuate itself only in the midst of society' (1973: 84).

The material basis of social organisation

> . . . *relations of production which correspond to a definite stage of development of their material productive forces. The sum total of these relations of production constitutes the economic structure of society, the real foundation on which rises a legal and political superstructure and to which correspond definite forms of social consciousness.*

Here we approach the heart of historical materialism. Marx claims that the pattern of social organisation in any society is linked to, indeed depends on, 'productive forces'. Forms of social life are ultimately shaped by material economic processes, and as these latter change so do the culture and the institutions of society. By 'material productive forces' Marx means more or less what we would understand by technology. This can be very simple, such as the axes and spears of hunting and gathering societies, or as complex as automated factories or satellite communications. For Marx, it is technology which is the crucial link between humans and the natural environment, and as technology changes so too do the forms of society. While we shall have more to say on this aspect of Marx's position later, it is worth emphasising that Marx offers a theory of society which claims to have identified the basic forces which give rise to particular patterns of social organisation. The economic base generates a particular form of 'superstructure' and a corresponding mode of 'social consciousness'. In more contemporary terms, the idea is that both the institutions and culture of a society take their form from underlying economic processes.

Economic production and social organisation

> *The mode of production of material life conditions the social, political, and intellectual life process in general.*

This states the connection between economic production and social organisation: the former 'conditions' the latter. The interpretation of the word 'conditions', however, is fraught with problems. Does it mean, as some have assumed, that the characteristics of culture and social institutions are *determined* by the nature of production technology, or does it mean that it *sets limits to* the range of variation in patterns of social organisation? Or does it simply suggest that the nature of economic activity will always exert some influence on the rest of social life? This is an issue to which we shall return.

The shaping of consciousness

It is not the consciousness of men that determines their being, but, on the contrary, their social being that determines their consciousness.

Once again here Marx emphasises the connection, as he sees it, between the social situation in which people find themselves, which is, as we have seen, 'conditioned' by the 'relations of production', and the kind of ideas and beliefs they develop. In short, human cultures are shaped, ultimately, by the nature of the economic processes which sustain them, and human individuals themselves formed by the cultures into which they are born. Human experience is, in other words, profoundly social.

The way Marx puts this is intended as a counter to those who, like the Hegelians of his day, believed that human consciousness exists in an independent and autonomous realm which cannot be explained in terms of social or economic forces. The life of the mind or of consciousness, they believed, is free and undetermined: human beings have the capacity to think and believe what they may. For Marx, however, this is an illusion. As thinking beings, we are deluded into believing that we can think independently of our social circumstances. In reality, the very concepts and categories which allow us to think at all are themselves derived from 'the ongoing confrontation between man and the intrinsically practical problem of sustaining his own existence' (Poggi, 1972: 94).

As we shall see, there are all kinds of difficulties associated with Marx's view of the social origins of consciousness. However, it is undeniable that the view has been enormously influential in the human sciences, emphasising, as has already been suggested, both the ways in which humans are socialised into culture and society, and the ways in which cultures themselves may reflect specific modes of economic production. As a more general sociological perspective, it offers an approach to understanding why the knowledge, beliefs and institutions of the range of human societies can be so different. From the materialist point of view, the source lies in the mode of production and in its transformations.

The sources of social change

At a certain stage in their development, the material productive forces of society come into conflict with the existing relations of production or – what is but a legal expression for the same thing – with the property relations within which they have been at work hitherto.

Here Marx moves from a concern with the fundamental organising principles of societies to a consideration of how social change occurs. Once again, the 'material productive forces' are at the heart of things: human history is seen as essentially the process by which productive forces develop. Marx held that there was no fixed limit to human wants. Once one need has been satisfied, another arises: consider the invention of theauto-mobile, which created new demands for raw materials, new inventions, new techniques of manufacture, new research, and so on. Thus, there is a persistent pressure to develop productive forces which, in capitalism, reaches its apogee as firms are compelled by competition to constantly innovate and rationalise their productive processes.

Inevitably, changes in the 'material productive forces' create a pressure for wider social changes, or, as Marx puts it, the forces of production come into conflict with the 'existing relations of production'. As we have seen, the argument is that for any particular production process, at any level of technological development, there will be a corresponding set of social relationships, a division of labour generated by the requirements of the process itself. Thus, the earliest automobiles were largely hand-built by small teams of craftsmen, much as horse-drawn carriages had been built. The craftsmen were largely displaced by the invention of mass-production and its requirement for large numbers of relatively unskilled workers. In turn, they may also disappear as production becomes more and more automated. Recently, we have become familiar with the effects of 'new technology' displacing old skills and jobs as new ones emerge. Sometimes such changes can be catastrophic, as in the notorious case of the English hand-loom weavers of the eighteenth century who were reduced to starvation by the introduction of powered looms in factories. On the other hand, new inventions can create wholly new areas of economic activity, as in the case of electronic information and communications technologies. Whatever the effects, however, a degree of social disruption is involved which, in Marx's terms, may be understood as the persistent conflict between changing productive forces and established social relations.

It is clear, however, that in talking of the social relations of production Marx meant much more than simply the division of labour, the specialisation of tasks which accompanies any productive activity. To this must be added the 'property relations' linked to the productive forces. In conditions of 'primitive communism', for example, both the division of labour and the change due to technical innovation were minimal. Accordingly, production was genuinely communal and, he argued, private property did not exist. With the development of the division of labour, however, and the increased productivity which ensued, this situation was irrevocably altered. For Marx, the progress of the division of labour goes hand in hand with the processes already referred to and through which the modern notion of the individual emerges from the 'sheep-like or tribal consciousness' of social existence in primitive society. The 'division of labour' and 'private property' amount to no more than different ways of looking at the same process, Marx argues, with the former referring to productive *activity*, and the latter to the *product* of that activity. As the division of labour progresses, stimulated by increasing population, new human wants, as well as its own productivity, it is accompanied by the growth of private property and the ability of some to appropriate the labour of others. In *The German Ideology* Marx and Engels speculated on the origins of the division of labour, locating it initially in the 'sexual act' and in the male-dominated family with its 'latent slavery' in which the father controls the activities of his wife and children. As with all slaves, they are the property of their master (1974: 51-3).

One of the most celebrated passages in Adam Smith's *Wealth of Nations*, using the example of the manufacture of pins, extolled the benefits of the division of labour in terms of the vastly increased productivity which could be achieved and the consequent advantages for both individuals and society. For Marx and Engels, however, the very notion of such advantages was itself ideological, serving to justify the domination of the many by the few. Marx and Engels preferred to speak of the exploitation and the degradation of human beings which occurs when, through the division of labour, they are reduced to performing elementary tasks, endlessly repeated, and they thereby become mere appendages to machines. Marx's reference to 'property' in the context of the 'relations of production' is intended to convey the idea that the whole process in which economic activity is fragmented and property created is socially divisive. As social production is turned into the appropriation of private property and then into the production of commodities for the market, there is an increasing separation between the interests of individuals and those of the community as a whole. Initially, it may have been simple physical advantages which enabled men to achieve a position of dominance in relation to women, but other forms of social division followed whenever an economic surplus was generated. In any territory it would be inevitable that some families or tribes would acquire more property than others, and that such inequalities could be reinforced through inheritance. Economic surplus also allowed for the emergence of a priesthood which, by virtue of its claim to speak with the authority of the sacred, could also ensure a position of dominance for itself. It is in this context that Marx and Engels speak of the 'division of material and mental labour', with priests as the 'first form of ideologists' (ibid.: 51), which eventually led to the false belief on which idealist philosophy came to be based, that is, that 'consciousness' or 'spirit' is independent of the material world.

An historically important basis of social division occurs whenever a specialised group of warriors emerges. Initially formed to protect a tribe and its territory, and supported by the labour of others, this group, by its access to weapons and the means of coercion, is in a favourable position to dominate the rest of society, especially if it can also secure the support of the priesthood. With the development of agricultural production based on the regular cultivation of a settled territory, the social role of the military becomes even more important, both in protecting existing land and in conquering that of others. It is in such activities, Engels argued, that we can detect the origins of the modern state. State power develops not as a means of defending the community as a whole, even though it may legitimise itself in this way, but out of the efforts of dominant groups to protect their land and economic interests in a situation where class divisions are developing (Engels, 1884: 205–6). An important aspect of this argument is the assumption that social power is a result of control over the forces of production, which in this case are agricultural. The organisation of society will reflect the division of labour necessary to carry out effective farming, whether this is animal husbandry, cultivation or whatever. But these technical relations of production are themselves formed in the context of a more fundamental relationship between the mass of people who simply work on the land and the relatively small number who are in a position to control its use. Land, the most important factor in the production process, has become property, and there is an inherent conflict of interest between those who produce wealth and those who live off the surplus the producers generate. The social relations of production are, above all, relations between dominant and subordinate social classes; between those who own or control the forces of production and those who do not. As the forces of production develop they transform the relations between classes.

The nature of social change

> *From forms of development of the productive forces these relations turn into their fetters.*

Historical change has its source in the development of the forces of production, and the growing incompatibility between these and existing social relations of production. The latter, though at one time promoting economic and social development, inevitably become more and more anachronistic. In real societies, the increasing tension between the forces and relations of production is experienced as a conflict between social *classes*; between a dominant class which controls the existing forces of production, and a subordinate but challenging class which draws its growing strength from the new developing forces. The idea of class conflict is, thus, at the heart of the materialist conception of history and is expressed forcibly at the beginning of *The Communist Manifesto*: 'The history of all hitherto existing society is the history of class struggles.'

In *The German Ideology* Marx and Engels had already put forward an analysis of the course of human history in terms of 'stages of development in the division of labour' which, in their view, were 'just so many different forms of ownership'. In *tribal* forms property in the modern sense did not exist. In the *ancient city-states* the division of labour was more advanced and the gradual development of private property gradually eroded communal sentiments and institutions. Major social division arose, based on conflicts of economic interests, such as those between town and country, between manufacture and maritime commerce, between citizens and slaves, and there were the beginnings of the transformation of peasants into wage-workers. In *feudalism* the nobility dominated the peasants through their possession of landed property. In the towns, small-scale production was carried on by guilds.

These stages of the division of labour are marked by a gradual increase in the significance of private property with its corrosive effect on communal life and the intensification of class conflicts. Marx and Engels' account of the process of social change, however, is best exemplified in their discussion of the transition from feudalism to the fourth form of the division of labour, *capitalism*. In their analysis, the major institutions of feudalism, which were once appropriate to a predominantly agricultural society, come to be 'the fetters' inhibiting the development of new forms of production which, eventually, will break them asunder. The essence of capitalism is the dominance of private property in the production process, and thus of society as a whole. Its origins lay in the craft production and commercial activities typical of the medieval towns, and carried on by the 'bourgeoisie'.

In *The Communist Manifesto* Marx and Engels provide a dramatic account of the expansion of commerce and manufacture and the resulting destruction of feudal society. The commercial activities of the 'chartered burghers of the earliest towns' were, at first, limited in scale. Nevertheless, they constituted the 'revolutionary element in the tottering feudal society'. Gradually, stimulated by increasing population, access to raw materials, precious metals and overseas markets, better communications and new inventions, commerce became more and more significant. With this development of the forces of production came corresponding changes in the relations of production. The medieval guilds could no longer meet the expanding demand and were an obstacle to the growth of free markets. Eventually, the 'guild masters were pushed to one side by the manufacturing middle class', who, in their turn, had to give way to the 'industrial millionaires, the leaders of whole industrial armies, the modern bourgeois'. It is this latter class who become dominant in capitalist society, owning and controlling the forces of production which have been revolutionised by 'steam and machinery' to become the most powerful and productive technology ever available in human society.

There are strong echoes here of Engels' awe at the sheer productive capacity of the immense new factories he saw in Manchester, an experience which fed both Marx and Engels' realisation of the enormous social consequences of industrial production. For them the history of the modern period was one in which the bourgeoisie sought and achieved a political power commensurate with their growing economic dominance. By contrast, and as a direct result, the institutions of feudal society, which at one time had been the 'fetters' – the monarchy, the church, the guilds and so on – restricting economic development, were no longer the authoritative forces they had once been. Although they might remain in place in one form or another, the economic basis of their power had gone forever, dissolved by the transition from agricultural to industrial production. Historically, particular momentous events symbolised the transformation of social power, notably the French Revolution of 1789, which temporarily put an end to the monarchy, and the British Reform Bill of 1832, which gave parliamentary representation to men who owned substantial property.

Once again we see the rejection of Hegel. The modern state does not, cannot, embody the whole society and the general interest. On the contrary, the state's role in actuality is to pursue and defend the interests of the dominant class. The point is bluntly stated in *The Communist Manifesto*: 'The executive of the modern state is but a committee for managing the common affairs of the whole bourgeoisie.'

What we have here is Marx and Engels' account of how the development of the forces of production brings them into conflict with the existing relations of production. The conflict is expressed as a conflict between dominant and challenging social classes; a conflict in which established institutions protecting the property and the power of the dominant class become 'fetters' inhibiting the growth and development of the challenging class. But not for long. Simply by acting rationally in pursuit of their economic interests, individual members of the bourgeoisie bring about the development of its triumph as a class and, as a consequence, capitalist society. The activities of the class bring about a revolution:

> The bourgeoisie, wherever it has got the upper hand, has put an end to all feudal, patriarchal, idyllic relations. It has pitilessly torn asunder the motley feudal ties that bound man to his 'natural superiors', and has left remaining no other nexus between man and man than naked self-interest, than callous 'cash payment'. (ibid.: 223)

Social revolution

> *Then begins an epoch of social revolution.*

For Marx, social change occurs as a result of the growing tension between the forces of production and the relations of production. Taken together, the forces of production and the relations of production constitute the *mode of production* of a society. Change is regarded as the normal condition of human society, and the great events of human history are the revolutionary transformations in which modes of production, no longer able to contain the increasing contradictions within them, collapse and give way to new ones. As we have seen, this is how Marx and Engels account for the transition from feudal to capitalist modes of production, with the growing power of the bourgeoisie making it the revolutionary agent. But, just as the contradictions within feudalism eventually led to its demise, so, they argued, will capitalism sow the seeds of its own destruction. Although the bourgeoisie is dominant in the capitalist mode of production, simply by continuing to pursue their individual interests its members will collectively bring about capitalism's downfall, since these interests stimulate the rise of a new revolutionary agent, the proletariat: 'What the bourgeoisie produces above all, therefore, is its own gravediggers. Its fall and the victory of the proletariat are equally inevitable' (ibid.: 231).

The emergence of the working class   One of the important preconditions
for the development of modern capitalist industry was the emergence of a
class of labourers no longer tied to the land by feudal custom and
tradition,legally free of any bonds to the landowners and so available for
hire for wages. Such a class had begun to develop during the Middle Ages,
swelling the population of the towns. In England, during the eighteenth
century this group grew rapidly in size. New techniques of agricultural
production had greatly increased productivity and enhanced the profitability of producing for a market rather than for local consumption. Open
fields were enclosed by landowners and, by the practice of 'engrossing',
several small farms were combined into larger units. Some contemporary
observers worried that now only the relatively rich could be independent
farmers: 'Now only men with capital could provide the stock and meet the
rent demands for large undertakings. All others were forced downwards
into the pool of wage-paid labourers' (Langford, 1989: 453).

It was this group of wage labourers, Marx believed, that would become
the revolutionary class of capitalist society. The proletariat and the
bourgeoisie confront each other as the embodiment of the social relations
of production; a confrontation which will eventually lead to the destruction
of capitalism:

> In big industry and competition the whole mass of conditions of existence,
> limitations, biases of individuals, are fused together into the two simplest forms:
> private property and labour. (Marx and Engels, 1974: 91)

The imperatives of capitalist competition would lead to the concentration
of wealth and power in the hands of a small bourgeoisie, with the
simultaneous creation of a much larger class of propertyless wage workers
whose interests were contrary to those of their capitalist masters. A
growing awareness of their true situation, encouraged by political activity,
would lead to a revolutionary *class consciousness* and the transformation of
the proletariat from a class 'in itself' to a class 'for itself'.

The 'era of social revolution' is the period in which the dominant class is
overthrown and replaced by another. However, according to Marx, the
proletarian revolution will be the final, ultimate transformation ushering in
the last phase of human development, the non-alienated, non-antagonistic
communist society in which the separation between the individual and
community is transcended. Initially, the revolution would involve the
workers' seizing power from the bourgeoisie and establishing 'a dictatorship of the proletariat' in which the priorities of the people would be
imposed. This would give way to a period of socialist reconstruction, but,
eventually, with the abolition of private property and the reconciliation of
individual and collective interests, the institutions of capitalism would
disappear. In particular, the state, seen by Marx as the means by which
capitalist domination was secured in the guise of representing the interests
of all, would 'wither away'. Human beings would once again be able to
realise their essential humanity.

Marx's conclusion that the proletarian revolution would be the final one is derived from his conviction that each stage of human history represents a progressive increase in the division of labour, a corresponding increase in the importance of private property in determining the social relations ofproduction, and a consequent growth in the extent of human alienation as people become dominated by 'things'. This process, he contends, reaches its limit in capitalist society, where all is decided on the basis of the calculation of profit. The 'cash nexus' determines everything and everyone. Social life is dominated by market forces. The worker, though legally a free agent, is forced to work for the capitalist or starve. The capitalist is compelled to obey the dictates of the market. Production is determined not by the use value of what can be produced, but by the exchange value of objects in the market. People are sacrificed for profits. Human freedom gives way to enslavement by capital. Thus, in liberating itself, the proletariat brings about the emancipation of all humanity.

> All previous historical movements were movements of minorities, or in the interests of minorities. The proletarian movement is the self-conscious, independent movement of the immense majority, in the interests of the immense majority. The proletariat, the lowest stratum of our present society, cannot stir, cannot raise itself up, without the whole superincumbent strata of official society being sprung into the air. (Marx and Engels, 1948: 230)

The economic sources of social change

> *With the change of the economic foundation, the entire immense super-structure is more or less rapidly transformed.*

In this and other passages, Marx explicates the relationship between economic activity and social organisation in terms of the metaphor of 'foundations' and 'superstructure'. What seems to have been intended is a conception of the structure of society as composed of two levels: the economic *base*, that is, the stage of development reached by the forces of production and the relations of production, and the social *superstructure*, that is, the institutions and cultural forms which correspond to the mode of production. The essential point is that the metaphor locates the fundamental organising principle of society in its economic foundations: as these change so will the social superstructure.

It would be difficult to underestimate the influence which this metaphor has had as a means of understanding the transition of European societies from feudalism to capitalism. As the economic base changes from traditional agriculture to capitalist industrial production, so the culture and the dominant institutions of the societies are also transformed. The political power of the monarchy and the nobility is destroyed and replaced by the modern bureaucratic state with its representative democratic institutions. The power of the church also declines in the face of the 'cash nexus' and the secular values it embodies. The traditional division between nobility and peasantry gives way to a class structure determined by the relation to the means of production, that is, whether people are owners of capital or whether they must sell their labour to survive. The extended family appropriate to subsistence agricultural production gives way to the small, independent nuclear family more compatible with individualistic patterns of work and their separation from the home. Education becomes more formalised and, with increasing industrialisation, is provided on a mass scale, inculcating the populace in the skills and compliance that capitalist production requires. The message is reinforced, in modern times, by the various media of mass communications which, from a Marxist perspective, are seen as effective means of producing passive workers and eager consumers, respectful of employers and loyal to the system which exploits them. It is through the activities of such institutions that the 'ideas of the ruling class are in every epoch the ruling ideas. . . . The class which has the means of material production at its disposal has control at the same time over the means of mental production so that, thereby, generally speaking, the ideas of those who lack the means of mental production are subject to it' (Marx and Engels, 1974: 64).

Historical materialism and the critique of Hegel

This development of a materialist conception of history starts from the premise that individual human beings are the creations of their societies. It relates the organisation of society to the ways in which human beings secure their conditions of life in their natural environment. It relates human culture, patterns of ideas and beliefs to the ways in which such economic activities are conducted. It lays claim to explain the interrelationships among the institutions of society in terms of its economic base and to show how social change is not random or haphazard but systematically related to this base.

It was also the outcome of Marx and Engels' comprehensive criticism of Hegelian philosophy. Although their aim was to reveal the errors and delusions of idealism, and replace them with what they regarded as the objective analysis of materialism, important elements of Hegelian thought remained. Marx's view of social development, like that of Hegel and most social philosophers of the period, was that historical change had a pattern and that societies developed from 'lower' to 'higher' forms. But Hegel and Marx differed from most of their contemporaries in their insistence that this movement was not a simple process of evolution but one of successive conflicts and contradictions which can be understood as a dialectical process. Marx's interpretation of the transition from feudalism to capitalism, to take the most obvious example, involves a conflict between the feudal nobility (thesis) and the rising bourgeoisie (antithesis) which is resolved by the victory of the latter in a new social order which retains the progressive elements of the old (synthesis). In turn, the new bourgeoisie, now dominant (thesis), is challenged by the proletariat (antithesis) and the eventual revolution transcending this opposition in the emergence of a classless society (synthesis) which will, nevertheless, incorporate progressive elements of past eras, not least the techniques of agricultural and industrial production. Without this implicitly Hegelian framework, it is difficult to understand quite why Marx and Engels regarded revolution as inevitable, or even historically necessary, and why, in *The German Ideology*, they described the proletariat as the 'universal' class which would liberate humanity. Such a conclusion follows from Marx's analysis of capitalist society as the total negation of genuine human social life and its overthrow as the 'the negation of the negation'. As he put it in one of his last works, the posthumously published third volume of *Capital*, human freedom 'cannot exist of anything else but of the fact that socialised man, the associated producers, regulate their interchange with nature rationally, bring it under their common control, instead of being ruled by it as some blind power'. The less people are ruled by this 'realm of necessity', says Marx, the more they can experience the 'true realm of freedom' (1909: 954–5).

This passage also indicates another Hegelian theme, namely, the over-coming of alienation. We have seen how Marx, following Feuerbach, inverted and extended Hegel's notion of alienation, applying it not only to religion but also to the state and, above all, to economic production. As the division of labour proceeds, so too does the creation of private property and the domination of people by things. This is the essence of Marx's notion of alienation, what he was later to call the 'fetishism of commodities', in which inanimate objects come to control the lives of real people. The ultimate form of alienation is capitalist society in which 'market forces' both pervade every area of social life and determine how people live and what they do. Profits come before people, exchange value before use value, as people obey the dictates of the market, however destructive they may be of human life and the natural environment. We have lost control of our lives; we must do what the market tells us, just as we once believed that our purpose on earth was to do God's will.

While many later social theorists have shared Marx's bleak assessment of life under industrial capitalism, not all have had his faith in the emancipatory potential of dialectical change. Max Weber, as we shall see, firmly rejected the idea that history had some ultimate end and seriously doubted the possibility of human liberation through a socialist revolution. For him, the 'iron cage' of bureaucracy, itself the result of industrialism, would stifle distinctively human qualities, irrespective of whether the society was capitalist or socialist. Weber's contemporary, Georg Simmel (1858–1918), argued that the very process of creating human social life involved a form of alienation, since we must conform to the established cultural and institutional forms of life. How could we communicate, for example, if not in a language which confronts us, as individuals, as an objective reality, and which influences the very processes of our thought? This, for Simmel, was the 'tragedy of culture' from which there is no escape. Similar pessimism is evident in the works of the much later Frankfurt School of critical social theorists, who shared Marx's belief in the alienated character of modern life, but lost his faith in the possibility of revolutionary social change. Adorno and Horkheimer, for example, emphasised a 'dialectic of alienation', namely, the process by which the powers of science and technology, originally offering the possibility of liberating societies from material want and intellectual darkness, had turned into forces whichimposed a mindless, conformist existence on the mass of the population in the interests of rationally planned production and consumption. The project which began with the Enlightenment had become a means whereby humanity oppressed humanity (Adorno and Horkheimer, 1979). However, like Marx, and Hegel before them, such theorists maintained a distinction between a possible free and fulfilling human existence, and the alienated conditions of life as experienced in most present societies.

Issues of interpretation

The writings of Marx and Engels between 1844 and 1848 developed the major ideas which have come to be regarded as the foundations of Marxist thought. It is important to recall that much of this work was not published during their lifetimes. As we earlier pointed out, later generations of scholars, such as Max Weber, were acquainted with only a fragmentary version of Marx's thought. Not unnaturally, as more and more of the works became available, issues of interpretation became more pronounced. The 'conservative' view can be represented by Kolakowski, who concludes that with the appearance of *The Communist Manifesto* in 1848, 'Marx's theory of society and his precepts for action had attained completion in the form of a well-defined and permanent outline. His later work did not modify what he had written in any essential respect' (1978: 233).

Others, however, reject such a conclusion, stressing, instead, the development of Marx's thought from an early phase, in which his concerns were primarily humanistic and philosophical, to a later, more mature period, in which his commitment was to economic analysis. The most prominent advocate of this view was the French Marxist philosopher, Louis Althusser (1918–90), who spoke of an 'epistemological break' between the thought of the early Marx, with its Hegelian concern with human alienation, and his later development of the science of historical materialism (Althusser, 1969). This view is drawn upon by Rattansi, who also speaks of an 'early stage' when Marx was concerned with alienation and human emancipation, a 'transitional stage' represented in the *Poverty of Philosophy* of 1847, and the 'mature writings', beginning with the *Grundrisse*, in which Marx focused on the analysis of the production process and the development of the theory of surplus value (Rattansi, 1982: 59).

Acknowledging the dynamic aspects of Marx's thought does help resolve some of the inconsistencies and other problems of interpretation which have emerged. It has been suggested, for example, that Marx's assumption of a human essence from which, in capitalist society, we are alienated is inconsistent with his more sociological observation that people are, above all, the products of the societies in which they live. This disappears if it is argued, as Rattansi does, that 'the concept of alienation . . . loses its centrality in his discourse' when Marx's more sociological ideas are read as a criticism of his own earlier humanism (ibid.: 73).

Similarly, critics of Marx have detected an incompatibility between his emphasis on the 'two great classes' and the simplification of the social structure in the *Manifesto* and in the *German Ideology* and, on the other hand, his recognition in Volume 3 of *Capital* that 'middle and transition stages obliterate . . . all definite boundaries' (Marx, 1909: 1031). There is also the recognition, most notably in *The Eighteenth Brumaire of Louis Bonaparte* (1852), of the role which could be played in the political process by social groups and interests not directly reducible to the 'two great classes', such as the 'lumpenproletariat' of Paris, the financial aristocracy, the industrial bourgeoisie, the state bureaucracy, the army, the peasantry, and so on. Once again, the apparent contradiction between the two-class model and the range of social interests which could coalesce in any real society is removed if the first is regarded as part of Marx's earlier phase and the latter a product of his more 'mature' thought.

The case for a separation of an early and a later Marx rests, to a considerable extent, on Marx's increasing preoccupation with economic analysis from the 1850s onwards and the disappearance of Hegelian terms from his writings. Yet, despite this, it is not so easy to conclude that these represent any fundamental reorientation of his thought. Consider the following passage:

> The capitalist mode of appropriation, the result of the capitalist mode of production, produces capitalist private property. This is the first negation of individual private property, as founded on the labour of the proprietor. But capitalist property begets, with the inexorability of a law of Nature, its own negation. It is the negation of negation. (Marx, 1954: 715)

The language here is definitely Hegelian, as is the idea of the 'inexorability' of the contradictions which will eventually bring about the collapse of capitalism. Indeed, the passage could fit comfortably into the *Paris Manuscripts*. In fact it occurs near the end of Volume 1 of *Capital*, first published in 1867 and regarded, by those who stress the distinction, as the great work of Marx's 'mature' period. Such passages do not convey much sense of a basic change in Marx's ideas.

Indeed, it seems that both Marx and Engels displayed a renewed interest in Hegel in their later years (Rigby, 1992: 97ff). This is most evident in Engels' development of what came to be called dialectical, as opposed to historical, materialism; a perspective which saw dialectics as 'the science of the *general* laws of motion and development of nature, human society, and thought' (Engels, 1878: 180). Marx, too, made his respect for Hegel explicit, notably in the 'Afterword' to the second German edition of *Capital* in 1873, where he makes a sharp distinction between the method of dialectical analysis and the mystification which it suffered 'in Hegel's hands'. His own task, Marx goes on, was to extract the 'rational kernel' from the 'mystical shell'; all the same, he declares himself still a pupil of Hegel, 'that mighty thinker' (1954: 29).

As we have pointed out, historical materialism departed from the speculative metaphysics which constituted most social philosophy up to that time. However, it generated its own problems as well as drawing a great deal of criticism. It is to some of these that we now turn.

The material foundations of social life and ideology

We have seen how Marx and Engels explained the nature and the development of societies in terms of economic activity, the 'social production' which sustains human life, and the levels of technological development which progressively bring about social change. We have also emphasised that this materialist conception of history was formulated as a critique of contemporary idealist philosophy and political economy. Against the political economists, Marx argued that people were not naturally competitive individuals but were, above all, shaped by their society. It was capitalism that made competitive individuals. This claim about the essentially social nature of human consciousness, along with its criticism of individualistic theories of social order, has been an important theme of subsequent sociological thought. However, historical materialism goes beyond this, arguing that the cultures into which people are socialised are themselves shaped by the processes of production. Taking these points together we arrive at the proposition that human consciousness is ultimately a reflection of economic processes, of the 'pragmatic confrontation of man with reality' (Poggi, 1972: 94).

Clearly, the primacy given to economic factors has to be understood as a counter to the German idealists with their mystical notions of Mind or Being as the origin of human existence. However, for some, Marx and Engels' materialism goes too far in reducing mind to matter and giving human ideas no independence from determination by the forces of production. Even some who would not accept the grandiose Hegelian scheme argued, with Hegel, that what is distinctive about human beings is their ability to engage in creative mental activity. Only humans, for example, can engage in the symbolic communication which makes language possible, and it is language which is an essential condition for culture. It is one thing to assert that our thoughts and ideas may be powerfully influenced by the mode of production, but quite another to say that they are conditioned or determined by it. This issue forms an enduring debate in the interpretation of Marxist thought. Many critics have interpreted Marxism as offering a deterministic explanation of all aspects of history and culture. But both Marx and Engels, and many later Marxists, deny this, stressing that their main objective was to criticise idealist explanations while recognising that, in any real situation, there will be an interplay between cultural and material factors.

The notion that the ideas and beliefs which become established in a society are, ultimately, a reflection of its predominant mode of production has been a highly influential one. Religion, legal codes, philosophic and artistic productions, for example, have all been examined in such terms. Critics, however, have pointed out that there are a range of different religious belief systems, for example, evident in societies with very similar modes of production. Others, Max Weber being the most prominent, have argued that certain kinds of religious belief can contribute to the process of economic change rather than simply reflecting it. Others have claimed to detect a confusion in Marx's notion of the forces of production as the motive power of social change, not least because their development requires, above all, the application of ideas and reason to the process of production. In which case, it becomes difficult to give explanatory priority to material forces.

Much debate has also been stimulated by the claim that the 'ideas of the ruling class are in every epoch the ruling ideas' (Marx and Engels, 1974: 64). The idea here is that members of the dominant class are likely to accept ideas which reflect and promote their material interests and so 'regulate the production and distribution of ideas'. Thus, in modern societies, it has been argued that by virtue of their possession of television networks, news media, the entertainment industry and so on, the dominant capitalist class is in a position to create a cultural climate which legitimates its interests. This need not occur through direct coercion, censorship or interference, but simply by encouraging some ideas and trivialising or marginalising others. In such ways, it is argued, the ruling class can establish and sustain a dominant ideology which will inhibit members of the subordinate class from developing an awareness of their real interests. However, the concept of a coherent 'dominant ideology' has been criticised, partly because its proponents have as yet been unable to specify how it works in practice, and partly because 'it tends to produce an over-integrated view of society, in which ideology forges a seamless whole' and which 'underestimates the power of oppositional or subordinate cultural patterns' (Abercrombie et al., 1980: 159).

A related notion is that of *class consciousness*, through which, in Marx's view, members of social classes come to have an awareness of their real collective interests through the experience of conflict. Thus, bourgeois consciousness was forged in the long struggle with the aristocracy, just as the class consciousness of the proletariat will develop as the basic contradictions of capitalism become more evident. In this way, a class 'in itself' becomes a class 'for itself' as the distortions of 'false' consciousness give way to a more accurate reflection of its interests. The problem here, however, is the apparent failure of a working-class consciousness to emerge in the mature capitalist societies of the West. Moreover, many theorists have pointed to the persistence of powerful but non-economic influences on collective action and the formation of individual identities: gender, ethnicity, religion, nationality and so on, remain significant sources of social differentiation which are not easily reconciled with the basic class division of Marxist theory.

Base and superstructure

The metaphor which depicts society as having a fundamental economic base on which its social and cultural institutions rest is an important one. Inevitably, this image has been much criticised for reasons we have already outlined, namely, that it may lead to a deterministic view of social life and social change, denying the autonomy of human consciousness. Some theorists, notably Althusser, have also rejected the image on the grounds that it presents a rigid and oversimplified version of what is a subtle and complex theoretical perspective. Nevertheless, the conceptualisation of the relationships between economic and social factors remains an issue. As we have suggested, in his analysis of actual social situations, Marx did allow for the importance of non-economic factors in contributing to the course of events, most notably in his interpretation of Louis Napoleon's *coup d'état* in France in 1851, *The Eighteenth Brumaire of Louis Bonaparte*.

In this he offers an explanation of 'how a nation of thirty-six millions can be surprised and delivered unresisting into captivity by three swindlers' (Marx, 1852: 304). He emphasises not only long-term economic trends, but also the independent and unpredictable sequence of political events which allowed Louis Napoleon to draw support from such diverse sources as the Paris lumpenproletariat, the 'financial aristocracy', as well as the unorganised mass of peasants. Some have regarded this analysis as evidence of the need to draw a clear distinction between, on the one hand, Marx's purely theoretical writings and the political polemics in which he emphasises economic factors and the inexorable destiny of the proletariat, and, on the other, his subtle and sensitive interpretation of real sequences of events which allow for the independent effects of political, cultural, personal and even contingent factors. The *Eighteenth Brumaire* has also, as we have seen, been read as an indication of Marx's move away from historical materialism and class reductionism, toward a recognition of 'the relative autonomy of superstructures, and especially of political bureaucracy' (Rattansi, 1982: 107).

Certainly the analysis of the *Eighteenth Brumaire* seems far removed from, say, some of the famous passages in *The Poverty of Philosophy*, written some five years earlier, in which Marx claimed that the 'hand mill gives you society with the feudal lord; the steam-mill society with the industrial capitalist' (1847: 95). However, the replacement of the base–superstructure metaphor by the notion of 'relative autonomy' brings its own problems. How autonomous are such elements? And if the 'super-structure' can influence the 'base', what is the point of the distinction?

Engels, in an attempt to overcome such difficulties, denied that he and Marx saw the former as determined by the latter, and spoke, instead, of a dialectical 'interaction' between them in which economic factors prevail only 'in the last resort' (Rigby, 1992: 167).

Neither Marx nor Marxists have an agreed commitment to a simple model in which the economic 'base' determines the social 'superstructure'. Indeed, much attention has been paid to their reciprocal effects, in particular to the influence of the state, and the effects of ideological factors on economic activity. What is less certain is whether such analyses have overcome the problems just identified. As Rigby puts it:

> The dilemma for Marxism is to maintain a middle course between the perils of an economic reductionist philosophy of history on the one hand and, on the other, an analysis which gives so much autonomy to the social superstructure that it ceases to be recognisably Marxist. (ibid.: 177)

In emphasising the fundamental importance of a society's mode of production, Marx and Engels made an immense contribution to sociological thinking, but the precise nature of the relationship between economic and other institutions remains a problem for sociology more generally as well as for Marxist social thought. It is also a problem that preoccupied Max Weber, as we shall see.

A final question concerning the 'base' and 'superstructure' metaphor, and historical materialism more generally, is the idea that ultimately social change is the consequence of technological change. We have already noted the argument that since technological developments are normally the result of intellectual work, the distinction between the 'material' and the 'ideal' may be hard to sustain. It has also been objected that, historically speaking, many of the social institutions and cultural developments which Marxists have seen as consequences of capitalist industrialisation were in fact evident prior to it. MacFarlane's (1978, 1986) influential analysis of parish records, for example, shows, contrary to some established beliefs about feudal society, that not only were 'modern' patterns of marriage and kinship much in evidence by the thirteenth century, but even at this time there was a widespread market in land.

The implication here is that the individualistic, economically rational orientations which are held to have been the result of competitive capitalism, and the antithesis of feudal life, were well established some time *before* the 'industrial revolution'. As we shall see, Max Weber viewed the transformation of religious ideas in Europe from the sixteenth century not as a consequence of economic change, but as a coincident factor which had a significant part to play in allowing the development of capitalistic economic activities. Others have suggested that, far from industrialisation being the driving force propelling capitalism forward, capitalist institutions were well developed before the industrialisation of production. Braudel, for example, concludes his massive study of everyday life in fifteenth- and eighteenth-century Europe by warning that it is a 'mistake' to see the development of capitalism as a series of ordered stages – mercantile, industrial, financial, and so on – with 'true' capitalism emerging 'only at the late stage when it took over production': 'The whole panoply of forms of capitalism – commercial, industrial, banking – was already deployed in thirteenth-century Florence, in seventeenth-century Amsterdam, in London before the eighteenth century' (Braudel, 1984: 621).

Moreover, when, as a result of increased competition, the first great profits 'boom' attributable to industrial production came to an end in the early nineteenth century, there was a 'return' of the finance capitalism which had characterised earlier periods with market speculation, trading, colonial exploitation and so on (ibid.). From this perspective, the connection between capitalism and industrialism is a great deal more complex than Marx's historical materialism allows. The relationship is even more uncertain if we accept the arguments of economic historians that during the first great phase of the 'industrial revolution' the rate of technological change was in fact quite low.

In general, what emerges from these debates is the conclusion that the capitalist was around before the steam mill, and that the social relations of capitalist society may well have developed prior to the transformation of the 'mode of production'. It may be that as a theory of history which sees technological change, expressed as class struggle, as the ultimate source of social change, historical materialism is 'unsustainable' (Kolakowski, 1978: 369), though most Marxists would reject this. None the less, as we know from our ordinary experience, it is not unreasonable to hold that the patterns of social life are shaped in some fundamental ways by the mode of production and technological change. The sociological problem is how to specify the connections. This is a theme which is also, of course, of considerable concern for Durkheim and Weber.

Historical change as a dialectical process

The dialectical method was one of the elements of Hegel's thought which remained central in Marx's work. History is seen as a dialectical process in which humanity is first subject to the power of nature, then struggles to overcome it, and finally achieves liberation by gaining control over nature. Within each of these stages, there is conflict between opposing classes and through this a transcendence to the next stage. Not surprisingly, one of the main objections is that this dialectical pattern does not fit the historical record: history cannot be reduced to a pattern of contrasting stages. Moreover, there are scholars, again Weber is one of these, who reject the idea that history reveals any pattern at all, progressive or otherwise.

Other critics see Marx's, and particularly Engels', account of history as involving a deterministic view of social change in which the major events, and the path of history itself, are determined by economic forces. There are, as we have seen, Marx's own references to the 'inexorability of a law of Nature' in his discussion of social development. Such a view, it is claimed, is a denial of free will, just as the materialist account of human consciousness denies the autonomy of the mind. On the other hand, many Marxists deny that historical materialism has such an implication and claim textual support in Marx and Engels' writings.

The significance of the role of revolution in social change has also been disputed. As we have pointed out, the notion that a total transformation of society will bring about a transcendent era of human liberation derives from the dialectical account of history. But why should history reach an ultimate stage, and why should it have a happy ending? There can be little doubt of the appeal of such a vision to oppressed and impoverished people in much the same way that religions have so appealed by promising redemption in the next world, liberation at the millennium and so on. But it has been suggested that this belief in the inevitability of revolution is more of an article of faith than a rigorous implication of the theory (Kolakowski, 1978: 373). Marx and Engels were, moreover, vague about just when and how a revolution would occur; certainly their early belief that it was imminent faded in later years. Showing that capitalism is an inherently unstable economic system does not entail that its collapse is inevitable or that such a collapse would lead to the establishment of a communist society.

But even if the inevitability of capitalism's collapse is granted, it is not clear what kind of society would succeed it. Marx's vision of communist society was not that of a bureaucratic state controlled by a single party: on the contrary, he envisaged a reconciliation of the individual and the communal interest, and the kind of free existence where people, largely freed from the drudgery of work, would be able to express their own authentic selves. Critics have, however, regarded this picture as just as utopian as those of the socialist thinkers whom Marx bitterly attacked. Others have questioned the practicality of a society in which the division of labour has ceased, the state has 'withered away' and private property has been eliminated. How would production and distribution be carried out? How would such a society be organised? Who could ensure that the principle 'from each according to his ability, to each according to his needs' was actually adhered to? For Marx, all these things would come about with the cessation of human alienation; a notion which derives from a prior philosophical commitment rather than an empirical analysis.

Capitalist society

During the winter of 1857–8, in London, Marx produced an outline of his projected critique of political economy, the *Grundrisse*. Although not written for publication, it is an important document providing not only a link between the more philosophical concerns of his early work and the economic ones of the later, but also a plan of Marx's intended *magnum opus*. The introduction to the *Grundrisse* contains some of Marx's most sociologically significant writing as he forcefully contrasts his own approach with that of the orthodox political economists. He begins by emphasising the *social* nature of all production and, in doing so, attacks the political economists for taking for granted such basic concepts as that of the independent, individual worker. This is a theoretical fiction as well as an historical impossibility. Other concepts, such as capital, private property, wage labour, prices, exchange, and so on, are neither objective nor universal but relate only to a particular mode of production, namely, capitalism. All such 'abstract categories', Marx concludes, despite their apparent generality, must be understood as 'a product of historic relations, and possess their full validity only for and within these relations' (1973: 105).

The ideas of the political economists were products of a particular time and place, and a specific form of society, namely, capitalist. By the 1850s, it is clear that the nature of Marx's interest in capitalism had changed. The early concern with alienation and its consequences had given way to an increasing preoccupation with exploitation, though, as we have seen, there is some debate about the significance of this shift. For Marx the fundamental feature of a capitalist economy is that it involves the production and exchange of *commodities*; that is, goods are produced so that they can be sold on the market. The measure of their value is money: commodities of equivalent value can be sold for equal amounts of money, their exchange value. It is exchange value which distinguishes commodities under capitalism from the kind of useful objects produced in other societies. Exchange value presupposes certain sets of social relationships, such as organised production, markets and so on. In capitalism, considerations of exchange value will come to outweigh those of use value, as production is dictated by the demands of the market, rather than what people actually need or want.

The theory of surplus value and exploitation   What determines the exchange value of objects on the market? As we have seen, in general Marx accepts the solution of the political economists of his day: the source of the value of a commodity is the amount of human labour that is required for its production. This presupposes a set of social relationships through which production can take place and, once again, Marx detects in capitalist production a tendency for the real relations between people and things to become reversed: 'the social character of men's labour appears to them as an objective character stamped upon the product of that labour' (1954: 77). Although it seems that commodity prices express their intrinsic values, in fact their value reflects the social relations of production. It is for this reason that Marx speaks of the 'mysterious' and 'mystical' qualities of objects once they become commodities; 'a definite social relation between men . . . assumes . . . the fantastic form of a relation between things' (ibid.: 76–7). The situation is analogous, Marx continues, with the world of religion in which the creations of the human mind become treated as living, independent beings which must be obeyed. There is, in fact, a parallel here between his early ideas about alienation, formulated in response to Feuerbach's critique of religion, and his discussion, at the very start of *Capital*, of the 'fetishism of commodities' (ibid.: 77). Once commodity production is established, people 'consent to be enslaved by human power instead of wielding it' (Kolakowski, 1978: 277). The market is allowed to dictate what, when and how things get produced, and rational human activity comes to be defined in terms of obedience to market forces. By allowing such forces to operate unhindered, human beings surrender control of their lives and societies.

In capitalist production, then, the source of the value of commodities is the 'socially necessary' labour which they embody even though it *appears* to be intrinsic and independent of human activity. Further consequences follow once it is realised that labour itself has become a commodity. As with all commodities, there is a market in labour in which the demands of the capitalists are met by the supply of the workers. The price of labour is the wages paid by the former to the latter in return for specified services. For the orthodox political economists, the wage-bargain is a market transaction like any other, in which case, if what the capitalist buys and what the worker provides are of equal value, what is the source of profit? It is here that Marx departs from the political economists, arguing that the 'use value' of labour, its particular and specific property, is its capacity to produce new value to add to the value of the raw materials through the production process (Mandel, 1983: 191). But the exchange value of labour, like that of all commodities, reflects the cost of the socially necessary labour taken to produce and reproduce it. Workers must be born, raised, fed and clothed, housed, educated and so on before their labour can be of any value to the capitalist. All this is paid for out of the wages received by the worker. However, and this is perhaps the crux of Marx's economic theory, the 'use value' of labour, its capacity to add value in the production process, is typically greater than its exchange value as represented by its price, or wage. There is a difference, then, between the cost of hiring workers and the value of what they produce. Marx calls this difference the *surplus value* and points out that it is *all* appropriated by the capitalist, since whatever is produced becomes the private property of the capitalist.

Through the theory of surplus value Marx believed that he had identified the source of profit in capitalist production. Clearly, surplus value is not the same as profit, since the goods produced must be sold on the market, with inevitable costs of distribution, advertising, administration, and so on. Moreover, the goods may not fetch the desired price, or remain unsold. Nevertheless, in general products will yield a profit on the market which is taken by the capitalist. Just as in his earliest writings, Marx assigns a special place to human labour in the theory. Now, however, his principal objection to capitalist production is not only that people are dehumanised, but that the relationship between capitalist and worker is *inherently* exploitative, since the surplus value created by the labour of the proletariat becomes the property of the capitalist. The political implications are summed up in Proudhon's slogan 'property is theft'.

In capitalism, exploitation is, therefore, seen as an inherent element in any wage-bargain, irrespective of the actual level of the wage or salary in question. So the theory does not simply suggest that exploitation is a matter of the capitalist keeping the workers in poverty, though this may well occur. The point is that even highly paid managers and professionals are, from this point of view, being exploited because they are paid less than the value of their labour. Furthermore, the wage-bargain is not a contract freely entered into. Quite simply, workers whose only property is their labour power must sell it to the capitalist or face starvation. The basis of economic life, and hence of social organisation, is not free choice but, though often covert, coercion and alienation.

The hidden dynamic of the structure of capitalism   Inevitably Marx's model of the economic basis of capitalist society has attracted much criticism. His techniques of analysis are widely regarded by more recent economists as outmoded and suspect. The distinction between use value and exchange value, for example, is hard to maintain in practice. It rests, like the labour theory of value, on a presumption that things have a real or essential value. Just because two commodities have the same market value, it does not follow that they share some common quality of which that value is an expression. It simply means that under certain particular social conditions people are prepared to exchange them for equivalent amounts of money. Kolakowski, for example, suggests that the very idea of 'real value' is an echo of medieval thought, and metaphysical in the sense that 'it claims to reveal the "essence" hidden beneath surface phenomena, but provides no way of confirming or refuting what it says' (1978: 327).

Others, however, have been attracted by Marx's distinction between the *appearance* of capitalist society, as depicted by bourgeois economists and political philosophers, as a society of free and fair exchange, individual liberty and human fulfilment, and the *reality* as revealed by his analysis which strips off capitalism's 'mystical veil' to reveal exploitation, coercion and dehumanisation (Marx, 1954: 84). If things were as they appeared to be, Marx remarks elsewhere, there would be no need for science to discover the truth: it would just be apparent to us. So it is with human society. The implication, which has been highly influential in twentieth-century social thought, is that in order to understand the workings of society we must go beyond immediate experience and seek the real, underlying structures and processes which determine its appearance and form. As Godelier has put it: 'For Marx, the scientific understanding of the capitalist system consists in the discovery of the internal structure hidden behind its visible functioning' (1978: 78).

The best and most important example of this contrast between appearance and reality is the wage-bargain through which capitalist employers pay for the workers' labour. As we have seen, the appearance – taken for granted by the bourgeois economists – is of a fair exchange, with each class taking, in the form of profits or wages, what it is entitled to. For Marx, of course, the reality is quite different. The social relations of production involve the systematic exploitation of the workers by the capitalists through the appropriation of 'surplus value'. The concepts of the orthodox political economists are shown to be mystifications obscuring the real social relations, and ideological in that they serve to sustain the interests of the dominant class.

The idea that there is a hidden, inner logic or underlying structure to social life has given rise to a whole school of social thought. 'When Marx assumes that structure is not to be confused with visible relations and explains their inner logic, he inaugurates the modern structuralist tradition' (Godelier, 1978: 80). The first major manifestation of this tradition, and still one of the most influential, was Ferdinand de Saussure's study of language, published in 1916. From linguistics, structuralist ideas spread gradually, though persistently, to anthropology, literary theory and cultural studies, and among Marxist scholars there was a significant revival of structuralist thought in the work of the French philosopher Louis Althusser during the 1970s. As mentioned earlier, Althusser insisted that there was a clear division, an 'epistemological break', between the work of the earlier and of the later Marx; the first humanistic and speculative, the second properly scientific. It was in this second, mature phase, Althusser believed, that Marx began to develop the principles of the scientific analysis of society, or 'social formations'. These principles involved the identification and examination of the deep structures which are held to govern the formation of patterns of social life. Thus, for Althusser and the structuralists, the reality which is the object of study of the social scientist is not human beings and their familiar everyday world, but rather the underlying, hidden structures which produce the familiar world of appearances.

A number of major theoretical consequences follow from this. First, emphasis is firmly placed on the notion of society as a totality, a complex of interrelated parts, the form of which is determined through their interaction with each other. Second, scientific interest is directed at the whole, and at the structures that generate it, rather than individual human beings. Indeed, the individual 'subject' of Western social, political and philosophical thought is seen as the consequence of rather than a cause of 'social formations'. As social beings, we are the products of social formations. Third, in Althusser's formulation of structuralism our actions and thoughts are determined by those underlying structures of social life.

Althusser's idea of the social totality, however, moves significantly away from that of Hegel, who saw social wholes as the expressions of an essence. For Althusser, there is no single core, and he rejects those readings of Marx which give ultimate priority to the 'base' over the 'superstructure' in giving precedence to economic factors in the explanation of social life. Rather, Althusser's view of society is a conception of the 'totality' as a multi-layered complex of structures, which may well not be consistent with each other, in which the form of each is affected by the action of all the others, or, to use a term which Althusser borrowed from psychoanalytic theory, 'over-determined'. The social formation is, then, 'decentred'.

However, at any particular time there will be a 'structure in dominance', and in modern capitalist societies the most effective structures are the economy and the state. The state controls by means of a 'repressive state apparatus', such as the army, the police and the courts, and an 'ideological state apparatus', in particular the church, the family and, above all, the educational system, which does not simply transmit knowledge but does so in a way which 'ensures subjection to the ruling ideology or the mastery of its "practice"' (Althusser, 1971).

An example of the kind of analysis generated by structural Marxism is provided by Nicos Poulantzas' work on the state. Opposing both the bourgeois notion that the state in capitalist society is a neutral referee ensuring fair play among competing interests, and the Marxian contention that it simply reflects the interests of the capitalist class, Poulantzas (1973) argued that the function of the state is to ensure both the political unity of capital, which is always threatened by a tendency toward fragmentation, and the corresponding disorganisation of the proletariat by counteracting the class consciousness which might occur as a result of the increasing concentration of production. To achieve this, the state must be relatively autonomous from the capitalist class. That is, in order to protect the general, long-term interests of capital, it must not be too closely linked to the immediate, short-term interests of particular individuals or groups within the class. In Poulantzas' analysis there is a distinction between the 'objective' character of the state, that is, its functioning to protect the capitalist mode of production, and its 'subjective' aspects, the particular people who operate and control the state agencies, their class origins and affiliations, and so on. In this respect, the theory is dismissive of those, such as Miliband (1969), who sought to explain the pro-capitalist nature of the state in terms of the social background of its top officials, interpersonal links between élite members and so on.

For some critics, the emphasis on structures reproduces idealism by holding that reality is ultimately to be found in intangible, invisible 'structures' to the neglect of the purposive actions of real people (Thompson, 1978: 196). Indeed, in much of this criticism there are echoes of Marx's own impatience with the Young Hegelians for their preoccupation with ideas and theories and their failure to engage with issues of the real world: 'the Althusserians' navel-gazing seldom led theory to engage with actual history, past or present. In the end, their theory of history as science produced neither' (Merquior, 1986: 155). In dismissing the actions and beliefs of real people in real societies as, at best, secondary in the analysis of social formations, the approach devalued or ignored real political struggles, conflicts and contradictions. Moreover, the emphasis on structural 'over-determinations' and the reproduction of social classes, it was argued, resulted in an essentially static model of society. It was hard to see where social change, let alone revolutionary transformation, would come from. In this respect, argued Thompson, structural Marxism had, ironically, come to resemble the functionalist sociology of the late 1950s and early 1960s, which was strongly criticised as an ideologically loaded perspective which served to justify the existing social order with all its injustices and inequalities. The source of social change, says Thompson, lies not in either self-regulating systems or 'over-determined' structures, but in the actions of real people as they pursue their interests. What the structuralists had done is reduce class, 'a self-defining historical formation, which men and women make out of their experience of struggle', to a 'static category, or an effect of an ulterior structure, of which men are not the makers but the vectors' (1978: 238).

The development of capitalism   Marx retained his firm belief in the transformation of capitalism, with class playing the major role in bringing this about. In capitalist production, he argued, the general relationship between money and commodities is reversed. In pre-capitalist production, producers would bring goods to the market, sell them for money, and then spend the money on other goods to sustain themselves and their families in a recurring circulation of commodity>money>commodity. Money does not function as capital; it is simply a means of exchanging commodities of equivalent values. In capitalism, however, the relationship is the other way around. Money is advanced by the capitalist to produce commodities which are sold at a profit to produce more money; a cycle of money>commodity->money. In the capitalist mode of production, and hence its name, money is capital since it is invested in the production process in the expectation of yielding profit, that is, increasing itself. This is the incentive and motive for the capitalist. This profit involves, as we have seen, the appropriation of surplus value; a unique consequence of the capacity of labour to produce a value greater than the cost of its own reproduction.

In the process of realising profits, however, capitalists are inevitably drawn into two fundamental conflicts. First of all, they are faced with the inevitable competition with other capitalists and, second, they are involved in an equally unavoidable conflict with workers, the providers of the labour on which they depend.

Competition among capitalists   For orthodox political economists the dynamism of capitalism was one of its strengths, ensuring that consumers could expect an increase in their standard of living through improvements and innovations. For Marx, however, the situation was much less benign. When investment in production is governed solely by the criterion of profitability, there is always the possibility that the production of certain commodities will outstrip the capacity of the market to absorb them. It is the first producer who will tend to have the advantage as far as profits are concerned, but this is only temporary. Once more competitors enter the market, the average rate of profit for the commodity concerned will tend to fall. So rather than seeing the market as an effective regulator ensuring that human needs are met, Marx viewed it as 'anarchic'. The direct link between producer and consumer is broken, with production controlled only by the search for profit. Thus, as we have seen, in a capitalist economy exchange values will drive out use values; what is produced depends simply on profitability rather than need.

The capitalist economy is also prone to overproduction. The search for profits will draw producers toward particular sectors of the economy. Given the scale and the productivity of modern enterprises, demand is soon met and, accordingly, producers must either become still more competitive or look elsewhere for their profits. In this way, according to conventional political economy, supply and demand are generally kept in equilibrium. Marx scorned this idea, viewing it as no more than a theoretical possibility which usefully legitimised the capitalist market. In real-world capitalist economies, crises of overproduction are inevitable, and an excess of supply, and the consequent collapse of profits in one sector of the economy, produces instability and loss of demand in others. The result is a general reduction in economic activity – a 'slump'. Just as with the tendency of the rate of profit to fall, the occurrence of successive crises of overproduction is not, from the Marxian viewpoint, a departure from normality or the result of the capitalist's greed or incompetence, but an inevitable result of the normal operation of the system as capitalists make rational decisions about investment for profit.

It is this relentless drive to remain competitive that sows the seeds of the system's destruction. Chief among the consequences of the declining rate of profit and the periodic crises of overproduction is the concentration of capital. From its earliest stage, when large numbers of individual entrepreneurs carried out their activities more or less independently, the logic of capitalism has been to reduce the number of individual capitalists while greatly increasing the amount of capital owned and controlled by each. The process of competition eliminates the weaker and less successful enterprises, so giving larger shares of the available market to fewer producers. The losers are reduced to the condition of propertyless proletarians with only their labour to sell, and the development of capitalism progressively eliminates the 'petit bourgeoisie' as an intermediate class between capital and labour.

Competitive capitalist production favours larger producers who can achieve economies of scale, and thus lower unit costs. The increasing scale and technical complexity of production encourages, indeed necessitates, the formation of large-scale enterprises in order to carry out 'those immense industrial undertakings which require a previous centralisation of capital for their accomplishment'. Such undertakings are only possible with the corresponding development of large-scale banking and associated financial institutions, or, as Marx referred to it, the 'credit system'. Originally formed as a means of facilitating commercial transactions, the credit system as 'the humble assistant of accumulation' soon becomes a 'new and terrible weapon in the battle of competition and is finally transformed into an enormous social mechanism for the centralisation of capitals' (Marx, 1954: 587). For Marx, competition and the credit system were 'the two most powerful levers of centralisation', that is, the 'concentration of capitals already formed, destruction of their individual independence, expropriation of capitalist by capitalist, transformation of many small into few large capitals' (ibid.: 586).

The history of modern societies demonstrates, according to Marx, that new methods of production almost invariably involve the deployment of more capital, and less labour, than old ones. Agriculture, for example, which once employed virtually the whole population, now yields vastly more with only a tiny fraction of the previous workforce. In the twentieth century, the demand even for industrial manual labour has shrunk as people are replaced by machinery. Clerical and administrative work, too, which once absorbed millions of 'office workers', is increasingly handled by computerised systems. From Marx's point of view, this is all in accordance with the rationality of capitalist production: if the cost of labour is the highest single item of expenditure, then it makes sense for a firm to replace people by machines to lower production costs. As the level of wages and salaries rises, the incentive to mechanisation and automation is greater. In the economic terms in which Marx expressed it, the process is one in which there is a relative increase in the amount of constant capital, that is, plant and machinery, employed in production, and a relative decline in the amount of variable capital, or labour, so named because it is capable of producing surplus value (ibid.: 202). That is to say, there is a change in the ratio of constant to variable capital employed in production as the former increases at the expense of the latter; a change in the 'organic composition of capital' (ibid.: 574).

The increasing ratio of constant to variable capital, widely observed as a feature of industrial capitalism, has momentous consequences, if we accept Marx's claim that human labour is the ultimate source of surplus value. If the proportion of labour, as variable capital, in production is decreasing, then so is the source of surplus value and, eventually, profit. This conclusion Marx expressed as the law of the falling rate of profit.

> Since the mass of the employed living labour is continually on the decline compared to the mass of materialised labour incorporated in productively consumed means of production, it follows that that portion of living labour, which is unpaid and represents surplus value, must also be on the decrease compared to the volume and value of the invested total capital. Seeing that the proportion of the mass of surplus-value to the value of the invested total capital forms the rate of profit, this rate must fall continuously. (1909: 249)

This is the basis for Marx's claim that capitalism, as an economic and social system, was doomed. Simply by pursuing their own interests, the capitalists would bring about its collapse.

Clearly, Marx's conclusion depends upon accepting the proposition that human labour power is ultimately the sole source of profit; a proposition which, as we have seen, a number of critics doubt. It is equally clear that Marx's apocalyptic conclusion about the final collapse of capitalism is consistent with his earlier, and more philosophical, judgement that a revolutionary transformation would inevitably bring an end to human alienation and usher in a new, and final, era of human liberation. Despite the considerable differences between the earlier, more philosophical analyses and the later, economic phase of Marx's work, both point to the collapse of capitalism through revolution and the establishment of a new social order. To Marx and Engels, it may have seemed that this co-incidence of their critical philosophy and their economic science could only strengthen their case: for many, it is this promise of social transformation which has given Marxism such a powerful appeal as a political ideology and crusade.

Certainly, it would be hard to find a more influential doctrine in the twentieth century than Marx's account of how the demise of capitalism would come about. It is an account which, in broad terms, outlines the main forces which, he believed, would shape the development of entire societies. As such, it is hardly surprising that it is mistaken in some respects and inadequate in others. What is impressive, however, is how clearly he grasped, even at a comparatively early stage in the development of modern capitalism, the fundamental forces it would generate. More than a century after his death, his ideas still provide a framework for the analysis of both modern and modernising societies.

Changes in the nature of capitalism

Not surprisingly, Marx's conclusion about the inevitable self-destruction of capitalism has been disputed. Few, however, doubt the tendency towards the concentration of capital in ever larger enterprises controlled by an ever smaller number of huge business corporations and financial institutions. These ideas were significantly developed by the Austrian economist Rudolf Hilferding in his book *Finance Capital* (1910), in which he argued that the banks and finance houses, once the servants of industrial production, had now become their masters. This suggested the emergence of a new phase in the development of capitalism, in which banks and financial institutions rather than manufacturing entrepreneurs had come to dominate economic life. Through their involvement with financing commerce, they could generate vast profits and make significant investment decisions. Moreover, with the development of joint-stock companies in the latter part of the nineteenth century, banking and financial institutions came to be increasingly represented on the boards of industrial companies.

The influence of Hilferding is apparent in Lenin's influential book *Imperialism: The Highest Stage of Capitalism* (1916), in which he argued that finance capitalists had replaced entrepreneurs at the heart of the capitalist class, and that competition was giving way to monopoly as the inevitable consequence of centralisation. Moreover, and as Marx envisaged, capitalist exploitation had now become global in scale as the leading capitalist states, increasingly militarised, sought to secure by conquest new territories as sources of raw materials and labour. Such themes have been echoed in much of Marxist thought during this century. Indeed, in some accounts, the original emphasis on the exploitation of the proletariat by the bourgeoisie has given way to a primary focus on the conflict between the few rich nations of the developed world and the mass of the world's population in the impoverished countries of the 'Third World'.

Subsequently considerable attention has been paid to the nature and consequences of the development of 'finance capital' as, first, family businesses gave way to joint-stock companies in the leading sectors of the economy and, second, the latter were themselves swallowed up by national and multinational corporations. Some authors have argued that the character of capitalism was radically changed by the decline of individual entrepreneurs who owned and controlled their own firms, and the rise of salaried managers who exercised control on behalf of an often anonymous group of shareholders. Whereas the former were primarily interested in the maximisation of short-term profitability, the latter saw the long-term prosperity of the firm as more important in securing their own careers and prosperity. The effects of this 'managerial revolution' were considered by Burnham (1941), who originally coined the phrase, and by Berle and Means (1991). Others, however, have argued that the 'separation of ownership and control' has involved no fundamental change in the operation of capitalist economies. Managers, after all, are accountable to boards of directors who are legally required to pursue the best interests of the shareholders, and such boards often include directors placed there by banking and financial interests whose major concern is to secure a maximum rate of return on capital invested. In short, and consistent with Marx's basic argument, both independent entrepreneurs and salaried managers are subject, directly or indirectly, to the disciplines of the market. From this point of view, it is misguided, or at least premature, to conclude that the 'managerial revolution' has ushered in a post-capitalist era.

There is more agreement among Marxist and non-Marxist theorists that the centralisation of capital has led to a decline in competition. For Baran and Sweezy (1968), for example, the salient characteristic of modern capitalism is the tendency towards monopoly, that is, a few very large enterprises effectively dominating whole sectors of economic production, progressively eliminating small firms and preventing new competitors from getting a foothold in the market.

> Today, the typical economic unit in the capitalist world is not the small firm producing a negligible fraction of a homogeneous output for an anonymous market but a large-scale enterprise producing a significant share of the output of an industry, or even several industries, and able to control its prices, the volume of its production, and the types and amounts of its investments. The typical economic unit, in other words, has the attributes which were once thought to be possessed only by monopolies. (ibid.: 19)

If huge corporations can eliminate competition, they are also freed from the disciplines of the market and can, as Baran and Sweezy suggest, set their own price levels. The implications for orthodox Marxian theory are clear: if large corporations can effectively set their own prices, they can extract ever higher profits and the 'law' of the declining rate of profit begins to look suspect. In a situation where only a few large enterprises provide goods and services, the competitive pressures which Marx regarded as relentlessly driving profit margins down no longer have this effect. The 'price war' is replaced by 'tacit collusion' in which the large corporations agree to set price levels. Thus, it becomes 'relatively easy for the group as a whole to feel its way toward the price which maximises the industry's profit'. If this occurs, 'we can safely assume that the price established at any time is a reasonable approximation to the theoretical monopoly price' (ibid.: 71). Although strictly speaking the situation is one of oligopoly, that is, a situation in which there are a few large players rather than a single monopolistic one, Baran and Sweezy's conclusion is that the result is the same. Marx's arguments about the declining rate of profit are not so much mistaken as outmoded, since the competitive market economy on which it was based has been replaced by monopoly capitalism (ibid.: 80–1).

For Baran and Sweezy, and some more recent authors, capitalism has entered a new phase in which gigantic, often multinational, corporations dominate whole sectors of the economy and are no longer responsive to the disciplines of the market. The economist J.K. Galbraith, for example, has described the 'new industrial state' in which the technical and administrative complexity of production, its sheer scale and the vast amounts of capital required to finance it mean that large corporations can no longer take the risks involved in producing for markets, and so use all available means to remove such uncertainties. His thesis, in brief, is that planning replaces the market (Galbraith, 1967: 26). Indeed, some projects are so large that they must be financed or guaranteed by states rather than by individual corporations. This is particularly the case in respect of military production, where national governments are the only customers. Others have followed the lead of C. Wright Mills (1956: 224) in viewing modern industrial economies as dominated not by a market but by a 'power élite' based on the tightly interlocking relationships between industrial corporations, the military and the state bureaucracies.

It has also been suggested that the state itself has changed in modern capitalist societies, and it is no longer, if it ever was, the neutral referee of liberal theory, guaranteeing the free operation of the market. Nor is it simply the partisan committee for managing the affairs of the bourgeoisie that Marx depicted. States have become by far the most important actors on the economic stage as significant producers in their own right, often the largest providers of services, and the largest employers and consumers. In these circumstances, the state's combination of political and economic power may be sufficient to outweigh market forces, replacing decisions about the investment of capital by bureaucratic planning.

In democratic countries, such planning is, in theory, controlled by politicians responsive to the electorate. However, it has been argued that in practice the scale and complexity of these processes means that effective power is increasingly concentrated in the hands of state officials who are closely linked to the senior managers of large corporations. In Britain, for example, Scott has argued that the power of the traditional and informal 'establishment' – the economic, political and cultural élite which coalesced with the rise of Britain as a capitalist power – has been supplanted by a more formal and more formidable combination of interests. In the 1970s formal bodies facilitated regular consultation and negotiation among industrial leaders, financial institutions, government departments and, to an extent and variously, trade unions (Scott, 1991: 148). This 'corporatism' seemed to many Marxists only to confirm their view of the extent to which the state and monopoly capitalism are now inextricably linked. Corporatism was also denounced by the radical right, precisely because it represented the elimination of market forces (Friedman, 1962; Hayek, 1949). The Thatcher governments in Britain during the 1980s, for example, declared their intention to 'roll back the frontiers of the state'. However, efforts to reduce the state's role in the economy produced relatively modest results. For some this is evidence of the extent to which the corporatist state has become the political expression of monopoly capitalism.

A great deal has been written about the transition from competitive to monopoly capitalism and the rise of the corporatist state. For present purposes, however, we wish to emphasise the implications of these developments for Marx's account of the development of capitalism. As we have seen, it was fundamental to his economic analysis that enforced competition among capitalists would, ultimately, lead to a decline in the rate of profit and, finally, to the collapse of capitalism. If, on the other hand, the claim is correct that market-oriented competition has been replaced by monopoly capitalism, and if the institutions of the corporatist state have developed as a consequence, then the process depicted by Marx will no longer be as effective. In this case, far from being doomed by its inherent contradictions, the capitalist system might well be self-sustaining. This is a point to which we will return.

The conflict between capital and labour

We now want to turn to one of the other processes which Marx argued would bring about the collapse of the capitalist system, namely, the fundamental conflict between capital and labour.

Consistent with his method of analysis, Marx held that the development of the conflict between capital and labour was the outcome of underlying economic processes. In the process of realising profits, capitalists must resist the claims of workers for higher wages, for the higher the wage bill, the less the surplus value that will be created, and the lower the eventual profit. To this end, capitalists will seek to maintain a 'reserve army of labour', as Marx put it, of unemployed people whose availability for work will act to restrict wage demands. This 'reserve army' is likely to increase as production becomes more mechanised. In general, firms will always seek new sources of cheaper labour, to the extent of encouraging immigration and 'guest workers' who will take low-paid jobs, or relocating production to regions or countries where wage rates are low. Such processes have been much in evidence since the 1950s' with the increasing 'globalization' ofcapital. The essential point at present, however, is that in Marx's view there is an inherent conflict of interest between workers and capitalists arising from the exploitation of the former by the latter.

It was also part of Marx's argument that the very conditions of capitalist industrial production would transform an unorganised mass of propertyless labourers into a politically conscious class which would eventually rise up and overthrow its bourgeois oppressors. These conditions included increasing urbanisation which crowded workers together in huge cities, and the increasing scale of factory production. Both processes served to make the workers more aware of the collective nature of their oppression and exploitation. In *The Communist Manifesto*, Marx and Engels had written of the way in which 'collisions between individual workmen and individual bourgeois take more and more the character of collisions between two classes' (1848: 228). Gradually, the workers organise themselves to resist the capitalists by forming trade unions, using the instabilities of the system as a lever to win some political and economic advances and, in so doing, begin to develop a revolutionary consciousness. During times of economic 'boom', for example, when labour is scarce, the workers may achieve better conditions. Such successes will, however, be only temporary for the inherent tendency of capitalism is to reduce the mass of workers to poverty. The real benefit of such struggles is only apparent in the longer term, namely, as the 'ever-expanding union of workers', itself facilitated by advances in communications, and leading to the emergence of an organised, politically experienced working class, fully prepared to assert itself 'when the class struggle nears the decisive hour' (ibid.: 229).

By pursuing its own interests, as it is forced to do by the logic of its economic situation, the bourgeoisie will inevitably bring into being the class which is destined to bring about its downfall, and the final liberation of humanity from domination by private property. 'All previous historical movements', wrote Marx and Engels, 'were movements of minorities, or in the interests of minorities. The proletarian movement is the self-conscious, independent movement of the immense majority, in the interests of the immense majority' (ibid.: 230). The logic of capitalist development, then, results in the 'polarisation' of society into two opposed classes. The remnants of the old feudal order, such as peasants, craftsmen, small tradesmen, and so on, are forced into the ranks of the proletariat, as are the artisans, self-employed and the proprietors of small businesses who might have flourished in the early days of capitalism. With the rise of large-scale production such persons cannot compete. Their response is to cling to conservative political ideas as they try to 'roll back the wheel of history'. However, the vast majority are doomed, like their feudal predecessors, to be reduced to the ranks of the propertyless.

From an historical point of view, of course, their fate is only temporary since the ultimate victory of the proletariat is 'inevitable'. It is important to note, however, that Marx and Engels stipulated two conditions necessary for the development of a revolutionary situation: first, the development of class consciousness among the proletariat, that is, an awareness of collective oppression and a realisation that all workers have common political interests which override individual, sectional and local ones; second, the fullest development of the capitalist forces of production. As Marx wrote later: 'No social order ever perishes before all the productive forces for which it is broadly sufficient have developed' (1859: 4).

The problem of class consciousness

Inherent in Marx's thesis is the idea that there is a 'growing polarisation of society between a declining number of buyers of labour power and a constantly growing number of sellers' (Mandel, 1983: 199–200), and that this *economic* relationship will lead to the formation of *social* classes and, further, a revolutionary class consciousness among the proletariat. However, it was argued as long ago as 1899 by Eduard Bernstein that, rather than disappearing, the middle class, intermediate between capitalist and workers, was in fact expanding in advanced capitalist countries.

The rise of the 'new' middle class has been a preoccupation of Marxists and their critics ever since. It is clear, however, that Marx himself did not subscribe to any simple version of the 'polarisation thesis'. As we indicated earlier, in a now famous passage at the very end of the third volume of *Capital*, he refers to the 'middle and transition stages' which obliterate definite class boundaries, although adding, significantly, that 'this is immaterial for our analysis' (1909: 1031). Elsewhere in the same volume, and in *Theories of Surplus Value*, there are passages which make it clear that 'Marx was aware that the "middle classes" would increase in size, both absolutely and relatively' (Abercrombie and Urry, 1983: 50). The ever increasing size and complexity of industrial production necessitated the employment of greater numbers of administrative and managerial staff whose work did not conform easily to the image of the unskilled proletarian manual worker. Marx was much too shrewd an analyst to have missed these developments which have continued apace as the numbers of managers, administrators, scientists, teachers, technicians and professionals of all kinds has expanded to the point where manual workers are now in a minority in advanced industrial countries. It has been argued, accordingly, that instead of polarisation, increasing industrialism has entailed a convergence around the *middle* of the class structure. Moreover, the expansion of the non-manual sector of the labour force, it is suggested, has produced a sizeable proportion of the population who, although employees dependent on selling their labour, are relatively affluent and secure in their work, and who have both formal qualifications and skill. Such groups are unlikely to develop a common class consciousness with the proletariat; on the contrary, the evidence suggests that the middle classes are likely to support right-wing or centrist political parties. In which case, the economic development of capitalism has produced not an inexorable march toward class polarisation and revolution, but a relatively stable social structure.

Marxist theorists have, in various ways, tried to reconcile Marx's ideas with the evident failure of a class-conscious proletariat to emerge in modern Western economies. For a time it was argued, following some remarks of Engels, that most workers live in a state of 'false consciousness' in which alternative, erroneous beliefs prevent them from realising the true nature of their exploitation. Later work has sought to understand the relationship between social position, belief and action in more sophisticated ways. In this respect much attention has been given to the ideas of the Italian scholar, Antonio Gramsci (1891–1937).

Gramsci was imprisoned by Mussolini's regime in 1926, and between 1929 and 1935, while still in prison, he produced a series of notebooks which, on their posthumous publication, did much to reorient Marxist thought on the nature of advanced capitalism. For Gramsci such societies could not be understood simply in terms of a small capitalist class subduing a hostile proletariat by sheer economic power or physical coercion. On the contrary, it seemed that the dominant class ruled by the consent of the majority. Their rule needs to be understood as *hegemony*, that is, and in simple terms, a combination of power plus the organisation of consent. While the capitalist state enacts and enforces the law which upholds the social order, and can use physical force if necessary, for most of the time this exercise of power is unnecessary because people have been led to accept the prevailing ideas, values and beliefs which include, above all, beliefs about the rightness of the prevailing social order. The implication is that the dominance of a ruling class derives not only from its control of material production but also, and crucially, from its ability to control *cultural* production, so echoing Marx and Engel's claim that the 'ideas of the ruling class are in every epoch the ruling ideas' (1974: 64).

Gramsci's ideas also anticipate some of the ideas of the Critical Theorists of the Frankfurt School and their claim that the 'culture industry' turns workers into docile and pliable consumers. Althusser drew on Gramsci in his analysis of the role of 'ideological state apparatuses', particularly educational institutions, in ensuring the conformity and quiescence of the working class. Gramsci's ideas have also had an influence beyond the small circle of Marxist theorists in providing a stimulus for much sociological research in the field of culture, broadly defined, and focusing on institutions and practices not normally considered specifically economic or political. 'Privately owned television stations, the family, the boy scout movement, the Methodist Church, infant schools, the British Legion, the *Sun* newspaper; all of these would count as hegemonic apparatuses which bind individuals to the ruling power by consent rather than coercion' (Eagleton, 1991: 113–14). The general idea is that our taken-for-granted ideas and beliefs are permeated by notions which implicitly give sanction to the existing social order. It follows that to challenge and change that order would involve more than bringing about changes at the level of material production. 'What must also be contested', writes Eagleton, 'is the whole area of "culture", defined in its broadest, most everyday sense' (ibid.: 114). In recent years such ideas have been influential in stimulating a range of sociological investigations into the impact of mass culture on working-class lives, lives that are not necessarily poverty-stricken. For Marxists, of course, the question has remained as to 'how the working class might retain the resistance that was at least a potential of class difference' (Nelson and Grossberg, 1988: 4). Thus, for example, rock and roll music has been interpreted as inherently oppositional, with a capacity to expose the 'alienation' of contemporary everyday life (Bradley, 1992: 174), and, more generally, working-class youth cultures have been seen as organised around 'resistance through rituals' (Hall and Jefferson, 1976).

Other studies of the mass media have argued that they present people with a selective image of reality which has the effect of legitimating the political and economic status quo. Analyses of television news, for example, have emphasised the ways in which the production of 'news' marginalises and excludes ideas and issues which might challenge the dominant ideology (Glasgow University Media Group, 1980). During the 1980s there was a notable increase in the attention paid to the cultural, as opposed to the economic, aspects of Marxian thought. The most general effect of the renewed interest in Gramsci's work was the abandonment of the assumptions, first, that cultural practices and forms are always to be regarded as dependent on or secondary to basic economic processes, and, second, that beliefs and values can ultimately be reduced to class interests. This focus on 'ideological struggle', or the politics of meaning, has inspired work in the field of cultural studies which examines, on the one hand, the ways in which dominant institutions, aided by the mass media, attempt to organise the consent of the masses and, on the other hand, ways in which aspects of 'popular' culture express resistance to the dominant symbolic forms.

We have been considering some central aspects of Marx's argument that the inherent economic logic of capitalism would lead towards disintegration and collapse, and that the social consequences of this process would bring about the formation of a revolutionary working class. These developments need not be regarded as automatic. On the contrary, Marx's analysis remains consistent with the principle he and Engels laid down in *The German Ideology*, namely, that the process of history is nothing more nor less than the actions of real people in pursuit of their interests. What his analysis identifies are the conditions which, he believed, would lead rational people to behave in ways that would lead to the collapse of the system. Even capitalists, who have most to lose, are forced into competition with their fellows, a process which, according to Marx, would in the long run lead to their eventual ruin. Workers, too, are compelled by their impoverished conditions to enter into conflict with their capitalist employers and, thus, initiate the process which leads to the emergence of a revolutionary proletariat.

It is possible, however, that capitalism does not engender these conditions; that competitive capitalism has been replaced by monopoly capitalism; that instead of an angry and hungry proletariat, there is an acquiescent middle class and a mass culture which inculcates consumerism and sells escapist fantasies. Certainly, more than a century after Marx's death, capitalism seems more securely established than even in his time. Though aware of developments such as the ideological power of the ruling class, and the rise of the new middle class, Marx never lost his conviction that capitalism would eventually collapse through the pressure of its own internal contradictions. In a passage in Volume 1 of *Capital*, he outlined these processes in terms similar to those of *The German Ideology* and *The Communist Manifesto* written two decades earlier:

> That which is now to be expropriated is no longer the labourer working for himself, but the capitalist exploiting many labourers. This expropriation is accomplished by the action of the immanent laws of capitalist production itself, by the centralisation of capital. One capitalist always kills many. Hand in hand with this centralisation, or this expropriation of many capitalists by few, develop, on an ever-expanding scale, the co-operative form of the labour process, the conscious technical application of science, the methodical cultivation of the soil, the transformation of the instruments of labour into instruments of labour only usable in common, the economising of all means of production by their use as the means of production of combined, socialised, labour, the entanglement of all peoples in the net of the world market, and with this, the international character of the capitalist regime. Along with the constantly diminishing number of the magnates of capital, who usurp and monopolise all advantages of this process of transformation, grows the mass of misery, oppression, slavery, degradation, exploitation; but with this too grows the revolt of the working class, a class always increasing in numbers, and disciplined, united, organised by the very mechanism of the process of capitalist production itself. The monopoly of capital becomes a fetter in the mode of production, which has sprung up and flourished along with it, and under it. Centralisation of the means of production and socialisation of labour at last reach a point where they become incompatible with their capitalist integument. This integument is burst asunder. The knell of capitalist private property sounds. The expropriators are expropriated. (Marx, 1954: 714–15)

Conclusion: Marx's legacy

Marx died in London on 14 March 1883. He had been in poor health for some time and his energies ebbed away following the death of his wife, Jenny, in 1881. The subsequent death of his first daughter, also named Jenny, in January 1883, aged 38, was a blow from which he never recovered. While these sorrows and some disillusionment marked his last years, he retained his belief in the inevitability of revolution and his commitment to its cause. In the years that followed Marx's death, until his own death in 1895, Engels was energetic in editing Marx's papers for publication and in responding to the enormous wave of interest in Marx's ideas which developed with the growth of the socialist movements at the end of the nineteenth century. There are those, as we have seen, who believe that the version of Marxism which flowed from Engels' pen was considerably at variance with Marx's ideas. What is not in dispute is that in the years after his death Marx became much more famous than he had ever been in his lifetime.

Whether or not it is accepted that there were fundamental differences between Marx and Engels' interpretation, and most recent commentators have been dubious about this, any general assessment of Marxist ideas must take account of the fact that during the period when these were first popularised much of the writing which is now considered central to Marx's theories was either undiscovered or unpublished. This is important, as we have already noted, because the relatively simple form of historical materialism which came to be regarded as fundamental to Marx's thought is not easily reconciled with the more sophisticated and certainly less materialistic arguments of the *Paris Manuscripts* or *The German Ideology*. Neither of these was published until well into the twentieth century. Moreover, there seems little doubt that, as Rigby (1992: 8) argues, the vast writings of both Marx and Engels contain enough inconsistencies and contradictions to support a whole range of interpretations. While it is no longer plausible to regard Marx as having identified the 'laws' of history, it is not particularly useful to regard Marx's ideas as simply a theory which has been falsified by subsequent events, as Dahrendorf (1959) did. In the present context, our main concern must be to identify those elements which have proved durable in the sociological analysis of modern societies.

Accordingly, it is important to emphasise Marx's view of human beings as social producers; social because there is no such thing as an isolated human being totally independent of society, and producers because human beings act to create both material and cultural objects. Without these there would be no society. Indeed, as Marx himself pointed out, what we call our consciousness is itself the result of our social being. This basic perspective has become central to modern sociological thought, and serves, in important ways, to distinguish sociology from the other human sciences, which have often presupposed an independent, pre-social individual, existing prior to social experience. Following Marx's lead, most modern sociologists accept that the acting individual must be the starting point for any understanding of social order, and also seek to show how such an individual always acts within the context of existing institutions and cultural patterns which, although they are the outcome of the actions and interactions of many people, nevertheless seem objective and immutable. As Marx put it, 'circumstances make men just as men make circumstances' (Marx and Engels, 1974: 59). In other words, it is people who make history, but they do not make it as they please.

The question of making history, however, has figured prominently in many debates about Marx's analysis of the dynamics of capitalist societies. The persistent failure of a class-conscious proletariat to appear, and the absence of signs that a revolution is imminent in advanced capitalist societies, have given rise to many attempts by Marxist authors to revise the original ideas in an effort to make them more compatible with recent historical developments. Their claim is that Marx's fundamental perspective retains its validity even though the forces of production, and capitalism generally, have developed in all kinds of unforeseen ways since Marx's time. This view had considerable influence among sociologists during the 1970s and 1980s. An important contribution then was Braverman's argument in *Labour and Monopoly Capitalism* (1974) that the labour force, in conditions of monopoly capitalism, was not, as was conventionally held, becoming increasingly skilled and differentiated. On the contrary, Braverman's contention was that economic rationalisation and the automation of production had contributed to a general deskilling, just as Marx had implied. It is true that there are more technical, scientific and engineering specialists at the heart of industrial production in advanced capitalist societies, but such groups constitute only a small percentage of the whole workforce (ibid.: 242). And while new skill requirements have emerged, many of the old ones, such as crafts of various kinds, have been virtually destroyed. Above all, the great majority of the working population, whatever their level of skill, income or lifestyle, remain employees at the mercy of the labour market and, as such, are in the 'dispossessed condition of a proletariat' (ibid.: 403).

Earlier theorists had talked of a process of 'embourgeoisement' in which working people were increasingly adopting the values and consumer lifestyles of the middle class, thus explaining the frequent failure of left-wing political parties to win majorities in Western democracies. Sociological studies, however, found little evidence of embourgeoisement and, following Braverman, it was argued that the class structure of advanced societies is undergoing a process of proletarianisation; a notion that seemed consistent with the evident effects of the 'electronic revolution' in which not only factory work, but also office and administrative work of all kinds was increasingly carried out by machines, particularly the computer. There was, it seemed, no need for the army of clerical workers which had once formed the core of the 'new' middle class. Those who remained in such jobs were reduced, just as Braverman, and earlier Marx, had predicted, to the status of 'appendages to the machine'. So not only the working class but the middle class, too, were vulnerable to the relentless processes of economic rationalisation and technological innovation.

Objectors to Marx's analysis have often pointed out that the workforce of modern capitalist economies is becoming increasingly educated, and differentiated in terms of its formal credentials. Capitalist production, it has been claimed, has produced not a mass of mindless machine-tenders but a well-educated population equipped with the knowledge and skills demanded by the increasingly sophisticated methods of production. The implication of Braverman's analysis, however, is that education in capitalist societies primarily serves as a means of social selection rather than training; a case developed in relation to American society by Bowles and Gintis in *Schooling in Capitalist America* (1976). For these scholars, as for Althusser, the main function of schools and colleges is to reproduce the existing class structure rather than to encourage a meritocratic matching of individual talents to occupational requirements. As evidence they point to the well-established and persistent finding of sociological studies that there is a strong positive correlation between students' social class background and their final level of educational attainment. This is not, they argue, a matter of schools reflecting differences in individual abilities but the result of a system which appears to be fair and equal, but which is, in practice, far from this.

Just as Braverman argued for the continuing relevance of the idea of the proletariat, others have suggested that the kind of bourgeoisie envisaged by Marx does, in fact, retain ownership and control of the dominant sectors of the economy. It is a relatively small group which, by virtue of its wealth and location at the heart of economic decision-making, exercises power and influence out of all proportion to its numbers. 'Britain', writes John Scott, 'is ruled by a capitalist class whose economic dominance is sustained by the operations of the state and whose members are disproportionately represented in the power élite which rules the state apparatus. That is to say, Britain does have a ruling class' (1991: 151; for international comparisons see Bottomore and Brym, 1989).

In the present context our purpose is not to enter into the debate about whether modern capitalist societies do or do not conform to the model outlined by Marx. Rather it is to emphasise the persistence of this framework as a basis for debate and research and, for some, as a theoretical method intended to inform praxis. It remains a vital agenda for research and theorising about the nature of contemporary societies. Both the 'embourgeoisement thesis' and the idea of 'proletarianisation', for example, with their widely differing perspectives on the nature of modern industrial societies, are nevertheless formulated in terms of Marx's ideas and concepts. Moreover, many of the developments which have often been argued as invalidating Marx's perspective – the rise of the 'new middle class', for example – are processes which may be understood through the application of his basic method, namely, seeing changes in the forces of production as producing changes in the social relations of production. In this case, briefly, the introduction of advanced technologies and larger-scale production encourages the growth of specialists and administrative staff, and a decline in the need for manual workers.

More recently, Marxist analyses, drawing on the distinction between appearance and reality, have argued that apparent differences between the middle class and the working class, such as income, attitudes and lifestyles, are essentially secondary in comparison to the fundamental fact that they are both employees of capitalists or dependent on the system for their livelihood. As Marx himself argued, the existence of 'middle classes' and 'transition stages' was 'immaterial for our analysis' since the fundamental 'tendency and law of development of capitalist production is to separate the means of production more and more from labour' (1909: 1031). This process, Marxists argue, will continue to operate despite the apparent affluence of sections of the middle class, who also are ultimately dependent on the vicissitudes of the market. Moreover, as the global economy, another development foreseen by Marx, stagnated in the early 1990s, many observers, not by any means Marxist in outlook, commented on the ways in which not only individuals and their families but also governments and whole nations were at the mercy of the international money markets and the search for profit out of currency movements. The young Marx would have described all this as the condition of alienation. It is also consistent with the older Marx's expectations about the likely centralisation of capital and the increasing power of the 'credit system'.

We have suggested that there are major fields of sociological inquiry in which Marx's ideas have stood the test of time and continue to provide a framework for research. There are, of course, various ways in which Marx's expectations have not been fulfilled by subsequent events, but even here it would be unwise simply to dismiss the body of his work. As Carver has argued, Marx's ideas, like those of Darwin, may be regarded as 'general hypotheses' rather than specific, testable propositions. They are no less scientific for that since they act as general and productive guides to research.

> These views or theories function as hypotheses in the most general sense, in that they define entities for study and suggest in general terms what relationships are *likely* to obtain between them. Whether or not such relationships exist in any particular case is precisely the point to be investigated. (Carver, 1982: 35)

Furthermore, there can be little doubt as to the range and the utility of Marx's work:

> The grand themes of modern sociology – industrialisation, urbanisation, secularisation, rationalisation, individualisation, state formation – are all addressed by Marx. . . . So is the darker face of modernity: the ephemerality and insecurity of modern life, the disintegration of community and susceptibility of society to its ideological substitutes, the anomic isolation of the rootless individual, the 'disenchantment' of the world, the iron cage of an enveloping rationality in which means usurp ends. (Sayer, 1991: 12–13)

For the sociologist what Marx provided was a coherent perspective and a powerful method of analysis which has served as a guide to significant research traditions in the discipline. It is a *model* rather than a set of falsifiable hypotheses about the empirical world and, in this respect, closely resembles that created by the classical political economists whom Marx so derided. There never was, and never will be, a society with free markets and perfect competition, populated by wholly rational individuals consciously seeking to maximise their returns. But much useful theory may be based on such a model. As we have seen, Marx rejected the economists' individualistic assumptions and replaced them with much more sociological ones and, in doing so, elaborated a body of theory which has not only shaped our understanding of capitalist societies but also confronted us with 'the darker face of modernity'.

Select bibliography and further reading

There is a vast literature on Marx and Marxism which cannot be fully represented here. What follows is a selection of accessible texts which should be of interest to the sociologically minded.

There are a number of short introductions to Marx's life and thought, including the long-established *Karl Marx: His life and environment* by Isaiah Berlin, (Oxford University Press, 1963, 3rd edn). More recent works are Peter Singer's, *Karl Marx*, (Oxford, 1980), Peter Worsley's *Marx and Marxism*, (Tavistock, 1982) and David McLellan's *The Thought of Karl Marx: An introduction* (Macmillan, 1980). Jon Elster's *An Introduction to Karl Marx* (Cambridge University Press, 1986) presents a reading of Marx influenced by 'rational-choice theory'.

Leszek Kolakowski's *Main Currents of Marxism*(3 vols, Oxford University Press, 1978) is a comprehensive account of the origins and development of Marxist thought. *Volume 1: The Founders* places the central ideas of Marx and Engels in the context of European philosophical traditions. Peter Singer's *Hegel* (Oxford University Press, 1983) is a clear introduction to the main themes in Hegel's thought, while Fred R. Dallmayr's *G.W.F. Hegel: Modernity and politics* (Sage, 1993) contains a sympathetic reading of Hegel's political philosophy. Charles Taylor's *Hegel and Modern Society* (Cambridge University Press) is also a clear introduction. Hegel's *Elements of the Philosophy of Right* (Cambridge University Press, 1991) is worth a try. Karl Popper's *The Open Society and its Enemies, Vol. II* (Routledge, 1945) is a very unsympathetic reading of Hegel and Marx. Friedrich Hayek's *Individualism and the Economic Order* (Routledge, 1949) and Milton Friedman's *Capitalism and Freedom* (University of Chicago Press, 1962) represent celebrations of the capitalist market system that Marx attacked.

Marx's social thought is also considered in Shlomo Avineri's *The Social and Political Thought of Karl Marx* (Cambridge University Press, 1968), Raymond Aron's *The Main Currents in Sociological Thought, Vol. 1* (Pelican, 1968), Terrell Carver's *Marx's Social Theory* (Oxford University Press, 1982) and Anthony Giddens' *Capitalism and Modern Social Theory* (Cambridge University Press, 1971), which also considers Durkheim and Weber. Others worth looking at include G.A. Cohen's *Karl Marx's Theory of History: A defence* (Oxford University Press, 1978) and P. Thomas' 'Critical reception: Marx then and now', in Terrell Carver (ed.), *The Cambridge Companion to Marx* (Cambridge University Press, 1991).

David McLellan's *Karl Marx: His life and thought* (Macmillan, 1973) is a thorough intellectual biography, while S.H. Rigby's *Engels and the Formation of Marxism* (Manchester University Press, 1992) is useful on the contribution of Engels. A contrasting interpretation of their relationship is to be found in Terrell Carver's *Marx and Engels: The intellectual relationship* (Wheatsheaf, 1983), where it is argued that the standard interpretations of Marx's thought, for example its Hegelian aspects, are largely the construction of the elderly Engels. J.D. Hunley's *The Life and Thought of Friedrich Engels: A reinterpretation* (Yale University Press, 1991) is useful because it focuses on Engels.

There are various relevant selections from the works of Marx and Engels, most notably David McLellan (ed.), *Karl Marx: Selected writings* (Oxford University Press, 1977), which is a good source for the following writings by Marx referred to in the chapter: 'On the Jewish Question', 'Critique of Hegel's Philosophy of Right', 'Towards a Critique of Hegel's Philosophy of Right: Introduction', 'Theses on Feuerbach' and 'The Eighteenth Brumaire of Louis Bonaparte'. Also important in this collection is Engels' 'Outlines of a Critique of Political Economy' and, with Marx, 'The Holy Family' and 'The Communist Manifesto'. A shorter collection is Lewis Feuer (ed.), *Marx and Engels: Basic writings on politics and philosophy* (Anchor Books, 1959). Tom Bottomore and Maximilian Rubel (eds), *Karl Marx: Selected writings in sociology and social philosophy* (Penguin, 1963) arranges key extracts according to topic, as does Derek Sayer (ed.), *Readings from Karl Marx* (Routledge, 1989).

Tom Bottomore (ed.), *Dictionary of Marxist Thought* (Blackwell, 1991) contains authoritative discussions of important people and ideas. Useful surveys of current academic thinking are to be found in Terrell Carver (ed.), *The Cambridge Companion to Marx* (Cambridge University Press, 1991) and Bob Jessop and Charlie Malcolm-Brown (eds), *Karl Marx's Social and Political Thought: Critical assessments* (Routledge, 1990). Critical surveys of modern Marxist thought can be found in Leszek Kolakowski's *Main Currents of Marxism, Vol. 3: The breakdown* (Oxford University Press, 1978) and J.G. Merquior's *Western Marxism* (Paladin, 1986).

Ferdinand Braudel's *Civilization and Capitalism, 15th–18th Century* (3 vols, Collins, 1984) is a broad historical examination of everyday life, economic forms and perspectives in Europe prior to the nineteenth century and is a useful perspective against which to judge the historical basis of much of Marx's writings. Alan Macfarlane's *The Origins of English Individualism: The family, property and social transition* (Blackwell, 1978) illustrates the existence of capitalist economic forms prior to the nineteenth century.

Sources for the Frankfurt School of Critical Theory include David Held's *Introduction to Critical Theory: Horkheimer to Habermas* (Hutchinson, 1980), Susan Buck-Morss' *The Origin of Negative Dialectics* (Harvester, 1977) and Martin Jay's *The Dialectic Imagination: A history of the Frankfurt School and the Institute of Social Research, 1923–1950* (Little Brown, 1973). Theodor W. Adorno and Martin Horkheimer's *Dialectic of Enlightenment* (Allen Lane, 1979) and some of the work of Jürgen Habermas, such as *Knowledge and Human Interests* (Heinemann, 1971) and *Legitimation Crisis* (Heinemann, 1976), are also important sources.

The recent influence of Marxist ideas on literary and cultural studies owes much to Terry Eagleton's *Marxism and Literary Criticism* (Methuen,

1976), Raymond Williams' *Marxism and Literature* (Oxford University Press, 1977) and Gary Nelson and Lawrence Grossberg (eds), *Marxism and the Interpretation of Culture* (Macmillan, 1988). See also Stuart Hall and Tony Jefferson (eds), *Resistance Through Rituals* (Hutchinson, 1976). Gramsci's writings are published in *Selections from the Prison Notebooks* (New Left Books, 1971). Nicholas Abercrombie, Stephen Hill and Bryan Turner's *The Dominant Ideology Thesis* (Allen and Unwin, 1980) explores the idea of a dominant ideology.

Structuralist interpretations of Marx are to be found in: Louis Althusser's *For Marx* (Allen Lane, 1969), and 'Ideology and ideological state apparatuses', in his *Lenin and Philosophy and Other Essays* (New Left Books, 1971, pp. 121–73), Martin Godelier, 'System, structure and contradiction in "Capital"', in D. McQuarie (ed.), *Marx: Sociology, social change, capitalism* (Quartet Books, 1978) and Nicos Poulantzas' *Political Power and Social Classes* (New Left Books, 1973). Counters to this interpretation include Ralph Miliband's *The State and Capitalist Society* (Weidenfeld and Nicolson, 1969) and E.P. Thompson's *The Poverty of Theory* (Merlin Press, 1978).

There is, of course, no substitute for reading Marx and Engels in their own words. Newcomers could start with their *The German Ideology*, *The Communist Manifesto* and passages from the *Paris Manuscripts*. These are available in various editions and there are edited versions of each in David McLellan (ed.), *Karl Marx: Selected writings* (Oxford University Press, 1977). Marx's major works, including the *Grundrisse: Foundations of the critique of political economy* and the three volumes of *Capital*, are published by Penguin (1973 and 1976).

References relevant to the development of Marxist and Marxist-influenced analyses of modern industrial societies include Rudolf Hilferding, *Finance Capital* (Routledge, 1910) and Adolf Berle and Gardiner Means' *The Modern Corporation and Private Property* (Macmillan) which, though published first in 1932, is still worth reading, as is Paul Baran and Paul Sweezy's *Monopoly Capital* (Penguin, 1968). James Burnham's *The Managerial Revolution* (Doubleday, 1941) was a classic attempt to update Marx's analysis in light of the managerialist developments in the large corporation. J.K. Galbraith's *The New Industrial State* (Hamish Hamilton, 1967), though not a Marxist account is a useful resource in the context of the Marxist analyses of industrial society, as is C. Wright Mills' *The Power Elite* (Oxford University Press, 1956). Ralf Dahrendorf's *Class and Class Conflict in an Industrial Society* (Routledge, 1959) was an important attempt to blend Marx's analysis of class with that of Weber. Samuel Bowles and Herbert Gintis' *Schooling in Capitalist America* (Routledge, 1976) applied a Marxist framework to the educational system in capitalist society. Henry Braverman's *Labour and Monopoly Capital* (Monthly Review Press, 1974) eloquently developed a Marxist analysis of the erosion of skill in work under capitalism. More recent efforts to address the issue of class are Olin Wright's *Classes* (Verso, 1985), Frank Parkin's *Marxism and*

Class Theory (Tavistock, 1979), Gordon Marshall, David Rose and Howard Newby's *Social Class in Modern Britain* (Unwin Hyman, 1989) and, for international comparisons, Tom Bottomore and Robert Brym (eds), *The Capitalist Class: An international study* (Harvester, 1989). John Scott's *Who Rules Britain?* (Polity Press, 1991) is a recent analysis of interests and power in Britain.

3

Max Weber

Both Karl Marx and Émile Durkheim were relatively optimistic about the prospective achievements of social theory; by comparison, Max Weber was a pessimist. Both Marx and Durkheim were inspired by the theoretical achievements of the natural sciences into envisaging social sciences that could match the former in their scope and power by providing a general theory of human society and history. Indeed, in his youth Marx had compared his own intellectual ambitions with the achievements of Prometheus who, in legend, had stolen fire from the Gods. Both Marx and Durkheim were convinced that the development of scientific knowledge would provide unparalleled opportunities for social improvement. Marx, for example, supposed that his work would contribute to the complete emancipation of the whole of humanity; somewhat more modestly, Durkheim's interests were in directing social scientific knowledge toward the amelioration of some of the 'pathologies' of modern society. Weber, however, while confident that sociology could develop as a sound science, had far lesser expectations than Marx and Durkheim as to what this could amount to, and certainly did not expect that it could overcome the basic conflicts in human life, let alone achieve the emancipation of all humankind. It need not even necessarily ameliorate the condition of modern society. Sociology might develop generalisations, but it could not expect to develop general theory in the way that natural science (or at least physics) has, and it would, in many ways, have its main role in supporting historical inquiries.

Though Weber believed that scientific knowledge was of practical value and that social science could provide such knowledge, he also argued that expanding scientific knowledge did not automatically bring benefits; it could also produce disillusionment. As Weber saw it, the practical value of scientific knowledge depends not upon the quality of the knowledge itself, but upon the purposes and the spirit in which it is applied, and there was no guarantee that the application of scientific knowledge would be benignly motivated. Indeed, there was much to fear from the experts, who often believed that their intellectual pre-eminence entitled them to a privileged position in deciding human affairs. Though Weber opposed what we might nowadays characterise as 'technocrats', he did not thereby dismiss the value of expertise, but demurred, rather, at the idea that the possession of expertise is any kind of qualification for political leadership. When it comes to political questions, the scientific expert is no more qualified than the rest and is not, therefore, entitled to any privilege in these matters.

So, Weber was much more sceptical than either Marx or Durkheim about the capacity of sociology to contribute to the continual progress in society and was less optimistic about the possibility that sociology could provide ultimate knowledge of social reality. He repeatedly emphasised the limitations upon the capacity of the human mind to know reality, a view that, as we shall see, derived from his philosophical inheritance, which insisted that reality can never be known 'in itself'. Weber maintained that external reality is far more complex and detailed than our thought is capable of apprehending, and that, therefore, the latter can never represent the former in other than a highly selective and, therefore, partial way.

Though Weber was 'pessimistic' in these respects, this does not mean that he was offering only a counsel of despair with respect to either social science or politics; far from it. Weber saw both value and purpose in the pursuit of scientific work and political engagement, but also insisted that the difference between the two must be kept clearly in mind. In Weber's eyes, the pursuit of knowledge was worthwhile for its own sake, and a life seriously devoted to scholarship could be a worthy and dignified one. Though we might never arrive at an understanding of the ultimate nature of reality, this does not mean that we cannot improve the understanding that we have, and this can be both intellectually rewarding and, possibly, of practical value. The political activist, too, has an important part to play, for the activist's role is to join in the struggles that take place over the significant choices that necessarily confront human beings and which decide the directions in which society will go. Weber was pessimistic, for example, about the political prospects of the Germany of his time, as part of his gloom about the future prospects of the entire Western world, but the whole point of politics is to fight for what one believes in, and the fact that one's own beliefs are under threat does not mean that one should give up the fight.

The most effective way in which we can present Weber's scholarly work is by separating it into two parts, the 'substantive' and 'the methodological'. These represent two strands in Weber's work in that they involve two distinct sets of writings, one of which consists of historical and sociological studies, the other of philosophical essays. But there is, none the less, a sense in which the separation is an artificial one. The philosophical essays are on the 'methodology' of the social (or, as they were often called in Weber's time, the 'cultural') sciences and debate those perennial questions about the general manner in which these sciences are to be pursued – should they follow the method of the natural sciences, or do they require a very different method? Weber regarded such debates as a waste of time, though this did not prevent him from being intensely involved in them. These issues were a matter of fierce controversy in the Germany of Weber's time, and it would have been near impossible for him to avoid engagement in them. None the less, he held the clear view that the real business of the social scientist was to engage in productive empirical investigation, rather than in speculative controversy about the scientific status of the social sciences. If methodology must be discussed then let it be in a way that involves the spelling out of the methods that have actually been employed in social and historical studies along with an awareness that this is very much a secondary activity to the making of the investigations themselves.

The question of whether Weber's writings (which were often, like Marx's, unfinished and unpublished during his lifetime) constitute a unified body of work is a controversial one, though there is nothing like the debate that there is over the unity of Marx's thought. For a long period, Weber's work was made available in English through a string of partial translations, and it is this which gave rise to the impression that it was a collection of studies of disparate topics such as 'bureaucracy', 'the law', 'the basic categories of sociology' and so on without any thematic coherence. In reaction against this situation, it was eventually argued (Tenbruck, 1980) that there was a pervading unity to Weber's thought, though the precise nature of this inner coherence then became a focus for further dispute (Hennis, 1988). Recognising that it is not unproblematic to look for connections amongst all the parts of Weber's work, we will none the less treat them *for the purposes of this exposition* as relatively unified, with very much of his work being centred on the two related preoccupations noted earlier.

The first of these, the emergence of capitalist business as the dominant form of organisation in the West, involves a concern to understand the origins, in its specifically 'rationalised' and moralised form, of the capitalist business organisation and the civilisation associated with it that was, at the time Weber was writing, becoming ever more thoroughly pre-eminent within Western Europe and the United States. The notion of 'rationalisation' refers to the proclivity to work things out systematically; a proclivity which Weber thought had been given freer rein within the modern West than elsewhere in human history. This was particularly manifest in the progressively pervading tendency for the business organisation systematically to work out its own internal organisation, by making as many of its affairs as possible calculable.

The second preoccupation concerns a basic sociological theme, namely, the relationship between ideas and interests in human action. This was a theme stimulated in significant respects by the Marxian analysis encouraged by the German Social Democratic Party. However, and as we have explained in the chapter on Marx, only a small part of Marx's own writings were available to Weber and, therefore, many of his ideas about Marx's teachings were derived from secondary sources. These were the work of what are often disparagingly called 'vulgar Marxists', interpreting Marx's theory as an 'economic determinist' one. This theory offered the view that the economic 'base' of society, that is, the organisation of its system of production, determined the nature of the society's 'superstructure', that is, the organisation of the other institutions of society – such as the family, the legal system – and of its belief systems, such as its religious and political ideas. The idea of 'economic determinism' further encouraged the view that the fundamental motivations of human actions are 'material' in character and essentially concerned with the advancement of practical, most particularly economic, interests, and that *all* conflicts in society, be they ostensibly over, say, religion or nationalism, are *really* about economic interests. This means that religious and political beliefs are conceived as *rationalisations*, that is, as justifying actions undertaken out of materialistic and self-interested motives in order to make them seem more palatable.

Whether or not such 'economic determinist' views are rightly ascribed to Marx, they were views that Weber flatly rejected. He did not necessarily reject them as *entirely* false, certainly not to the extent of denying that human actions could be motivated by economic interests. He rejected them because they were much too crude as a portrayal of human motivation and, therefore, of little use in analysing the complex causal conditions which give rise to actual historical situations. Weber's own background in economics gave him a strong interest in the role that economic motivation played in individual action as well as in the role that the economy played in structuring the society more widely. But a recognition of the real importance of 'economic' elements could not equate with the view that these were *primary* factors, explaining everything else about society. The very idea of a 'primary factor' was one that was also, in Weber's judgement, too crude for a real understanding of history.

The view of beliefs and ideas as 'rationalisations' is one that is present in both Marx and Durkheim. Both argued that in significant respects the members of society do not know what they do and need to have the true causes of their actions revealed to them by social science. Both agreed that the explanation of beliefs must be sought in the nature of social reality; a reality which is, again for the members of society, mystified and concealed. This applied not only to religious beliefs but to other kinds, too. As we have seen, Marx devoted considerable effort in arguing that the political economy of his day was nothing less than a rationalisation, an ideology, of capitalist economic relations.

On this point, Weber's views directly opposed those of Marx and Durkheim. For him people undoubtedly act on the basis of their beliefs and ideas, and the ways in which they conduct themselves follow from the religious and political conceptions to which they subscribe. Whether or not God exists does not matter, for the fact is that people who believe that God does exist are likely to act in certain ways because of their conviction that they are doing what God wants them to do. From the point of view of the sociologist analysing the way in which people's actions make up and affect the organisation of society, the fact that people hold to and, to a greater or lesser extent, act out the instructions of a religious doctrine will have a tangible impact upon the patterns of their conduct and upon the organisation of the social arrangements in which they live. Thus, the sociologist who wishes to understand people's actions must take into account the beliefs and ideas to which those people are attached, and seek to understand the way in which holding such beliefs and ideas leads them to act.

This was the basic presupposition of Weber's sociological approach, known as the '*verstehen*' (or 'understanding') method, which sought sociological explanation in prominent part through understanding the outlook – what might be called the world view, or basic system of beliefs – that people have. On such a basis, Weber rejected the 'vulgar Marxist' notion that actions are motivated by economic interests alone. *Some* actions certainly are motivated by such interests, but in Weber's view it would be a dreadful oversimplification to suggest that *all* or even *most* of them are, and that religious and political ideas just provide a 'cover up' for a more disreputable pursuit of self-interest. People are, to a varying extent, and in degrees which are themselves susceptible to sociological explanation, capable of genuinely believing and acting in terms of ideas other than those which concern their material self-interest, most particularly in terms of religious ideas and ideals. Understanding why they accept those ideas, and what it leads them to do, cannot be achieved through a focus upon economic interests alone. Both economic interests *and* religious ideas are at work in society. Both interact with one another and, along with many other factors, play an important part in the dynamic shaping the structure of society and the courses of action of its members. In Weber's view religious ideas and ideals arise out of a widespread human need to feel that human life and the world both have meaning, that is, they have some point, serve some purpose. There is a common need to feel that things in the world and one's life do not merely 'happen' by chance, but that they are part of some greater pattern and that one's fate is bound up with that plan. For example, Weber pointed to the importance of 'suffering' in many religions, arguing that it was eased if it was seen as being borne for something. Thus, religions sometimes explain that suffering in this life is borne in order to achieve salvation in the next. The needs to which religion speaks are, then, just as authentic as those which are satisfied by food, clothing or power over others.

It is not surprising, then, that such a major part of Weber's 'substantive' work should be devoted to studies of religion. The major project of his mature work was given over to a comparative study of the 'world religions', that is, those religions which had made a decisive impact on world history (and/or upon that of Western civilisation). Weber's agenda had included Christianity and Islam, but he did not make significant inroads into the study of these, though he did manage to generate large (though incomplete) studies of Confucianism (in *The Religion of China* (published in English, 1951)) and of Buddhism and Hinduism (in *The Religion of India* (published in English, 1958), as well as his *Ancient Judaism* (originally published 1922). He also produced a general account of the general 'evolution' of forms of religious belief and practice (*The Sociology of Religion* (1963)). It is through these studies, though not these *alone*, that Weber sought to examine the interplay between beliefs and ideas, particularly religious ones, economic interests and social conditions more generally, and it is because this takes up such a major part of Weber's writings that we can treat it as a strongly unifying theme.

The early career

Born into the well-to-do middle class in Berlin in 1864, Weber was the son of a lawyer who was politically active as a National Liberal parliamentarian. Weber was to have a lifelong interest in, as well as a strong desire to be influential upon, practical politics. His political outlook was strongly nationalistic, and his academic work was partially motivated by his concerns for the welfare of German society, which had recently been unified under the leadership of Bismarck's Prussia. Although Germany was politically modernised to some extent, and a major imperial power by the end of the nineteenth century, industrialisation had failed to establish a politically independent bourgeoisie, unlike in Britain, France and the United States. German liberalism, which had provided the intellectual underpinning for the unification and the modernisation of the German state, was under serious threat from the very creature it had helped to create. The rise of Bismarck's Reich saw the political defeat of the middle class that had most strongly espoused the values of respect for the individual, a concern for humanitarian learning, duty, personal integrity and the responsibility of the individual; values which were deeply entrenched in German Protestantism. The period of Germany's rapid industrialisation and urbanisation saw the demise of liberalism as the alliance of the state with the Junkers – the aristocratic landowning class – the army and the bureaucracy extolled and imposed the duties of deference to superiors, paternalism and service to the nation at the expense of individual autonomy. By the late nineteenth century Germany was governed by an authoritarian, militaristic state that regulated most aspects of social and economic life. Weber tended to support liberal policies while rejecting many of the elements of liberal political philosophy, such as a belief in progress. His own sentiments emphasised the virtues of individual autonomy and responsibility, the importance of doing one's duty and meeting one's obligations to the community; values which, he felt, and with good reason, were imperilled in the Germany of his day.

Weber's education at the universities of Göttingen and Heidelberg, interrupted by a year of military training, took him first into law and then into studies of law and legal history which, after 1886, he pursued at Berlin. Some of his earliest research, which included work on Roman law, was into the effects of industrialisation on the position of the Junkers in Germany. While political unification after 1870 had promoted rapid industrialisation, it was the southern and western parts of the country that had become economically strong, sucking in labour from the eastern agricultural regions – the sources of Junker wealth and power – which had, as a result, suffered a relative decline. Despite extracting more and more from their estates, the Junkers were increasingly unable to support their aristocratic position and pretensions by economic means and had to rely upon political power. This period also saw the appearance of what was then known as 'the social problem', namely, the rise of an industrial proletariat and the spread of socialist ideas. Bismarck had tried to solve the 'problem' by a carrot and stick combination of repression accompanied by welfare legislation (which was, paradoxically, to become the model for the modern welfare state).

The agrarian problem in Germany

The 'agrarian problem' of eastern Germany was Weber's first sociological study. In 1897, the previous free trade policy in grain had been abandoned under the threat of cheaper Russian and American grain imports. The Junkers, though highly nationalistic and protectionist, had encouraged the replacement of German farm labourers by foreign migratory workers. The problem of farm labour became the subject of a large-scale study conducted by an association of scholars, government officials and other specialists, the Verein für Sozialpolitik. In 1890, the association sent out a questionnaire to over 3,000 landowners throughout Germany, and Weber was given the responsibility of analysing the returns from provinces to the east of the Elbe. The study revealed considerable regional differences in the position of agricultural labourers. In eastern Germany the capitalist transformation of labour relations had tended to depress the workers' standard of living, partly because they no longer had quasi-feudal rights to depend on, and partly because of the influx of cheaper labour from Russia and Poland. For the first time Weber came face to face with a conflict between national values and economic rationality. The central issue, namely the replacement of German workers by Poles on the estates of eastern Germany, could not be understood in purely economic terms. Economically, Polish labour was cheaper than German, but, from the point of view of nationalist values, the influx exposed Germany's eastern frontier. Yet, as Weber realised, it was the eastern aristocrats who espoused loyalty to national values who were, in their economic life, pursuing an anti-nationalist course of action. Just as Marx was to realise after his study of 'timber thefts', capitalist economic relations were beginning to transform traditional rights and obligations and patterns of social organisation.

Weber began to take an increasing interest in historical and sociological studies. As he did not occupy a university position as a sociologist, this did not involve the same kind of struggle to legitimise his sociological inclinations that faced Durkheim at the beginning of his career. The intellectual climate within which Weber was educated, and to which he, in his turn, contributed, was that of a highly developed and widely respected scholarly tradition which identified itself with the well-being of the nation. Germany, with its rapid rise to cultural and intellectual eminence, buttressed by a well-developed educational system, had within a short space of time begun to make major contributions to natural science and industrial technology. Nor did German academia neglect 'the social' as a distinct sphere of inquiry. Rather unusually with respect to European countries, German scholars in general accepted that the social could be the object of academic, even scientific, study. Economics was well established in the universities, and legal studies embraced far more than the theory and practice of law, giving attention to the social and cultural settings within which the law had its place. Indeed, one of the most prominent pre-occupations of German scholarship during Weber's time was with the nature of the so-called 'cultural sciences', a collection which included, among others and as we now know them, economics, history, law, archaeology, etymology, linguistics, sociology and political science.

Weber's studies, then, began to concern themselves not just with the internal organisation of Germany society but also with the character, origins and prospects of the wide-ranging social and cultural transformation that was taking place throughout European and North American society. As Marx and Durkheim also saw, this was due above all to the spread of the capitalistically organised business venture. It was to understanding the character, origins and prospects of this new Western civilisation that Weber devoted the remainder of his scholarly career.

Weber and modern capitalism

Marx had already identified the business organisation, with its overriding compulsion for profit and expansion, as the most striking feature of the modern Western society which had developed in the nineteenth century. He had emphasised the way in which capitalist production endlessly reorganises itself as part of the mutually destructive competition in which capitalists seek to preserve their market advantage against encroaching rivals. As we have seen, the need to accumulate capital was, Marx maintained, imposed upon the capitalist. It was not any psychological trait of greed which mattered. The individual businessman might be a well-meaning and generous person, and genuinely concerned for the welfare of those he employed. But this did not mean that he could exploit their labour power any the less if he himself was to survive in business. Marx had also drawn attention to the way in which the 'capitalist class' was becoming not only economically but also politically dominant in Western society, not only influencing government policy, but also shaping the ideas and values of the wider society. Western society was developing a predominantly 'bourgeois' character.

Though, as mentioned above, Weber was in fundamental disagreement with Marx (or, at least, Marx as he understood him), he was in significant agreement with him that the development of the dynamic, dominant capitalist economy on a scale which extended its influence across the globe was historically unprecedented. The need was to understand this 'meteoric' rise. But whatever common ground there was between them was bounded by very different ideas of how this understanding was to be achieved. Particularly in his earlier work, Marx inclined toward connecting the development of modern Western capitalism with an account of the progress of the whole of human history, even suggesting that the developments in the West anticipated those which must take place throughout the rest of the world, thus seeing capitalism as a stage in the *general* development of the whole of history. By contrast, Weber had no regard for comprehensive accounts of history, seeing, instead, the contemporary developments as entirely distinctive to the history of Western Europe and the United States and unmatched elsewhere. Capitalist enterprise as such, however, was not the source of this distinctiveness. Weber argued that capitalist enterprise had often existed elsewhere. There had been profit-seeking organisations throughout history, and these could be every bit as ruthless and exploitative as ever might be the case in the industrial societies Marx wrote about. It was the *relentlessness* of the pursuit of profit which was the distinctive aspect in modern societies. In other societies the capitalist enterprise had tended to be a sporadic affair, with people organising a profit-making venture, carrying that through and, when sufficient profit had been made, at least temporarily discontinuing the venture. The modern business enterprise was, however, one which was remarkable for its continuity, seeking to sustain and expand its operations, shifting and adapting itself to change in market opportunities, competing in an endless cycle to outgrow other businesses.

Marx had been right to emphasise the extent to which profit-seeking in capitalism is dissociated from personal needs. The capitalist does not seek profit simply in order to improve his standard of living. Marx had attributed this endless pursuit of profit to the necessity of the survival of the business organisation. Weber, however, notes that from the point of view of the capitalist the pursuit of profit has become an end in itself. The very point of business activity in the modern world is to make greater profits and build larger and larger companies. The capitalist measures achievement by reference to the profits made and the companies controlled. Such a drive is not imbued with a purely pragmatic motive; it has a strong *moral* sense. Profit is perceived as the rightful reward for devotion to work.

When viewed against the attitudes toward work held throughout the historical range of societies, it is the moral injunction that hard work deserves reward which is most striking. Acquisitiveness and avarice are common throughout all societies. In other societies, work and the pursuit of wealth are regarded as necessary evils, as means which provide the good life; they do not themselves make up the good life. In modern capitalism, by contrast, work has a morally positive character. Holding a job, going to work regularly, working in a steady, disciplined and dedicated way, are all seen as essentials of a worthy way of life in our society. It is this attitude toward work as a worthy pursuit which is rewarded by economic prosperity that Weber termed 'the spirit of capitalism'; an ethic, he argued, which was an essential element in the nature of capitalism in the West, and which must have been a vital contributory element in the rise of the capitalist system. Without some motivation for determined, persistent work, and to work for its own sake, the economic and other opportunities which had brought the dynamic growth of modern capitalism to dominance would not have been seized and exploited as they were. Both the profit hunger of the capitalist and the disciplined devotion to work of employees had a strongly *moralistic* character, and this is a crucial feature which, in Weber's judgement, could not be accounted for by the Marxist scheme.

There is a further distinctive element to modern capitalism which we have already noted, namely, the extent to which it is 'rationalised'; that is, the extent to which people attempt systematically to work out the conduct of their affairs. 'Rationalisation' is, like profit-seeking, something which can occur in any society, and in any sphere of life. There are many instances in history in which people have attempted to work out their system of beliefs more systematically or have sought to consider the organisation of their practical activities in a more systematic way. What is distinctive in the modern capitalist West is the extent to which 'rationalisation', like the pursuit of profit, has become almost an end in itself, and an extensive and dominating aspect of our lives. There are two sectors of modern society which have most dramatically exemplified such rationalisation. One has been our understanding of nature. The modern sciences represent a most systematically worked out understanding of nature, one which enables the most finely calculated comprehension of its details. The other is, of course, the business enterprise, where there has also been a strong and continuing drive systematically to work out the most efficient means for organising the enterprise and delivering its product.

However, the drive toward further systematic working out of systems of belief and the organisation of conduct now enters into most spheres of our lives. As we have suggested, in the modern West there is a marked tendency to regard rationalisation, and still further rationalisation, as desirable in its own right, as an ideal of efficiency which should govern all activities. Certainly for Weber the intensity of the quest for rationalisation in modern capitalist society was historically quite exceptional and, thus, called for explanation.

The Protestant ethic and the spirit of capitalism

The main phase of Weber's work was initiated by the writing of a pair of essays – collected together under the title *The Protestant Ethic and the Spirit of Capitalism* (and published in 1904–5) – in which he set out a possible explanation for the origin of the spirit of capitalism with its moralistic view of work and its determination to rationalise all aspects of life.

The Marxist account, as Weber understood it, made the development of capitalism seem an inevitable outcome of a continuing, pre-destined development of history and also made the development of the beliefs necessary to the appropriate conduct of the capitalist system appear an automatic consequence of the development of its economic and political preconditions. The 'material base' was, in a schematic formulation of Marxism, the direct cause of the 'superstructure' of ideas, beliefs and values. Such a conception was unacceptable to Weber. The Marxist approach could not explain the origin of 'the spirit of capitalism' because it had misguided views about the nature of historical explanation in general.

First, there was nothing inevitable about the course of history, no necessity whatsoever that capitalism should have developed or, having developed, have taken the specific form that it now has. A whole complex of causal conditions converged in Western Europe to initiate and sustain the development and expansion of capitalism, but these conditions did not *have* to arise and converge as they did. Historical situations are always contingent, they could have been otherwise, and the contributory causes of modern Western capitalism need not have obtained. To understand why they did was a matter of identifying their particular causal preconditions, not seeing them as provided for through some guiding 'master plan' of historical development.

Second, even if the material conditions of capitalist development were present, it does not follow that what Marxists would term the 'super-structure' elements, the values and beliefs necessary to the exploitation of the opportunity for capitalist activity, would *inevitably* arise. The economic and political preconditions for industrial capitalism might have been present in Reformation Europe, but the presence of an opportunity does not ensure that it will be taken, that people will have, for example, the motivation to exploit it. It is possible that the values and beliefs of the Reformation might have developed in directions other than they actually did, and, as a result, the opportunity for industrial capitalism might not have been exploited, or that it might have been developed with quite a different 'spirit' than that which it now has. People's motivations, no less than anything else, require historical explanation for, as we have noted, the kind of motivation common in modern Western capitalism is very far from common or usual elsewhere. The question of the causal conditions of the 'spirit of capitalism' is, for Weber, *a separate question* to that of the causal conditions of capitalist industrial production.

All kinds of material preconditions were, therefore, necessary for the rise of capitalism, many of them already identified by Marx, such as the development of manufacturing technology, the urbanisation of the rural population, the growing political independence and power of the urban commercial classes, changes in law, the development of accounting systems, a free market in capital and goods, a division of labour based on skill and expertise rather than traditional, ascribed criteria, a legally defined notion of the citizen, and many more. But what had provided the initial motivation for capitalist activity of the kind familiar to us?

The source of that motivation, Weber surmised, was to be found in the transformation of religious ideas brought about by the Reformation, particularly the impact of Calvinist doctrines. There was, he argued, a resemblance between the 'capitalist spirit' and the attitudes of Protestants toward hard work and wealth, for the latter also emphasised duty and austerity, encouraged economic diligence and condemned laziness and wastefulness, and spread the virtues of thrift and productivity. The only real difference between the 'spirit of capitalism', on the one side, and this 'Protestant ethic', on the other, was that the latter spoke in the name of God whilst the former speaks in entirely secular terms. It was Weber's hypothesis that the 'spirit of capitalism' is the secularised successor of the 'Protestant ethic', and that the latter was a cause of the former. If true, then the Protestant ethic played a vital part in the rise of modern Western capitalism.

The role of ideas in history Weber is often taken to be saying that it is religious *ideas* which played a causal role, and it is on this basis that he is standardly contrasted with Marx – the one denying and the other affirming that ideas can play a causal role in social change. However, the divergence between the two is not actually of this kind. Weber was, in fact, no less of a 'materialist' than Marx. Certainly he was as deeply opposed to the Hegelian idea that social change could be understood as the 'emanation' of ideas working out their own internal logic. He rejected, too, just as vigorously as did Marx, the idea that the individual and ingenious thinker could, as an individual and just by coming up with new ideas, make a decisive impact on the course of history. For *both* Marx and Weber, historical change is not brought about by any unfolding of the logic of ideas but only through the activities of real, striving human beings acting in pursuit of their interests. However, Weber took it that these real, striving human beings are guided not only by their practical, particularly economic, interests, but also by, among other things, their beliefs and ideals, including their spiritual ones. Their attachment to these can be as real, intense and as important to them as their needs for animal sustenance and comfort. Individuals can, therefore, have an interest in realising their beliefs and ideals; an interest which can match, or even override, their material interests. For the deeply convinced believer in a religion that offers the concept of an immortal soul and its eternal salvation, the individual's concern to ensure that salvation can matter as much, and more, than everyday affairs. How can the transient discomforts and miseries of this life compare with the prospect of eternal damnation in the next? Weber, no less than Marx, saw individuals as acting in pursuit of their interests, but he insisted that the range of interests which governed actions was wider than that allowed in Marx's theory. People indeed do have economic interests and these play an influential, and sometimes the most influential, role in history, but they are neither the *only* interests people have nor *invariably* the most influential ones. In particular, for Weber's concerns, people's religious interests may be the most important thing in their lives and decisive in shaping the direction of their actions.

As mentioned, Weber was as sceptical as Marx of the effect on historical change of the ideas of individual thinkers *as such*. His account of the 'Protestant ethic' certainly gave great prominence to the teaching of John Calvin (1509–64) but only to argue that the ethic engendered the spirit of capitalism *despite* the official teachings and exhortations of the religious leaders. It was only because believers applied Calvin's religious teachings 'against the grain' of his thought that they were led into the actions that followed. Ideas could only have a decisive historical effect insofar as they came to comprise the interests of large numbers of individuals and, even more, the interests of groups of individuals.

Weber was determined to reject the idea that any single factor should be given general primacy in the explanation of human action, and his emphasis upon the role of religious ideas and the interests associated with them was not, therefore, meant to comprise a new single-factor approach of his own. Historical situations are *always* brought about by a multitude of interacting factors, and the emphasis on religious interests was, then, merely intended to provide a corrective to any unbalanced emphasis on economic ones. Religious ideas and interests are prominent in Weber's concerns merely to make up for the fact they had been unduly played down in other places, and not because he considered these the single most significant factors in history.

The idea that religious beliefs might have an influence upon economic activities is not, within Weber's conception, as attenuated as it might first appear. The fact that religious beliefs could have a direct and decisive influence on economic activity might appear unpersuasive in a society like our own where religion is very much 'marginalised' in our lives, but this is not a characteristic human condition. In other societies religion plays a very important, even dominant part, in social life. Weber's assumption was that all religions contain definite attitudes toward economic activity, toward the worldly business of acquiring a living, the ethics of trade, the legitimacy of usury and so on, and it was these 'economic ethics' of a religion which were of particular interest to him. Such ethics are an offshoot of the general orientation of religions to the meaning and value of life on earth. Many religions devalue work, regarding economic life as meaningless and empty. They accord little importance to economic activity and the pursuit of prosperity. The former is necessary to meet the needs of survival, but beyond that it is a worthless endeavour. The attitude of the medieval Catholic church was an example. Its ideal was to serve God through near full-time religious activity, with only the minimally necessary time given over to meeting the practical requirements of life. A monastic existence came closest to fulfilling this ideal. By contrast, the Protestant sects profoundly disparaged specifically religious ceremonials and practices in favour of carrying out one's practical, everyday affairs, including the making of one's living, in a spirit of service to God. Their ideal life was one of vigorous embrace of, not monastic retreat from, the affairs of the ordinary society.

Again like Marx, Weber recognised that modern capitalism was a destroyer of all tradition, an unprecedented revolutionary force within society. The drive toward rationalisation called into question any practice in its name. Thus, an account of the origins of capitalism's spirit must also explain how such a thorough rejection of tradition could arise in a society dominated by the deeply traditional institutions of crown and church. As we said earlier, the distinctive features of the 'spirit of capitalism' closely resembled the teaching of the Reformation's Protestant sects, especially in their attitudes to austerity, discipline and hard work. Accordingly, if we are looking for a motivational set that not only resembled the 'spirit of capitalism' but which could also have been a cause of it, then the ethics of these sects had not only a strong resemblance to that spirit, but also developed in just those places and at that time at which capitalism itself developed. How could they have provided the spur for capitalist acquisition when the teachings of the sects themselves emphasised the priority of spiritual ideals over material concerns, and were hostile to the pursuit and possession of wealth?

Weber's short answer was that in challenging the Catholic conception of the religious life the Protestant sects effected a profound change in the ways in which people led their lives in the world of ordinary affairs, one which also altered their orientation to work and business.

Ascetic Protestantism and social change   The first vital feature of the Protestant ethic Weber emphasised was the idea of 'the calling', that is, the idea that people have been 'called by God' to the position that they occupy in this world. The Catholic church's ideal was the monastic existence, but to the Protestants this was to withdraw from the position to which one had been called by God. Thus, a new ideal was created: to withdraw from or to fail to fulfil the responsibilities of one's position in the world of ordinary life was to show disrespect to Almighty God. Weber credited Martin Luther (1483–1546) with first giving voice to the idea that through fulfilment of the traditional requirements of our secular station in life we show devoted service to God.

The concept of 'the calling' as an obligation of individuals in their everyday life turned the task of earning a living into a religious duty. This was an important step, but as far as Weber was concerned Luther's teaching did not explain the rejection of all tradition which was to become a characteristic of the 'spirit of capitalism', for Luther encouraged compliance with traditionally defined obligations. Instead, for Weber, the explanation lay with John Calvin's teachings, which exhorted the rejection of authority and tradition as guides to one's duties in the practical world in favour of absolute reliance upon the individual's conscience, under God's guidance, as the measure of right action.

Calvin's teachings, however, involved a crucial inconsistency. He taught that since God was omnipotent and omniscient the whole pattern of creation must have been predetermined. There is nothing that a person can do to influence God to change things, since everything has already been settled. The rituals and 'good works' of the Catholics are just so much idolatry, and cannot influence God's will one jot. God's determination is final. He does not reveal His will, and though He has already decided which souls will be saved, there is no way of knowing whose these are. It makes absolutely no difference how we live in this world for it cannot change God's decisions, nor even show whether we are amongt his 'elect'. Before such a God, individuals stand alone.

For Calvin, as for Luther, service of God's greater glory is carried out in the everyday secular world. The crucial inconsistency in Calvinism was not within the system of teaching itself, but between the teachings and the religious *interests* to which they gave rise. The salvation of the soul must have been a matter of intense importance to the believer, for the glories of heaven and the terrors of hell were immense and awesome. Salvation was, therefore, an important, even the most important, interest of the believers. But it was one that the believer could neither achieve nor even know about. A position of unrelieved ignorance about something so important to them as their eternal salvation was one which was, said Weber, psychologically intolerable. The tension between the need for certainty about salvation and Calvin's official teachings must be psychologically resolved. Despite the doctrine of the invisibility of membership of God's elect, many followers convinced themselves that there were signs which showed who was, in fact, saved. Though the teachings said that how you actually behaved made no difference to salvation, believers convinced themselves that one's conduct must be a sign and that those who acted in a way pleasing to God were, in fact, of the elect.

The conviction that one could know that one was saved developed without corresponding modification of the belief that one's salvation could not be influenced by one's actions. If a person's conduct was the sign of his or her membership in God's elect, then any evidence whatsoever of deviation from God's ordinances would be a cause for doubt about his or her salvation, for such deviation could not be corrected by penitence and penance. The slightest departure from God's way was, then, to be avoided at all costs. This meant that individual believers were motivated to maintain the most stringent self-control, monitoring their conduct in the most systematic and rigorous way, most scrupulously conforming to their standards of behaviour, all in order to show not the slightest blemish – all the while, of course, living in the practical world of daily affairs with its endless demands for pragmatism, compromise and flexibility.

What was striking to Weber about the cumulative effects of Lutheranism and Calvinism was that they brought into the lives of ordinary religious believers demands for self-monitoring and self-control that had, hitherto, been asked only of the most advanced of religious practitioners or, as Weber referred to them, religious 'virtuosos'. Other, later, Protestant sects such as Methodism, Pietism and Baptism, whilst lacking Calvin's rigorous consistency, nevertheless held to the conception that salvation could not be attained by good works, sacraments or confession, and propounded the rational planning of life in accordance with God's will. What the Protestant sects collectively created was a new mentality which involved the thorough disciplining of every detail of practical life. It was through the formation of this stringently managed attitude to everyday activity that the Protestant ethic, Weber held, helped create the 'spirit of capitalism'. It was a further feature of that 'spirit' that it encouraged the extensive 'rationalisation' of life, the extension of calculation and control into all its sectors, but particularly into the sphere of economic action.

Although the Lutheran insistence that a person's calling demanded that an individual fulfil the obligations of his or her station in life, it could not explain how the pursuit of profit could rise above the demands of tradition, as it does in the modern world. Calvinism was significantly different. God's world gives to people opportunities to add to God's manifest greatness by doing well in their calling. It would therefore be sinful to fail to take even the smallest opportunity that God gives. There was, thus, no reason to regard oneself as prevented by the obligations of tradition from taking whatever economic opportunities life offered. To the contrary, it would be to reject something that God had given.

A good illustration of this relentless attention to even the smallest detail of economic affairs, and condemnation of the neglect of even the smallest economic opportunity, is provided at a key point in Weber's essays by the citation of Benjamin Franklin's condemnation of waste:

> Remember, that time is money, he that can earn ten shillings a day by his labour, and goes abroad, or that sits idle, one half of that day, though he spends but sixpence during his diversion or idleness, ought not to reckon that the only expense; he has really spent, or rather thrown away, five shillings besides.
> He that kills a breeding sow, destroys all her offspring to the thousandth generation. He that murders a crown, destroys all that it might have produced, even scores of pounds. (Weber, 1930: 48–9)

The inevitable result of such remorseless profit-seeking will be the prosperity of the business. But the seeking, as with Franklin, is expounded in terms of the sinfulness of waste, the wickedness of idleness and laziness combined in turn with warnings against the sinfulness that success and prosperity themselves could encourage. Business activity was worthy only where it was directed toward realising the glory of God. The motivation of business expansion and accumulation had been detached from those of the personal acquisitiveness and had become almost an end in themselves. The moral rightness of profit-seeking resulted from God's sanction and its sheer endlessness was a result of the necessity for unrelenting devotion to the ever greater majesty of God.

The Weber thesis: critiques and continuities

The Protestant ethic thesis remains a matter of sharp controversy, much of which continues to be over its interpretation as well as interpretation of the historical record. Pellicani (1988), for example, argues that the thesis is false because, first, the spirit of capitalism was found in medieval Europe and, second, the Protestant sects were opposed to the accumulation of wealth. Oakes (1988–9), however, accuses Pellicani of pointing to kinds of medieval capitalism which were adventurous ones motivated by greed as opposed to the sober, unheroic, duty-guided kind found in modern capitalism. He also reiterates Weber's point that the spirit of capitalism was an unintended, almost paradoxical, consequence of teachings which forbade the pursuit of wealth for its own sake. In the same volume, Dulman in attempting to summarise the difference from recent historical scholarship, asserts:

> Weber's thesis continues to be vigorously discussed, although no new productive starting points have taken up his initial ideas in all their fullness. No doubt today we see individual factors differently; no longer value Luther's conception of vocation so highly; distinguish Calvin's theology from Calvinism in important ways; see no direct connection any more between the active bearers of early capitalism and the propagandists of an ascetic Protestantism; and in general make more distinctions within the Calvinist–Puritan tradition and weight the Catholic contribution to modernity differently. Yet Weber's thesis is therewith not directly met, since he was primarily concerned with an analysis of the origin of the modern spirit not as an intellectual construction, but as a behavioural articulation. (1988–9: 80)

MacKinnon (1994) has provoked another round of controversy by claiming that Weber failed to understand Calvinist ideas and that subsequent developments in Puritan thought invalidate the entire thesis. Weber's case rests upon the claim that Calvin's doctrines engendered a psychological crisis in believers with respect to the 'proof' of their salvation; that is, they can neither do anything to influence their fate nor ascertain whether in fact they are saved. However, MacKinnon argues that in Calvin's thought provision was made for some self-assurance through 'good works', which could be of a spiritual kind, so providing an alternative to the need to seek self-assurance through disciplined application in worldly affairs. This was amplified by subsequent developments in Calvinist thought and so there was no need for believers to confront the crisis Weber identified. MacKinnon's critics claim, among other things, that he himself has misunderstood Calvin's theology and that he has failed to apply proper standards of textual scholarship to its interpretation (Zaret, 1994). Further, it is argued that MacKinnon pays too much attention to the official theological writings and makes too ready a connection between these and the actual beliefs of the followers. Even if MacKinnon is correct about Calvin's own teachings, this would not show that Weber's thesis was invalid. Although a way of avoiding the crisis may have been present in Calvin's thought, it may still have been true that believers did, in fact, face such a crisis (Oakes, 1994). The debate continues as to whether the whole 'Protestant ethic' question has been a complete waste of time or remains a provocatively fertile thesis (Moore, 1978; Poggi, 1994).

Weber himself did not suppose that the essays on the Protestant ethic had conclusively established his case for the critical causal role of the Protestant sects in creating modern capitalism. At most, he had shown that there was an affinity between that ethic and the spirit of capitalism, and had outlined a plausible account of how one *could* have led to the other. This account was plausible at 'the level of meaning'. It was an exercise in explanation which was meant to make the connection between the Protestant ethic and the spirit of capitalism 'understandable'. Weber attempts to show how it would make sense for the people concerned to act and react in the way that they did given their beliefs, ideals and purposes. However, showing that such a sequence of events was possible, and, therefore, a possible cause of the capitalist spirit, was not the same as establishing the case 'at the level of causality', that is, as demonstrating that this was, in fact, the causal sequence.

There was also some resistance to the idea that religious teachings could have such a decisive impact on socio-economic change. One way in which to reinforce Weber's argument would be through a general comparative survey showing the significant effect that the 'economic ethics' of major religions have had on the economic development of their respective societies. He therefore, began upon the study of the 'world religions', among which he numbered Confucianism, Buddhism, Hinduism, Christianity and Islam. Although he did not make substantial progress in the study of the latter two faiths, he did make a study of 'ancient Judaism' because of its formative influence on Christianity and, thus, upon the history of the Western world. The point of these studies was to reinforce the claim for the causal efficacy of religious ideals and, through this, secure his claim that the Protestant ethic was a causal factor in the origin of Western capitalism.

As the latter remark indicates, it was the rise of the civilisation of the West that remained the focus of his attention, with his study of other civilisations undertaken to enhance the understanding of his own. Further, Weber's concern to show the causal influence of the 'economic ethic' of religions upon socio-economic organisation was a self-consciously 'one-sided' one. He recognised that the description of the way religious ideas influence social life was a selective, partial story. In fact, Weber's comparative studies were by no means one-sided, for if Weber did draw out the economic role of religious ideas he placed at least as much emphasis upon the way in which socio-economic conditions shaped religious ideas and practices. Along with the studies of the religions of India, China and ancient Judaism he produced a general *Sociology of Religion* which provided an account of the evolution of religion, ranging over a wide range of topics including the conditions favouring the emergence of specific beliefs such as those of monotheism, the roles of prophets and priests, the relationships of religious leaders to their congregations, and the variable religious inclinations of diverse groups such as the peasantry, the nobility, the urban bourgeoisie and those he termed 'the non-privileged strata'. He also turned attention to the various forms that the idea of salvation has taken, and the assorted practices, such as ritual, good works, self-perfection, asceticism and mysticism, that have been used as techniques of salvation, all as aspects of his understanding of the relationship, often one of tension, between religious teachings and such 'worldly' matters as economics, politics, sexuality and art. Throughout, there was a combined concern with the way in which social conditions favoured the creation of certain kinds of religious ideas and the conditions under which different types of people lived, developed their religious dispositions (or lack of them) and made them more amenable to one sort of religious belief rather than another.

It is out of Weber's comparative study of religion that we can see his conception of the nature of sociology and of society. Though no theoretical system-builder, none the less Weber developed a set of analytical concepts which he used with great effect in the analysis of features of rationalisation in modern society.

The organisation of society

Weber was scornful of views, like those of Durkheim, which supposed that society existed as a reality above and beyond that of individual human beings and their actions. Durkheim had maintained that unless society was a reality in its own right, then sociology was without an independent subject-matter. Weber, on the other hand, argued that sociology had its proper subject in the actions of individuals directed toward other individuals.

Action

'Action' Weber defined as 'behaviour with a subjective meaning'. The idea of 'subjective meaning' is particularly difficult to explain clearly, especially in a succinct way, and it will suffice, here, to take it to mean something that is done with an intention or purpose in mind. Many of the actions which an individual performs are not directed toward others – someone who sits in his room riding an exercise cycle in order to make himself fit is engaging in action but not in social action. Someone who rides a cycle down the street, however, will engage in social actions. If she is to ride safely she must be aware of the presence and behaviour of others, must seek to anticipate how those others will act and adjust the course of their own actions in anticipation of and response to that behaviour. It is with those actions which involve people in taking account of and adjusting to each other that sociology is specifically concerned.

At the basis of sociology there must, Weber thought, be a conception of the basic forms that actions can take. He identified four such basic types.

Traditional social action. This includes actions which we do because we are accustomed to doing them, ones which have an habitual character, which we do thoughtlessly and automatically, and because it is the way in which such things are conventionally done. For example, we shake people by the hand in greeting because this is the established, *traditional* way friendliness is shown in many societies.

Affectual social action. This is conduct which arises from and expresses our feelings, particularly emotions. Thus, we rage and shout at people to show the anger they have provoked in us, or embrace and hug them because of the affection we feel toward them.

We have said that action is, for Weber, behaviour directed toward an end, and these first two forms of action come close to the borderline of his definition. To do something out of habit is not necessarily to have any purpose in mind, just as to react emotionally is to express one's feelings rather than to seek some objective. The other two forms in Weber's schema are the more central cases.

Instrumentally rational action. This is action which has an essentially practical purpose; that is, it is devoted to working out the means to get something done, such as, for example, calling in a technician to repair the television. This kind of action involves choosing means to meet an end. It is 'rational' in that it involves the search for the most effective means to the relevant end. It is the inclination of 'utilitarianism' (as we will see in our discussion of Durkheim) to conceive of the rationality of human action *exclusively* in terms of such instrumental, practical concerns. However, Weber, like Durkheim, recognised that not all action is of this 'instrumental' kind, and that, therefore, the logic of efficient means/ends relations does not represent the only kind of rationality.

Value rational action. This form of action involves conduct which is, to use Weber's own words, 'determined by a conscious belief in the value for its own sake of some . . . form of behaviour, independently of its prospects of success' (quoted in Käsler, 1988: 154).) In Weber's view, people's actions are guided by beliefs and ideals, by conceptions of how they would like things to be; these he calls 'values'. There are many things people do because they believe them to be right or desirable. The captain who 'goes down with his ship' is someone who, seen from a practical point of view, has needlessly given up his life, and in that sense this is an 'irrational' action. But it is one which, to someone who believes that there are more important things than practical outcomes, and that there are, indeed, more important things than human life, appears as a rational course of action, as the only one which can honourably be taken in such a situation. The behaviour of standing unrelentingly by one's responsibilities is, in such cases, valued for its own sake, regardless of its prospects of practical success, even at the cost of one's own life.

The distinction between these two latter types of action further exemplifies Weber's insistence upon the range of interests which human beings pursue, and the extent to which people can have an attachment to objectives which are in tension with, and which can, for them, rise above, practical, utilitarian and material considerations. Weber's very definition of 'value rational action' makes the contrast with those actions which are pursued out of concern for practical material interests, identifying those which can be pursued even despite such interests.

Both Marx and Weber view human beings as acting in pursuit of their practical interests, prominently their economic ones, and this is something that creates conflict for, of course, one person's economic interest can often only be advanced at the cost of someone else's. Weber viewed 'value rational action' as another common source of conflict. Someone who sees a particular form of behaviour as worthwhile for its own sake does not typically suppose that it is to be sought only within his or her own life, but is also eager that it should be pursued in others' lives, too. Thus, the Protestants, for example, were not content that their own lives were given to the service of God, leaving other people to behave in whatever ways they might wish. On the contrary, it was part of their idea of service to God that they should spread His Word and bring the conduct of others into line with His commandments. The values that people hold are very diverse, and acting them out ensures conflict as they try to impose their preferred ways of acting upon each other.

Marx had made economic conflict, in the form of 'class struggle', the driving force of social change, and Weber certainly did not intend to minimise the importance of economic conflicts, even of class struggles, but he was insistent that conflicts of economic interest were not the *only* sources of influential social struggles, and that many of these originated in differences of values. In Weber's view, the possibility of conflict pervaded social life and interpersonal relationships, to the extent that the conduct of social life was often a continuing struggle between individuals or groups of them. To use his own example, even a chess club can be the site of a protracted faction fight. It was this emphasis upon the pervasive nature of conflict, and the diversity of its sources, that led to Weber's nomination as the forerunner of a 'conflict' approach to sociology, about which we say more later.

Though Weber held that society was made up only of individuals and their actions, he did not think that single individuals themselves make much difference to the state and development of the whole society. A few leaders can make a difference, but it is usually only through collective activity that people make a significant impact upon the overall arrangement of social affairs, and Weber's sociological ideas were much concerned with the condition and character of *group* action, and his account of 'social stratification' was pivotal in this.

Social inequality: power, class and status

If Weber viewed social life as an intense competition amongst individuals with divergent economic and other interests, he did not imagine that this competition is conducted on equal terms. Power is by no means evenly shared out.

Power, in Weber's definition, is a person's capacity to get what he or she wants, even in the face of resistance by others. Social stratification is precisely about the unequal distribution of people's capacities to obtain things, and to prevail over others, and is, thus, essentially a phenomenon of the distribution of power.

Weber agreed with Marx that the possession of economic resources is vital for the achievement of ends. The extent to which people are unequally placed with respect to economic resources he was also prepared to characterise as their 'class position'. In line with his insistence that only individuals are real, however, he was not prepared to go along with any suggestion that might be found in Marx to the effect that a 'class' is a real entity with interests of its own, and which might differ from what its members believed their interests to be. For Weber, a class is not by its nature an actual group, it is only a category, or collection, of individuals who occupy comparable economic positions, and who need have no awareness of each other, or recognition of the fact that they are in the same position, let alone of the need to unite in pursuit of shared interests arising from that position.

The respect in which people are to be judged 'in the same position' in economic terms is, Weber argued, that of their 'life chances', that is, their prospects of leading a certain kind of life. The notion of life chances is a probabilistic one: how likely is it, given a person's current position, that certain things will happen to him or her in his or her lifetime? It is a fact about society, for example, that a person in a manual occupation is more likely to suffer from certain kinds of illness than someone in a non-manual one. Equally, it is less likely that someone born to a family of manual workers will obtain a university education than someone who is the child of professionals. The notion is probabilistic because, of course, people in working-class jobs do not necessarily suffer those illnesses, and some of their children do go to university. Yet it is an 'objective' rather than a 'subjective' fact of social life for it has nothing to do with what persons *believe* their class position to be. It is, rather, a property that needs to be calculated and determined for an individual without any reference to what he or she might believe.

The distribution of life chances is no random process. Marx argued that class membership is determined by one's position in the process of economic production, and Weber did not disagree with this. Marx proposed that one's position within economic production is fixed by one's relationship to the means of production. Weber made a slightly different proposal, though one which did not, in many respects, make for a significant difference. For Weber, it is one's relation to the market that is decisive in fixing class position: whether one buys or sells labour, as well as in terms of the labour one seeks to sell or to buy. Thus, a skilled worker comes with skills to sell, whilst the unskilled worker has only the raw capacity to work on offer. However, those who have skills to sell have different skills to dispose of, and this may put them at odds with one another. For example, a railway engine-driver and a truck-driver have different skills to sell and are in conflict with one another insofar as engine-drivers find that the transfer of goods from rail to road is taking their work away from them.

In deciding whether people stand 'in the same relationship' to the market there is an irreducible element of arbitrariness with which the criterion of sameness is to be applied. This is a matter on which the sociological analyst must finally take a decision. Thus, for example, it can be held that not even the members of the same occupation are in the same relationship to the market, for even though such capacities as they have to sell are broadly alike, there are still likely to be significant differences between them. Amongst ditch-diggers, for example, there is the difference between the young fit ditch-digger and the old wearied one, a difference which may in the end mean that the young one has a job and the old one does not. Applying the criterion of sameness very stringently would leave us with virtually an infinite number of classes. But such a finely discriminating classification would be beyond the practical resources of sociology and be of little practical use. For sociology's purposes, a much less stringent criterion, overlooking a vast multiplicity of intra-individual differences, is usually appropriate, one which sees not only the members of the same occupation but also those of broadly the same kinds of occupations as being in the same position in the market. Indeed, for many sociological purposes, it is sufficient to make the central difference of class on much the same basis that Marx did, namely that of ownership or non-ownership of property, for it is that which decides whether one comes to market to buy someone else's capacity to labour or whether one is there to sell one's own. It is this which characteristically makes a considerable difference to one's income and resources, and thus to one's capacity to lead a certain kind of life.

The formation of the class and status order   Though Marx and Weber more or less agree that, for many sociological purposes, 'class' is a matter of the ownership and non-ownership of property, they disagree about the import of class as a basis for collective action.

Marx took what would nowadays be called a 'realist' view of the theoretical constructs of science. Classifications are designed to capture divisions which are inherent in reality itself, and a 'class' is therefore something which actually exists independently of the theorist's conception of it. Given such a view, it makes sense to ask whether a proposed way of distinguishing one class from another is the correct way of doing so, and whether it actually does follow the line of division which exists in reality. For Weber, such a question makes no sense. There are lots of differences between individuals, but there is no dividing line built into reality which allocates them to different classes, and any proposed division between them is at the theorist's convenience. As mentioned earlier, we could devise virtually an infinite number of classes, but such discrimination would be too refined and inconvenient for the theorist when a crude division into two classes will often serve well enough. Weber is not being cavalier on this matter, but is, rather, pursuing the implications of his 'nominalist' views, which treat the theoretical constructs not as representing things inherent in reality but, rather, as devices to organise theoretical thinking.

Marx argued that the difference in economic interests arising from shared positions in the system of production would lead people to recognise their common interest and to unify in pursuit of it. This claim was one which Weber's approach eliminated. A 'social class' might become a group in that people in comparable positions might become aware of each other, see one another as having interests in common and set about organising more effectively to advance those interests. This could happen, but it was by no means destined to do so, and on the whole it is an unlikely development. It would require specific social and cultural conditions to encourage the recognition of similar situation, of shared interests and the need for action. Weber maintained that it is only relatively rarely in history that the members of social classes act together in a self-conscious way on the basis of their common economic position and associated interests. More often, the behaviour of members of a social class impacts upon society in the form of 'mass action'; that is, people who are in the same economic position respond in the same way to a particular situation, and do so just because people in the same situation tend to react in the same way. Accordingly, they act commonly but quite without awareness of each other.

Economic inequalities are not the only kinds of inequalities in society. There are inequalities in the value that people put upon each other, the esteem or honour in which they hold one another. People look upon each other as superiors, equals and subordinates, and their orientation to each other in these terms significantly affects the ways they behave. Indeed, people will often accept as associates only those whom they regard as at least their equals, rejecting those whom they think stand below them in the social order. Thus, social groups arise which are based upon the equality of regard in which their members hold one another. These Weber terms 'status groups'.

Such groups are ones which are defined 'subjectively' rather than 'objectively'. This does not mean that status groups are somehow less real than classes; on the contrary. A social class, in Weber's terms, has only the potential, often only the faint potential, to make up a real social group, but the status group is, by definition, a real group. The 'subjective' definition of the status group means that it consists in the reciprocal recognition of each other by the members of the group, an awareness of each other and an acting toward one another on the basis of that awareness of common position and interest.

Status groups, Weber held, form within the sphere of consumption rather than those of production and distribution, and it is 'lifestyle' rather than 'life chances' which is the criterion of membership. People recognise each other as equals on the basis of the kind of life they lead, feeling that certain patterns of life are to be looked up to or looked down upon. As Weber pointed out, it is not enough to have equivalent wealth to be recognised as someone's equal, it is what one does with the wealth which is decisive. Thus, the newly rich are often looked down upon and disparaged as *nouveau riche* by those who come from backgrounds of long-standing wealth and prestige because they lack the social connections, manners and polish and because they consume their wealth in ostentatious and 'tasteless' ways. It is the kind of house they buy, where they educate their children, the sorts of cultural activities they cultivate that are, in such cases, the marks which differentiate between inferiors and superiors. This was the kind of pattern Weber had detected in his early study of the agrarian problem, in which the high-status Junkers, whose economic advantage over the emerging bourgeoisie was being eroded, had sought to sustain their sense of *social* superiority over these economic rivals.

The basis for status differences is not an economic one, and people of comparable economic power can stand in differential status positions. But, of course, status inequalities cannot be entirely independent of economic ones if only because the maintenance of the consumption required for a superior 'lifestyle' demands, in the longer term, an appropriate level of prosperity. However, though there is a relationship between wealth and stratification in the case of status, just as there is in that of class, the relationship in the two cases is quite different, and, in important respects, antithetical. Stratification in terms of 'class' is based upon relationships to the market, but the development of strong status differentiation turns upon restricting the operation of the market. If the lifestyle characteristic of a status group could simply be acquired by being bought on the market, then one could become a status equal just because one had enough wealth. Thus, the kind of things which status groups make the criteria of membership are ones which characteristically cannot be purchased in the market. Thus, though one can buy big houses, hire servants and so forth, one cannot buy a long family lineage of wealth and influence, or retrospectively an education at the 'right' schools and universities. Status groups struggle to keep the things which are the marks of their status from the market, even to the extent of inhibiting the workings of the market itself.

The most developed example of a status system is the Indian caste system, which is divided into rigidly ranked, sharply distinguished and mutually closed groups in which a person's worth is decided entirely by heredity. Occupations are allocated on the basis of caste membership and marriage prospects restricted within the cast group. The development of a status system militates against the development of the class system, as must be the case if one is based upon the operation of the market and the other on its restriction. In the caste case, it is position in the status system which dictates one's occupation, rather than one's occupational position being the basic determinant. Weber conjectured that the two bases of society's organisation flourished under different conditions, with status groups tending to be more prominent in stable societies, and class stratification coming to the fore in times of more rapid social change.

Through the notion of 'status group', then, Weber opened up the possibility that social stratification can be organised around many different criteria of evaluation. Economic situation is certainly one basis upon which people rank each other, but ethnic origins, gender and religious affiliation are others which have been important. Though class membership can be the fundamental basis for ranking people in society, Weber does not have to assume, as Marx did, that it is the only, or even the primary, one.

Very often, then, the status group is more important in social organisation and social conflict than are social classes. The status group is, by definition, a real social unit which has some sense of solidarity. Its members recognise each other as equals and acknowledge a need to stand together against the depredations of rival groupings. It is easier for the members of such a group to act in a concerted way, although the basis of their joint action is likely to be a diffuse sense of mutual interest rather than a clearly calculated understanding of their common interests and of the most instrumentally rational means to achieve these. However, it is the reality of the status *group* as a basis for collective action which leads Weber to treat this form of stratification as central to his understanding of the economic ethics of the world religions, as we shall shortly see.

Power and forms of domination   A clear, self-conscious awareness of common interest and the calculation of effective means toward realising that interest is characteristic, again by definition, of 'the party', the third element in Weber's account of stratification. The status group is concerned about its position, its power over other groups, and it acts to sustain and develop that power position. But it is not, like the party, specifically formed in order to struggle for power. By 'the party' Weber does not only mean those organisations which are called 'parties' and which are the constituents of an electoral system, but any kind of organisation which is set up specifically to compete for power, and which organises itself primarily in pursuit of this. Thus, Weber observed, the kind of faction fighting which goes on in a chess club would comprise an instance of party organisation if those in the factions have set them up to fight for control of the club, to determine who shall occupy the administrative positions within it and what policy it will follow. The basis for party membership is, then, acceptance of its purpose, a recognition of common interest with other members. The members of a party can, but need not, be drawn from the same kind of social groups. A party can base itself upon a particular social stratum, can align itself with a particular social class or ethnic group, in which case it is likely to recruit mainly, if not exclusively, from that group. But parties need not identify themselves in that way and can also recruit a socially heterogeneous following, one which crosses class and status lines.

Social relations were, for Weber, essentially conflictual, and prominent social struggles were between social groups, sometimes social classes, sometimes status groups and sometimes parties. Of course, he did not imagine that social life endlessly involved overt conflict and outright struggle, with inequalities being endlessly, and in every particular, contested. This would simply be a false picture of historical reality for in very many historical situations people are quietly compliant in inequality and domination. They *accept* and do not contest the inequalities which confront them and are obedient to the commands of their superiors.

Power, in Weber's definition, is the capacity to achieve one's ends even over the opposition of others, but power is not always faced with opposition, nor is it always exercised over those who are resentful of and resistant to its imposition. The powerful often achieve their ends through the willingness of others to act as instruments of their projects. Weber marked a difference between the exercise of power as such, in which might alone achieves the objective, and situations of 'domination' (or, as it used to be translated, 'authority'), in which the entitlement of the powerful to the obedience of others is accepted by the latter. The domination of some individuals by others is regarded as something which is right, which is justified, and it was, therefore, important to Weber to identify the main bases which justified domination as legitimate.

Weber noted three main forms of domination, singling them out in terms of their primary justification.

Tradition was, historically, the most widespread and long-lasting of these, which is given leading example by the kingly ruler who holds the position through inheritance and is entitled to obedience entirely because the right has traditionally been in the hands of his family. The king's power to command derives not from any personal characteristics, but entirely from the fact that he is someone with the right kind of hereditary connection to his predecessors. The forms of domination are ways of administering social affairs, and each form is associated with a characteristic administrative arrangement: 'traditional authority' is typically operated through the royal court, with the king's personal following performing the administrative functions because they are connected to and trusted by the king, and carrying out their functions at his behest.

Charismatic leadership is contrasted with traditional domination, for the power of charismatics resides entirely in their personal qualities. Charismatics are those who, in the original meaning of the term, are gifted with 'holy grace', or, in Weber's usage, those who present themselves as people with special gifts – frequently supernatural – which entitle them to the obedience of others. Charismatics, accordingly, claim to have been sent by God or national destiny, and demand that others should follow them unquestioningly to realise what they ordain. Charismatics are an exceptional people in the sense that their personalities are such that they can impress themselves upon others powerfully enough to lead them to abandon their normal lives to follow their cause. Such figures are common in religious life, but are also to be found in the worlds of politics and warfare. One leading example of the charismatic is, of course, Jesus Christ, who claimed to be the Son of God sent upon a special mission of salvation, entitled to demand that others follow him to the extent of giving up their jobs and families to become his disciples. The charismatic is surrounded by an immediate personal following who act as the administrators of the movement, but the leader personally is typically contemptuous of regular organisation and worldly affairs, and tends, therefore, to treat matters of day-to-day administration somewhat whimsically.

The third type of domination Weber calls *'rational-legal'* to emphasise the fact that leadership is selected through the use of a procedure which is legally sanctioned. This is the kind of domination which we have in our own society, where the democratic electoral process is the means of choosing between rival leaders, and where entitlement to occupation of the position of leader and to our obedience are both due to the fact that he or she has been chosen for the leadership in this legally sanctified way. This type of leadership is associated with an administrative arrangement which is staffed by professionals, who have no personal relationship to the political leader, but who hold their jobs on the basis of their qualifications. They, too, have been selected for their positions by explicit procedures, most notably those of examinations, and their movement up the hierarchy of positions is based upon their supposed success in administrative work.

Charismatic leaders are the ones who, for Weber, have powerful potential in initiating important social changes, for they are typically disruptive and innovative. Charismatics can appear under either traditional or legal-rational domination, and characteristically confront and challenge the existing order. Religious prophets have often created and disseminated new ethical conceptions as, for example, Luther and Calvin did in Reformation Europe. However, whilst the charismatic leader can have a powerful impact, this can be short-lasting. It certainly cannot span the generations in the way that a dynasty of traditional rulers can. It is short-lived for two reasons: first, charismatics are constantly required to prove their powers, and, second, the charismatic's powers are purely personal and mortal.

The charismatic's position demands the continuing proof of his or her special powers. The prophetic leader can only convincingly claim special status so long as the prophecies are fulfilled, just as the military leader can only claim special powers if battles are won, and the leader is, therefore, vulnerable to a poor run of fortune. Even if events continue to 'prove' the charismatic leader's power, that leader will, sooner or later, die, so creating a problem of succession. Since the charismatic's powers are personal, they cannot be transferred to someone else. If the group the charismatic has founded is to continue, a successor must none the less be found. However, the selection of such a successor cannot be assured to find another equally dominating, powerful personality, and so the charisma of the deceased leader will be displaced onto the leadership position, rather than the person who occupies it. For example, the Pope is a special person not by virtue of his own awesome personal powers, but because he occupies a position as, so to speak, the successor to Christ. This transition from personal to positional power Weber termed 'the routinisation of charisma', marking the end of a period of charismatic leadership proper because routine is anathema to true charisma. Charisma is a disturbing and transitional force, lasting no longer than a single lifetime and either fading away or absorbed, at the moment of succession, into either one of the other two more stable types of domination, traditional or rational-legal.

During its lifetime the administration of the charismatic group is also unstable. The charismatic is surrounded by 'disciples', by personal followers who are chosen according to the leader's own decisions and who owe their loyalty to the leader personally. They are not usually chosen for their administrative skills, not least because the charismatic leader is typically indifferent to everyday matters, including those of running the routine affairs of his or her own group. Furthermore, the leader's decisions are often very changeable, and there is little stability in the direction in which the movement goes from day to day. Administrative decision will tend to be short-sighted and superficial, run by the dictates of someone with continually changing aims and with little interest in the details of how they are to be implemented, and carried out by trusted devotees rather than those chosen for any demonstrable administrative competence.

Bureaucracy, by contrast, involves the selection and promotion of administrators on the basis of administrative training and experience. It provides stability and predictability as an environment for decision-making, providing officials with life-long careers and, thus, some protection from the arbitrariness of superiors. The system of rules and hierarchy means that the individual's work is subject to impersonal regulation rather than personal behest. Because they are entirely dependent upon the bureaucracy for their income, the bureaucrats are thus insulated from external influences. They are not dependent upon the goodwill of others nor so amenable to bribes, and are less inclined to be suborned whilst making administrative judgements. In other words, the bureaucratic setting is one in which administration is a specialised task, in which expert administrative knowledge is concentrated, and in which decision-making procedures are stabilised and made independent of all kinds of exigent constraints. Therefore, it is not perverse to argue, as Weber did, that ideally such structures are superior for the administration of large-scale populations. Real bureaucracies of course depart in all kinds of ways from this ideal.

Weber perceived a political threat in the growth of bureaucracy, that there would develop a conflict between the administrative system and the political leadership which was supposed to direct it. Administration is a means not an end in itself, but the danger Weber saw is that the officials, by virtue of their administrative expertise, will be able to dominate their supposed leader, and will give priority to their own administrative preoccupations over the political objectives of the politicians who should be giving purpose to and controlling their work. It is the politicians' role, in

Weber's nationalistic conception, to lead the nation-state's pursuit of its destiny, not to be manipulated by civil servants.

The sociological concepts which Weber devised were numerous, but those for the analysis of stratification and domination were amongst the most significant in his comparative study of world religions, and have subsequently been most influential in sociology. The notion of 'status group' was particularly critical. If society is to be understood as a continuing struggle for domination among social groups, then those which have measure of internal solidarity and common purpose are more likely to be successful in the pursuit of their interests, and, as noted, the status group is much more likely to have these characteristics than are social classes. Further, what unites the status group is a 'style of life', and the style of life involves strong cultural elements, including values.

Religion, bureaucracy and the Chinese literati　We have mentioned that Weber saw ideas as having potent influence on socio-economic change only if they were involved with the interests of social groups, and thus, in his studies, he was alert to the need to identify groups which could act as 'bearers' of ideas and provide potentially effective vehicles for the introduction and transmission of values into society more generally.

In his studies of traditional Indian and Chinese societies Weber paid particular attention to pivotally placed status groups. In the Indian case, it was the Brahmins, a high caste of priests and teachers, in the Chinese, it was the Mandarins, who staffed the administration of the empire. What was particularly interesting about them was that though they were not dominant in society in political or economic terms, they were, none the less, immensely influential within the society, decisively shaping its culture and, in certain ways, even having power over those who were their political or economic superiors. The Brahmins, for example, had a crucial position within the caste system, and it was their authority in this respect which often placed them above those to whom they were in secular terms subordinate.

The Mandarins were at the centre of Weber's account of the religion of China, for they were the bearers of Confucian teachings which provided, for him, such a stark contrast with Protestant doctrines. Protestantism and Confucianism had systematically unified the relationship between God and the world, but with very different ethical consequences. Both of them provided rational systems of thought, each providing a consistent ordering of human life based on religious belief. Both encouraged sobriety and self-discipline and were compatible with the accumulation of wealth. The ends they espoused were, however, very different. Confucian ethics were aimed at creating 'gentlemen', people who were educated, cultured, with highly refined sensibilities, and who were devoted to their further self-cultivation, leading a life which took the traditional attitude of piety toward one's family elders as the model for conduct generally and, especially, meant respect for both propriety and for authority. The cardinal virtue for the

Confucian was that of consonance with the harmony of heaven and earth through fulfilment of the traditional duties of family and office and the requirements of ceremonial. This world and those in it were merely a part of the harmonious and beneficent unity of the entire cosmos, a view which contrasts with the Protestant image of both humanity and the world as inherently evil. Confucianism resembled Protestantism in the way in which it taught religious fulfilment through the discharge of one's secular responsibilities. The former, however, indicated that this should be done through acceptance of and compliance in the established order of things within the numerous constraints set down by tradition and ceremonial, whilst the latter came to reject all such restraint, including all sacraments and symbols that might distract an individual from the inward experience of God and guidance by His commandments. Obedience to those commandments stood above everything else, even the obligations of family.

The Mandarins, being officials in a 'traditional' bureaucratic structure, owed their powerful position as the effective rulers of the Chinese empire to qualification rather than wealth. They provided a sub-section of the wider status group of 'intellectuals' (termed 'literati' because of their possession of literary skills) and were capable of projecting a conception of themselves as the exclusive carriers of the culture of Chinese civilisation. Their success in projecting themselves thus made the figure of the gentleman engaged in educational and cultural pursuits, rather than economic or political ones, the ideal for the whole civilisation. The literati were strategically placed because of their administrative and political utility to the rival princes who were eventually included within the unified empire. For historical reasons, the literati were not inclined toward strong religious feelings. For them, religion was primarily of importance for its role in placating the masses, with the result that any religion which was likely to develop amongst them would be barely a religion at all. Confucianism was one such, placing its stress entirely upon the gratifications of this world, upon the benefits of long life, the family and some personal wealth rather than upon an afterlife and salvation. It was, further, one which contributed to the idea of the political status quo as sacred and, accordingly, to the sanctity of tradition.

The religious practice of the Confucians was directed toward 'self perfection' through the acquisition of the all-round virtues of the gentleman. The issue of the salvation of others did not arise. It was no business of Confucians to promote their own religion throughout the society and, in fact, the literati were highly tolerant of other religious and magical practices, limiting them insofar as they might present any threat to the interests of the state.

In this concise summary of Weber's treatment of the religion of China we can identify many of the themes that ran through his comparative studies. The concern was with the place of a crucial status group – the Mandarins – in 'setting the tone' for the civilisation's culture; upon the way in which they, through the political struggles leading to the formation of the unified state, had come into their powerful position; how the nature of their position shaped their religiosity and inclined them toward certain kinds of teaching; how they, as a group, sought to defend and advance their position against potential rivals. The situation of the Mandarins within their civilisation was understood in terms of a 'conflictual' conception.

The understanding of the religion of China was not, it must be recalled, for its own sake, but for its relevance to the understanding of the origins of the spirit of capitalism in Western Europe, primarily through *contrast* in the roles that the Protestant and Confucian religions could play in imparting economic dynamism. We have already indicated how the Protestant and Confucian world views differ, despite their common, highly rationalistic emphasis upon religious fulfilment through secular activity. In the characterisation of the role of the literati we have noted three things which Weber considered decisive in ensuring that the rationalism of traditional China took a very different direction to that of Western Europe. First, the literati's religious outlook bound them and their society ever more tightly to tradition rather than breaking away from it. Second, the tolerance and indifference of their religious outlook limited their effort to rationalise religious thought, and prevented them from seeking the elimination of magic. Third, the prevalence of the ideal of the educated gentleman, whilst it certainly did not inhibit the accumulation of wealth, prevented business activity from acquiring any inherent value of its own.

In addition to all this, the importance of 'family' in their lives was such that kinship dominated commercial transactions, voluntary associations, law and public administration. The stress on kinship led to a distrust of all persons outside the extended family, whereas Protestantism enjoined a trust of all persons who were of the faith. In Weber's view, the subordination of the demands of kinship to other, more impersonal requirements in many spheres of social life was vital to the development of the institutional setting within which the development of capitalism and the expansion of rationalisation could take place. Weber also argued that the most thorough development of bureaucracy was only possible in a society where there were legal codes based on the idea of 'citizenship'. This, he saw, resulted from the political independence of cities and, in important part, derived from their capacity to form armies based upon citizenship. Politically independent cities with their own armies were a tradition in the West that reached as far back as the Greek city-states and lasted through the cities of the Middle Ages. In the Orient, however, cities did not acquire this kind of independence because, for example, their development was under the aegis of a previously established military power or because they were dominated by religions or by kinship traditions which inhibited the idea of forming groups in association with strangers and, thus, of forming an army made up of those who had only location within the same city in common.

Capitalism, rationality and social change

It is a difficult task to summarise Weber's overall account of the rise of the modern capitalist system in the West. Much of his work was directed toward the comparative analysis of other civilisations, with a particular emphasis upon their religious traditions, and the way in which these engendered their own distinctive 'economic ethics'. Given the pivotal status of the *Protestant Ethic* within Weber's work and the predominance of studies of religion in the rest of that work, it would be easy, but mistaken, to suppose that Weber considered religion to be the most important causal factor in the emergence of capitalism. On such a view Weber would seem to be taking up a position at the opposite extreme to the Marx that he knew, and opposing the role of ideas to determination by economic and political factors. However, it was not Weber's purpose to challenge an extreme with another extreme, as though one or other of them must be the right one. Indeed, in his last lectures, in Collins' words, he 'reduces the ideal factor to a relatively small place in his overall scheme' (1986: 20–1). The characterisation of his own emphasis on religious interests as 'one-sided' recognises that this is a very partial account of the historical situation. Weber is as willing to recognise that economic organisation has causal consequences upon religion as that religion can have causal consequences for economic organisation. He is not arguing that religious causes be given as causes of capitalism *instead of* economic, political and other ones, but that they be given *as well*, as one of the numerous factors determining the course of a civilisation's development. The obstacle Weber perceived himself as overcoming was a view which denied religion any role at all, except as a 'rationalisation'. When Weber came to give an overview of the origins of modern, Western capitalism it ought not, therefore, to be surprising that 'the religious factor' was comparatively less prominent: it is, after all, only *one* amongst *many* factors.

Indeed, Weber argues that to trace the origins of modern capitalism requires a broader focus than that upon the Reformation period in Europe. The presence in Reformation Europe of many preconditions of capitalism, both 'material' and 'ideal', was certainly the immediate stimulus of capitalist development, but that combination of material and ideal conditions did not spring up overnight; it was itself the product of a long process of historical development of Western European civilisation.

The rationalisation which marked capitalist society, and especially its business organisation, could not have been possible if appropriate ways of thought and skills had not already been in place; if literacy, calculation and record-keeping, for example, had not already been developed and acquired social significance over many centuries. The Protestant sects played a crucial role but they themselves were the product of a reaction against the Catholic church. The Catholic church itself had a long history, one which owed its character to the nature of Christianity, a religion formed out of the legacy of two prior civilisations, namely, ancient Israel and Greece. Indeed, Weber saw some of the impetus for the strong development of rationalisation in the West originating in these civilisations. Ancient Judaism's conception of the relation to God, for example, gave rise to a religion, Christianity, which treated the prospect of salvation not as one available to a Chosen People but as available universally. This in turn fed into the idea of people as related to one another by universal legal membership. In addition, the general rationalism of Greek intellectual culture was a strong influence on the later culture of Western Europe and a potent inspiration to the growth of rationalisation.

Weber's comparative studies were intended to make sharp contrasts with the 'world views' of the Western tradition. He did not suggest that these other civilisations had failed to develop capitalism because they were inferior or incapable of rational thought. He stressed that the proclivity to rationalisation was a contingent feature of a culture. It was possible, for example, for Mandarin China to thoroughly rationalise its world view. But it had to be recognised that there was no necessary direction in which rationalisation had to go. The direction it took in Mandarin China was antithetical not to business and trade, but to the kind of spirit favourable to these activities. There was nothing inevitable about the rise of capitalism. It was the product of developments which could have taken a different direction. Had the reaction against the religious dominance of the Catholic church not taken place, then capitalism might still have developed, but, in Weber's judgement, it would not have had the compulsively rationalising impulse that drove it in the West.

The inexorability of rationality in the West

Weber's interest in the origins of modern capitalism was not motivated by purely antiquarian curiosity. It was also influenced by his political outlook and his concern to understand and take part in shaping the political future of his society. However, the political implications of his analysis depressed him. The forward drive of rationalisation seemed irreversible and meant a degradation of the quality of life.

The inexorability of rationality did not contradict the view that the rise of capitalism in the West was contingent. Weber's argument was that it had become so deeply entrenched in the organisation and culture of the modern West that everything, including its immense practical success, worked to encourage its further expansion into every sphere of life. However, though it had much to its credit, including providing material comforts unparalleled in history, it did not ensure the growth of contentment. For Weber, one of the problems of Western societies was the deep level of alienation and 'lack of meaning' for a great many people, and this was a product of rationalisation.

Part of Weber's interest in religion was motivated by the idea that religious ideas can provide 'meaning' to human lives, give them a greater purpose or significance by fitting them into a larger pattern. Religious beliefs often make the world 'enchanted' in that it becomes more than a sequence of purely empirical occurrences. Natural phenomena become more significant and awesome if they are understood as manifestations of God's purpose, for example. The effect of rationalisation was to 'disenchant' the world, particularly through scientific advance. The world came to be increasingly understood in terms of the purely causal connections of empirical phenomena. While this enhanced the practical exploitation of nature, it served to deprive life of any 'meaning', significance or value over and above its ability to satisfy material wants. For many, this is not enough and their lives can seem empty and purposeless.

Rationalisation also made relationships increasingly detached as in more and more areas of life they became governed by strict rules which applied regardless of personal relations, as, for example, between one bureaucrat and another, or between the bureaucrats and those they administered. Indeed, in Weber's eyes, it was the bureaucratic form of organisation which constituted one of the biggest threats of the inexorable march of rationalisation.

The iron cage of bureaucracy The organisational form of rationalisation is that of the bureaucracy and this, too, in Weber's eyes, contributes much to the meaninglessness of modern life. Within these vast administrative structures the individual becomes increasingly insignificant, a mere cog in an impersonal machine. Work within the organisation is subject to rules, as are those subordinate to its administrative enforcements. Life becomes conducted within an 'iron cage' of regulation and administrative oppression. The very workings of bureaucracy themselves come to be seen as pointless.

There are political dangers, too. The great power and efficiency of bureaucratic organisations means that they can effectively promote their own interests over and above those of others, including the interests of those who are supposedly their political masters. It was this tendency, Weber feared, which was one of the great threats to the political life of the modern world, leading him to stress the need for strong inspirational but democratic political leadership which could keep the bureaucracy under control and ensure that it served some meaningful political purpose not merely its own expansion and empowerment.

Weber was not hopeful that this drift toward the 'iron cage' could be contained. The political alternative was the socialist movement, but, as far as Weber was concerned, this would expand the extent of bureaucratic domination. The role that the socialists projected for the state would mean even more bureaucratic regulation. Although its intention would be to ensure liberation, it would almost inevitably ensure people's further subjection to senseless, self-serving bureaucratic rule. Weber's contemporary, Roberto Michels (1876–1936), in his classic study *Political Parties* (first published 1915), reinforced the point that more, not less, bureaucracy was to be expected from socialism, by noting how, within socialist parties, the need for an administrative bureaucracy led to a dilution of the political programme in favour of the expansion of the organisation.

For Weber, the political imperative was to resist this rising tide of bureaucracy, and to create the opportunity for a charismatic political leadership to arise and provide a sense of national purpose. As indicated earlier, this ought to be within a democratic context, though such a leader should be allowed considerable room for manoeuvre. Weber's politics were both democratic and élitist. He saw a need for exceptional and inspired leadership to provide a sense of purpose for the society of his day and to dominate the bureaucracy but within a broad commitment to democratic politics. However, the conditions which obtained in Germany did not, he felt, favour the realisation of such hopes. The 'iron cage' would remain firmly in place.

We have outlined Weber's views on the origins and nature of modern capitalism up to the point at which he gave them application to the examination of the political plight of his own society; a society whose problems were not untypical of comparable contemporary societies. Weber's approach to these matters was related to more general, underlying philosophical-cum-methodological preconceptions which specified what could be expected from social scientific activities, and it is to an exposition of these we now turn.

The methodological Weber

For Weber it was historical and sociological studies that were important, and methodological debates about the underlying principles of inquiry distinctly secondary. More particularly, speculative debate about methodology was unacceptable; if methods must be discussed, then let them be those which have proven successful in actual investigative use. This, at least, was what Weber preached: his disdain for methodological controversy did not, however, prevent him from vigorously engaging in it. In a sense he had no choice, for the intellectual environment of the Germany within which he worked was intensely preoccupied with the proper methodology of social and cultural studies, including that of sociology. The original *Methodenstreit* (the 'dispute over methods') arose within economics but there was a much more general debate into which a whole range of scholars was drawn, involving history, legal and language studies, as well as economics. Weber's own background in legal studies, economics and historical work ensured that he was aware of these controversies, and his own purpose in joining the dispute was to articulate a relatively coherent view of the methodology that was meant to inform his own research.

It should come as no surprise to learn that these methodological controversies were essentially about a question that is still debated, namely: can the social and cultural studies ever be true sciences? In the quarter century prior to the First World War this issue was the focus of a complex, many-sided dispute among often polarised positions. Weber sought to reconcile many of these, drawing heavily, as he freely acknowledged, upon the ideas of the philosopher Heinrich Rickert (1863–1936). Essentially, the debate was about the question of whether the social sciences could be like the natural sciences in their method and about the kind of knowledge they produced – whether they were methodologically distinct from the natural sciences or, even, whether they were sciences at all?

The nature of the social sciences

One approach to the question of the scientific status of the sociocultural studies, that was broadly adopted by Durkheim, is one which is often called 'positivist'. It holds that there is an essential unity to science. All sciences pursue essentially the same purpose, which is the formulation of general laws. There is only one way in which any discipline can become a science, that is, by following the general method which has already proven successful in the natural sciences. Accordingly, studies of social life should seek to transform themselves into full-blown sciences by implementing the general scientific method and studying the cultural lives of human beings in the same way as any other natural phenomenon.

Though the positivist position was powerfully sustained by the obvious success of the natural sciences, as a programme for the study of social life it was distinctly less effective, and by the end of the nineteenth century there was growing opposition to it. Influential thinkers such as Friedrich Nietzsche (1844–1900) and Sigmund Freud (1856–1939) were suggesting that the nature of human beings was much more 'irrational' than previously supposed, and that methodologies based upon positivist principles were too 'rationalist' to allow for the recognition of this irrationality. Within German philosophy, moreover, there was a well-established tradition of thought, mainly of an 'idealist' character, which opposed positivism, at least with respect to the study of human beings. This opposition owed much to Immanuel Kant (1724–1804), whose own idealism Hegel had both criticised and enormously extended, and so one important party in the *Methodenstreit* were the neo-Kantians who, though he did not share all their contentions, had a significant influence on Weber.

The Kantian strain in Weber's thought   Kant had explicitly sought to limit knowledge in order to make way for faith. Metaphysical philosophers made it their aim to know ultimate reality, an ambition which, if successful, would eliminate the need for religious faith. Kant found this aim appallingly presumptuous, and attempted to demonstrate that it could not possibly be fulfilled. It was not possible for human beings to know ultimate reality – reality as it is 'in itself' – for they could only ever be acquainted with reality as it appeared to them. It was not possible for reality to be known 'in itself' because of the nature of human knowledge.

Kant sought to unite two polarised philosophies – rationalism and empiricism – since they were, he maintained, complementary. They argued over whether knowledge arose from 'reason' or from 'the senses'. The rationalists insisted that knowledge was produced by the mind through the working of reason. The empiricists insisted that knowledge was produced through the contact of our senses with the external world. Kant claimed that knowledge involved a synthesis between the capacities of the mind and of the senses. The only evidence that we have about the nature of the world comes to us through our senses but, Kant argued, the input from our senses has no intrinsic organisation: it is only a flux of disconnected impressions, a chaos of meaningless sensations which do not, on their own, present us with a perception of the array of stable objects arranged in time and space that we do, in fact, experience. The mind must *impose* a pattern of organisation upon the torrent of sensory impressions. The relations of spatial distribution, temporal succession and causal connection, for example, are not ones which we discover in things in the world but are already 'built into' our minds and through which we interpret and order the impressions coming in through our senses. As Durkheim was to agree, the experience we have of temporal, spatial and causal order amongst things cannot be obtained by abstracting from the raw experience of the world generated by sensory input. (Durkheim, however, was to turn this point against Kant, and to insist that ideas of time, space and causality were not built into the individual mind at all, but supplied to it by society.) Thus, Kant could argue that we cannot know reality 'in itself', as it is independently of our minds, for an element in anything we can call 'knowledge' will always derive from the mind itself.

The Kantian idea that we cannot know ultimate reality was one which Weber accepted, and which was the basis for his insistence upon the limitations of the sciences, both natural and sociocultural. He also accepted the idea that the mind plays an active role in the production of knowledge, that it *imposes* an order upon the otherwise formless phenomena of experience.

In Weber's view, reality is made up of concrete, individual things, each of which has its own inexhaustible set of unique properties. We could never exhaustively describe any one such thing. The vehicles of human thought are, however, abstractions and, as such, can only selectively represent things in reality; they can only include mention of some few of the virtually infinite variety of characteristics that make up the thing in itself. In creating the abstractions with which to think, then, we are of necessity making a choice, singling out certain features of things as the characteristics by which we shall identify them, in unavoidable disregard of the innumerable other characteristics which the things have. The ideas – abstractions – that we have can, then, only be the faintest representations of the concrete, inexhaustible richness of the actual things in the world that they seek to capture. What decides *how* we think of things in the world, what characteristics we see them as having, is something that is determined by the needs of our thought. In identifying a thing we have an endless variety of characteristics which we could pick on as the ones to associate with it, but because we can only grasp some of those characteristics we must select certain ones, and the selection that we make will have to do with the needs of our thinking. For example, if we describe someone to the police we mention, typically, their skin colour, height, build, the possession of visible distinguishing features such as scars. We do not, and could not, describe all the other features they have: each and every hair upon their head, the shape and colour of their finger-nails, the cells which make up their skin and so forth and so on. The features that we describe are ones which actually serve a particular purpose. In this case they assist in the *recognition* of the individual by selecting features which will enable his or her identification on sight and from among other individuals.

We have mentioned how Weber's 'nominalism' contrasts with Marx's 'realism'. Weber held that the general, abstract terms of the sciences did not refer to any reality. They could not do so for there are no general, abstract things in the world. The world is made up of concrete, individual things only, and, though we may use abstract general terms to talk about those concrete individual things, the connection between the terms and the things we use them to talk about is essentially an arbitrary one, a connection which is made *for our convenience*. We *decide* to collect numerous concrete, individually unique things together under the same heading because it is useful for certain purposes that we highlight a few of the features which they have in common at the expense of all the other characteristics which they do not share.

There was a further aspect of Kant's arguments which deserves comment. The burgeoning natural sciences were proving so successful that they could claim that they would eventually be able to explain everything in terms of causal determination. Natural phenomena were being increasingly understood in terms of causal laws, their behaviour determined by physical causes. It seemed only a matter of time before human behaviour, too, could be explained in the same way. The effect of this would be to jeopardise our notions of 'moral responsibility' and 'free will'. If such causal explanations could be sustained, it would be irrational to blame people for actions which they are causally determined to undertake. Kant sought to argue against claims about the all-encompassing reach of the natural sciences, insisting that there was an inherent limit on their application. Human beings were resident, so to speak, in two realms. They were indeed subject to the laws of the natural, physical sciences for human beings are physical creatures, and, as such, their behaviour is causally determined. Our bodily movements are subject to the law of gravity, the working of our physiology depends upon causal conditions to keep it in operation. However, human beings also inhabit a 'realm of freedom', the domain of ideas, beliefs and reason, and this is separate from the physical world and exempt from its causal laws. Human beings *do* make choices and decisions, act on the basis of their ideas and beliefs, follow the dictates of their reason, and therefore they can – in Kant's view, *must* – be held morally responsible for their actions. Kant thus provided a particular cast to the debate about the scientific study of humankind: is the 'realm of freedom', the world of mind and ideas, amenable to scientific study?

Knowledge and the interests of inquiry   Some of Weber's predecessors had argued that inquiry into human life should be entirely separate from the sciences, for the phenomena being investigated were in the world of beliefs, ideas and values (or, as it is often convenient to call it, the world of meaning) and are completely different from the phenomena of the natural sciences. Accordingly, they require an essentially different method. One aspect of the stark contrast between natural sciences and sociocultural studies was made in terms of those investigations, primarily those of the natural sciences, which aimed at providing generalisations (the so-called 'nomothetic' disciplines) and those, such as historical studies, which were primarily devoted to studying particular, individual cases (the 'idiographic' disciplines). Weber, however, did not think that this distinction between the 'nomothetic' and 'idiographic' entirely equated with that between the natural and the social sciences. Economic and sociological theory, for example, were generalising pursuits in his view.

Another, similarly stark, contrast was made in terms of method: the natural sciences sought causal explanations while the historical ones pursued 'understanding' in trying to grasp the ways in which the ideas, beliefs and values of people guided their actions. This method, known as *verstehen*, was neither causal in intent nor subsumable under the rubric of the scientific method. Weber himself, following Rickert, accepted the Kantian view that human beings are different from other natural phenomena and that proper study of them requires the use of the *verstehen* method. However, Weber maintained that this method was used as part of a process of *causal* investigation and did not conclude, therefore, that there was an essential difference between the natural and sociocultural sciences. The latter had features which distinguished them from the natural sciences, to be sure, but they were subject to certain *general* requirements of scientific method.

Like Rickert, Weber held that the crucial difference between the natural and social sciences does not originate in the subject-matter or methodology of the respective disciplines, but in the interest which motivates our studies. The leading natural sciences offer highly generalised accounts of phenomena, and this is acceptable to us because we are not, on the whole, much interested in individual natural phenomena, in the differences between, say, one stone and another. Insofar as we are interested in a particular stone at all, it is typically in respect of some use to which it could be put – we find this stone useful because it is *a* stone, not because it is *this particular* stone. The natural sciences reflect this typical lack of interest in the individual character of natural phenomena.

Historical studies typically reflect the fact that when it comes to human beings that someone who is *this particular* individual is of interest to us, and we are interested in those things about them which are distinctive to them, which they do not have in common with others. Thus, we are not interested in, say, Napoleon in respect of those things which would make him just *an* individual like any other, that he must eat, breathe, can talk, etc. We are interested in him because he was *the particular individual* who led an army which vanquished large parts of Europe, and whose activities had exceptional consequences on the history of our own society. When Weber talks of 'individuals' he does not necessarily mean individual people, but sometimes is talking of a whole people and their civilisation. Thus, part of our interest in Napoleon, the individual person, is due not only to his outstanding feats, but also to the fact that those feats had an impact on the whole history of the part of the world *in which we live*. The complex of Western Europe and the UK (or even the wider civilisation including that of North America) can constitute an 'individual' in this sense, and we are interested in the history of that individual in a way that we are less interested in the history of some other comparable, but geographically or historically remote, 'individual'. As we mentioned, the focus of Weber's work was upon the development of the 'individual' that was modern Western capitalist society, and Weber's study of more remote civilisations such as the Indian and Chinese was not undertaken because he had the same interest in them as he had in that of the modern West, but because he thought that understanding them would help in his understanding of the West.

The problems which sociocultural studies seek to solve are ones which arise from particular historical situations – why has the West taken a different road to that followed by other great civilisations? – and their solution, therefore, involves the investigation of those cases in all their specificity. The production of general laws is not the objective of sociocultural studies in the way it is the main objective of the natural sciences. But this does not mean that there is no point at all in developing general sociological concepts – Weber himself, in *Economy and Society* (published in English, 1968), did extensive if uncompleted work on such development. However, it was not the *primary* purpose of such investigative work. Its value must ultimately be judged in terms of what it contributes to the understanding of the 'individual' historical cases that are the principal focus of study. Sociology, for Weber, was not an entirely autonomous science but, rather, an adjunct to the historical disciplines. As McLemore points out: 'Weber was principally an historian, and it is perhaps too little appreciated that the primary aim of his early methodological writings was to defend the status of historical inquiry' (1984: 278).

Thus, Weber insisted that the difference between the natural and social sciences was due to the indifference that we have, on the one hand, toward the individuality of phenomena which make up the natural world, and the intense interest that we take, on the other, in the individuality of the fellow creatures that make up our social world. This latter interest is not, of course, evenly distributed but tends, rather, to be concentrated upon those who in themselves, or through the consequences of their actions, *matter* to us. To talk of what matters to someone is to speak of the *values* they hold, their ideas of what is important and worthwhile. Weber is, therefore, unequivocally saying that intellectual inquiry is no less governed by people's values than is any other activity. *Both* the natural and the sociocultural sciences are *value relative*. It is the difference between the value that individual natural phenomena and individual human beings have to us that makes the difference between the two kinds of inquiry.

Values and value freedom

The difference between the natural sciences and sociocultural studies is relevant to the extent to which they can develop general systems of concepts. There can be much greater continuity of purpose among natural scientists, and therefore a much greater coherence to the concepts they develop. Natural scientists are interested in natural phenomena only insofar as those phenomena are like one another, and thus the study of an individual instance is only a means of the studying of such phenomena in general. Thus, natural scientists studying different individual phenomena can have interests which coincide, allowing them to abstract mutually relevant aspects of the phenomena from their particular features. Individual instances of phenomena do not, as such, really matter to natural scientists. In the study of human beings, however, it is the differences between the individuals which is commonly of greater importance than what they have in common, and it cannot even be assumed that the way in which one individual will matter to one investigator will be the same as that in which it matters to a different one.

The interest that Weber had in Western civilisation owed everything to the fact that he was part of it, and that he was much concerned with its future and the fate that his own particular values would meet in the face of contemporary developments in Germany. A scholar with different interests and values might, therefore, find Weber's ideas, concepts and mode of analysis neither so interesting nor so useful as they were to Weber, and would need to set about studying the development of Western civilisation in a very different way. The *selective* nature of abstract concepts would ensure that those contrived by Weber would bear the mark of his preoccupations because they were the ones relevant to his problems, which arose out of his pervasive interest in the origin and fate of his own civilisation. Someone with a different general interest would have different problems and would need to make different selections in formulating their abstractions. In other words, all accounts of sociocultural life are *unavoidably* partial and reflect, in the end, the things that matter most to those who make them. Thus, if Weber's general ideas achieve any widespread acceptance it is not because they have captured indisputably general features of reality itself, but because of the widespread nature of the values and problems which motivated his work. Thus, though Weber's values were ultimately directed to the problems of the German nation-state and the responsibilities of the intellectual within that, his work can take on a much more general interest throughout the modern Western world because, of course, many of the problems of Germany are intertwined with those of the Western world as a whole.

Accordingly, there is a fundamental arbitrariness in the creation of abstract concepts of all kinds, though it is more marked in the social than in the natural sciences. The acceptance of abstract concepts depends upon their utility relative to a problem, and the validity of the problem itself is relative to values. However, this seems to make Weber's 'methodology' inescapably relativist, to the point at which anyone can proceed in whatever way they see fit.

Value freedom and politics   Weber maintained that, at bottom, intellectual inquiry is value-relative. Indeed, the acquisition of knowledge itself is a value, and not one that everyone shares. It is somewhat paradoxical, then, that Weber has sometimes been chastised for espousing an idea of 'ethical neutrality' or 'value freedom' in science which draws upon a simple-minded contrast between science and values. Weber did indeed maintain the importance of 'ethical neutrality' in science, but not on the basis of a naïve supposition that scientific work is unrelated to questions of value.

The idea that science is 'value-free' is often taken to mean that scientists can be entirely irresponsible with respect to the consequences of their work, and are free to pursue knowledge for its own sake without caring about what is done with this knowledge. Far from encouraging such irresponsibility Weber was concerned to advocate a 'responsible' and 'professional' approach to scientific work which was specifically concerned with controlling the wider consequences of science. His argument draws upon a familiar and standard distinction owed to David Hume (1711–76) between 'fact' and 'value', between empirical statements and the expression of evaluations. The former report how things are, the latter relate how things are to how they ought be, characterising them as 'good', 'bad', 'right', 'wrong', and so forth. Evaluative statements cannot be logically derived from factual ones, so Hume argued and Weber agreed. The breach of this principle is commonly termed 'the naturalistic fallacy'. This is taken to mean that it is possible only to prove the truth of empirical statements; one cannot equally conclusively demonstrate that some state of affairs is, say, 'bad'. This means that the difference between values cannot be *rationally* decided, that moral differences cannot be settled by argument, reasoning and proof. Values are, as a matter of fact, very diverse and are logically irreconcilable and, therefore, their diversity is logically irreducible. One person may believe that a certain course of action is 'right' and another person that this same course is 'wrong' and their disagreements *cannot* be settled by evidence and logic. Thus, there can be no *logical* basis for people to choose one set of values over another. None the less, people will have to choose. They will have to live in one way or another, that is, have to decide that one way is the right one for them to follow over another. All conceptions of what is right cannot be satisfied because these conceptions contradict one another. Thus, if confronted with a choice between two incompatible ways of life – such as the Catholic commendation of the monastic ideal and the Protestant condemnation of it – we will have to make an arbitrary decision about which one is right for us. This is why Weber's views are sometimes termed 'decisionist'.

Diverse values mean not only choices for the individual but also, importantly and as previously discussed, opposition between groups of individuals. We have already mentioned how a valued way of life often involves personal demands and commitments, but also demands about how others should live their lives, even if they do not agree. Such conflicts between values cannot be resolved through rational debate; they belong to the realm of politics. It is through conflict, struggle, confrontation and combat that the protagonists of one set of values seek to subordinate, perhaps even eliminate, the protagonists of some other set. The struggle may be for domination for its own sake, but it is often as much, and often even more, about ensuring the domination of certain values and their associated way of life as it is about the possession of power for its own sake.

There is an important difference between Weber and Marx that is worth noting at this point. As we have seen, the latter was a wayward follower of Hegel, whose dialectical philosophy had been specifically intended to show that, in the course of history, all the 'contradictions' which philosophy had made seem irreconcilable could be overcome. History was a 'working out' of contradictions. Marx adapted the idea to claim that it was through class conflict that such 'working out' took place, ensuring that contradictions of human life would be reconciled. In this respect, Hegel and Marx were optimists. Weber was not. There was, for him, no prospect that human life could change its basic nature with respect to the diversity and antagonism of values: the things which different people want are often in outright conflict, and their different demands cannot be 'reconciled' in any logical sense. Social conflict, arising from opposed values, would remain a constant feature of history. The idea that history has any kind of unifying purpose, let alone that this might be to overcome all contradictions of life, was utterly foreign to Weber.

Political struggle is the medium through which values contend with each other. It is the means by which we decide – or it is decided for us – which of rival 'Gods' and 'Devils' will rule our lives. Politics is about the question: how are we to live, what are we to do? This question is, in Weber's judgement, the most important one we can ask. However interesting and useful they might be, the empirical questions which science asks are not so important as those that confront politics, for these also include the question of the use we are to make of scientific knowledge.

Weber used such arguments as a basis for attacking what he saw as an undesirable state of affairs in the universities of his day, where many of his contemporaries were presenting their scholarly work as though it carried political implications. Since questions of fact and value are sharply distinct, there can be no question of one value being 'scientifically' shown to be superior to another. The choice between values is necessarily a matter of decision and of faith. Hence, however eminent scientists might be, they are authorities on the subject-matter of their specialism only, and have no special or unusual competence in connection with matters of value. When it comes to matter of 'right' and 'wrong' there are no experts, and therefore it just is not possible for one person to be more of an expert than another. Weber's essential complaint was that university teachers who pressed their political views from their academic position were abusing their authority, exploiting the opportunity that their authority as distinguished scholars gave them to impress their values upon their relatively susceptible students. They were collapsing the difference between their scholarly work and their ideological and political views, presenting the latter as though they were supported by the weight of the former when, as Weber saw it, this could not possibly be the case.

Weber's call for 'value freedom' was, in many ways, an attempt to prevent this abuse of scholarly and scientific mission by calling for acceptance and preservation of the distinction, and logical gap, between 'is' and 'ought', between empirical knowledge and value judgements, and, thereby, between the scientist's scientific work and political involvement. As should be clear, it was not a claim about the irrelevance of values to science, nor a demand that scientists should take no responsibility for the consequences of their work. What it does mean is that, first of all, there is a difference between a lecture and a sermon, between a sober presentation of the procedures and products of a piece of scholarly work conducted under the established standards of scientific inquiry, and an exhortation on behalf of a certain outlook. The scientist should respect that distinction, excluding the personal statement from the professional, particularly the teaching context, and making it in a more appropriate place, namely, the political forum. This did not deny the scientist a voice, nor an opportunity to say what, in value terms, his scientific work might mean. But it was meant to divest the scientist's voice of any particular privilege within the political forum. The scientist is, of course, 'privileged' with respect to the statement of what his or her work means *in scientific terms*. It is by this means that the scientist may have a part to play in the political process; but that part can be only an advisory one. The scientist can explain scientific work to laypersons and can use scientific knowledge to advise upon the empirical consequences of policy decisions. However, when it comes to establishing the *political* meaning of scientific work, then the scientist – *as scientist* – has no privilege whatsoever. In political debate the scientist's voice is no more important than anyone else's, for questions as to whether something is worth doing, whether it is more worthwhile than something else, are questions about which no one is more or less entitled to a view than anyone else.

Scientific inquiry itself, like all other forms of human activity, originates in 'irrational' considerations in the sense that it is motivated by values which cannot themselves be rationally chosen. 'Rational' is, in Weber's terminology, a term which applies to the selection of means not of ends. Scientific inquiries cannot, therefore, ultimately be objective, but this does not mean that they cannot be objective at all. It was part of Weber's argument on science and politics to call for a sober adherence to the established standards of scientific inquiry, for it was this which would ensure such objectivity as inquiries can have. Scientific research might originate in the personal motivations of the inquirer, but the activity of inquiry could be subjected to impersonal standards which apply across the sciences and which require, for example, logical consistency in argument, and the provision of sufficient and appropriate evidence in support of claims. Responsibility to such public standards of proof means that scientists are able to subject each other's work to careful and impersonal scrutiny, and thus to make a reasoned decision whether, given the initial problem, to accept a scientist's claimed conclusions.

The nature of sociology

Weber was far from regarding sociology as any kind of 'master science'. He generally held that the main concern of the sociocultural studies was with understanding actual historical situations, and thus the principal form of investigation was into the specifics of particular situations, and the kind of inquiry conducted by history. Sociology was an ancillary discipline. It was not that there could not be law-like generalities about social action, but that these could not, for the reasons discussed, be interesting for their own sake. Their value lies in their use in disentangling the complex problems of causality in historical investigations, much as Weber's own general ideas about 'stratification' and 'domination' had been intended to clarify the causal interactions, particularly between 'material' and 'ideal' interests, in the creation of modern capitalism; a problem which Weber had inherited from his historian predecessors Werner Sombart (1863–1941) and Ernst Troelsch (1865–1923). Indeed, and again as we mentioned earlier, Weber undertook, but did not complete, a major project, translated as *Economy and Society*, to work out a system of general sociological concepts, beginning from the categorisation of the types of social action we outlined earlier. In this work he continued his early interest in economics, and sought to elaborate a general account of the various forms that the relationship between economic and social organisational factors could take: the issue of the origin of modern capitalism is but an instance of that general relationship. In *Economy and Society* Weber reviewed, in a very general way and among other things, such topics as 'typical measures of rational economic action', 'the primary consequences of the use of money', 'the concept and types of profit-making', 'the concept of trade and its principal forms' and 'the financing of political bodies'.

Of particular concern to the 'methodological Weber' are his views on the nature of the generalities which sociology had to offer, views which followed from his ideas about knowledge and science. They were, in terms which he did not invent but did employ, 'ideal types'.

The ideal type   It was, recall, the role of the mind to impose organisation on reality. There is no abstract, general order intrinsic to reality itself. The mind must project such an abstract, general order, because concrete, individual reality is itself too complex for the mind to be able to represent in its totality. It is only by *simplifying* reality that thought can comprehend it. The interrelationship of elements in reality is a causal one, but that which connects ideas is a logical one, and it is the function of systems of ideas to provide the process of thought with organisation and structure.

The construction of concepts must of course be based upon the examination of reality, and Weber himself was assiduous in surveying the historical evidence. But the development of concepts is inevitably a process of 'idealisation', that is, conceiving things in terms which can exist only in 'the ideal' world of thought and not in reality. The notion of 'ideal' in the ideal type is the same as that involved in the natural scientist's idealisation of the 'frictionless engine' or the economist's notion of 'perfect competition'. There can be no such thing as a frictionless engine, but it is helpful to think through certain physical problems by imagining that there could be such a machine. In conceiving of a frictionless machine the scientist takes the calculations which show the consequences of reducing friction and extends these to the extreme, the case in which friction is reduced to zero.

Weber argues that the social scientist also takes things which one finds in reality and extends them to logical, and unreal, extremes. Thus, the ideal type of bureaucracy is based upon an examination of administrative organisations in societies as diverse as those of his contemporary Prussia and traditional Imperial China. In these Weber noted tendencies to put administration in the hands of administrative specialists. He is not, however, content to leave these as different, unrelated phenomena but seeks, rather, to achieve a level of generalisation which shows what they have in common. To do so, he projects the tendencies toward specialist administrators found in the historical materials in the direction of a logically coherent extreme. The full, 'pure' development of specialist administration would involve, for example, the administrator considering all problems from a purely technical administrative point of view in terms of their requirement for efficient solution, entirely without fear or favour. This would mean that the administration should be free of all influences which might interfere with such technical consideration. However, the principle of specialist administration will, in reality, always be taken less far than it can in the 'idealising' imagination. It might be, for example, that the principle of efficiency will conflict with that of tradition, and will, accordingly, be compromised to accommodate to this. The real administrator is, further, likely to be concerned for his own job security and advancement and may let these affect his technical judgement. Thus, we are unlikely to find anywhere in reality a 'full-blown' bureaucracy which has all the characteristics Weber listed. That the actual bureaucracies of Prussia and China do not correspond entirely with his type was no surprise to Weber, for his was only a theoretical model which *intentionally* misrepresents what things are actually like.

But what is the point of this elaborate, and seemingly roundabout, procedure? We must recall Weber's insistence that we are imposing order on reality through introducing order and discipline into our intellectual life, and the role of the 'ideal type' is to focus inquiry by providing coherence and direction.

One of the clearest illustrations of an 'ideal type' may be taken not from sociology but from economics. It is an ideal type known as *homo oeconomicus* (or 'economic man'). This conceives of a person who is exclusively devoted to extracting every last drop of satisfaction from their resources. It is assumed that this person will unrelentingly seek to maximise their satisfaction, that they will know exactly what they are doing, will have full knowledge of the situation under which they are doing it, and so forth. Many sociologists criticise economists because of the patent 'unreality' of this construction. For example, real people do not have full knowledge of their situation, put other things before material satisfactions, and so on. Nevertheless, people do engage in economic maximising. Confronted with two items of the same type which are identical in everything except their price, persons will prefer the cheaper of the two. Economists take this tendency to maximise and exaggerate it to a logical extreme.

By doing this, economics has made considerable gains, at least in respect of constructing itself as a logically coherent system. Because it has assumed that economic maximising is pursued unrelentingly, it is able to work out, with unrelenting thoroughness, how this might be done. The formulation of the problem in this way has provided a focus to the inquiries of many economists, working on the common problem of how economic maximising is to be achieved and what its consequences are. But of what value is such theorising if its central constructs bear no relationship to reality? On a Weberian view, the purpose of such constructs is to provide an aide for examining what people actually do. At its simplest, the ideal type provides some idea of where to look for explanations of how people do behave.

For example, other things being equal, people will prefer the most economically rewarding of two options. This is the premise of the argument. The economic model, then, tells us how, in pursuing the 'rational', that is, the 'ideally' most effective means, people should behave. In fact, they often do something other than the model predicts. This raises questions such as the following: in what ways do people depart from this ideal, rational course of action, and why do they do so? Is there anything which obstructs them from following the rational course? Are they, for example, following tradition, are they being coerced, were they ignorant of relevant considerations? In other words, by looking to see where the assumptions of the model do not obtain we are given some clues as to why people have acted as they did.

Weber's concept of bureaucracy is similarly developed on the assumption that there would be no practical problems in putting together the requisites of efficient administration, concentrating expertise and effectively regulating its deployment. Thus, it is assumed that the official is exclusively devoted to the ideal of administrative efficiency and puts this before personal interest, that the rules governing relations between officials are spelled out unequivocally and consistently. Such assumptions are quite unrealistic. However, constructing the type involves the logical working through of the organisational conditions for efficient, specialist administration. Having achieved this, one can then apply the conception to reality and determine how far, and in what ways, an actual bureaucracy departs from the 'ideal', and can thus point to aspects of the case which need explaining and in directions in which explanation might be sought. Thus, a source of a bureaucracy's inefficiency might be sought in a conflict between the requirements of good decision-making and the personal interests of officials. A further understanding of this conflict may then be looked for in the way in which the 'design' of the bureaucracy has failed to segregate personal and professional considerations and so on.

Thus, the ideal type explicitly distorts reality, giving a logically extreme, rather than an empirically generalised, depiction of the things it covers. Its role is to organise inquiries, giving focus to the questions they can ask and guidance as to where, in the unmanageable complexity of actual cases, to look for relevant causal connections.

It should also be recognised that Weber is not claiming that the production of 'ideal types' is a distinctive feature of his practice. Given his views on knowledge and science, his view must be that all general ideas are effectively 'ideal types' which must inevitably misrepresent reality, but, of course, in spelling out the idea and its logic Weber is suggesting that those who think otherwise are deluded about the nature of their concepts, believing that they have somehow captured the intrinsic nature of reality. This was a mistake he thought Marx had made in taking a 'realist' view of 'social classes' and other concepts. He also felt it important to encourage a greater self-consciousness, and therefore more systematic methodology, in the deployment of general concepts, such as ideal types, in social scientific investigations.

Weber's individualism

Reality is made up of concrete, unique individuals. There are no real abstract or general entities. We have referred to this as Weber's 'nominalism' and it applies to social life as it does to the rest of reality. Hence, social life consists of human individuals. These individuals may join together in large and complicated patterns of activity, which we term 'groups', 'societies' and 'civilisations', for example. However, only individuals really exist. The terms such as 'group' and 'society' cannot refer to any reality other than that of individuals and their actions.

On this point, then, Weber was sharply opposed to both Marx and Durkheim. As we have indicated, Marx supposed, for example, that 'class' was something which had real existence, and which could have interests different from those as perceived by its members. Durkheim argued that society must be more than the sum of the individuals composing it, analogically comparing society to an 'organism' with functional needs of its own. Weber forcefully rejected the idea that the interests of a social class could be anything other than the interests of its individual members, as they saw them, and rejected, just as firmly, an 'organicist' conception of society.

Weber's individualism does not mean that such terms as 'society' and 'class' should be eliminated from the sociological vocabulary, only that it should be correctly understood what they are referring to. Any temptation to think that they refer to a 'superhuman' phenomenon which plays a regulating role in human conduct must be resisted. It is, instead, to be recognised that they refer only to the actions of individuals. If we talk about the behaviour of 'the state', for example, we are in fact talking about the behaviour of politicians and/or civil servants and other state functionaries. If we say that the state has done this or that what we actually mean is that certain politicians or civil servants have done these things. Similarly, when we talk about the actions of 'the working class' we mean only the actions of, for example, plumbers, engine-drivers and so forth. 'The state', for example, is a complex of co-ordinated actions of many individuals and part of the sociological task is to understand how the patterns of action of those many individuals make up that complex.

Of course, such collective phenomena as 'society', 'the state' and 'the working class' are made up of very many individuals and one cannot describe the activity of all those who are involved in some pattern of action – one could not hope to describe the actions of all the soldiers involved in one side in a battle, though this is what one is talking about when one talks about, say, 'the advance of the British army'. Hence, what one is very commonly talking about when one uses such collective terms is the *typical* individual; thus, to say that 'the state' does certain things is, in effect, to speak of what the typical civil servant is doing. And this is, of course, what Weber was doing when he talked about 'the Calvinist' and 'the capitalist'. He was seeking to provide a generalised characterisation of such individuals, in full recognition of the fact that, of course, there is considerable variety amongst Calvinists and among capitalists, and all do not conform to the same degree to his depiction of them. None the less, his aim is to provide a characterisation of a representative figure, one who has characteristics that are common amongst Calvinists or capitalists and salient to their conduct as capitalist or Calvinist.

Weber's arguments prefigure the views of 'methodological individualists', such as the philosopher of science, Karl Popper, who sought to condemn 'holism', that is, ideas which claim the existence of real social wholes such as 'class' and 'society', views particularly associated with Marx. 'Methodological individualists' argue that holistic ideas are not only intellectually misleading in that they falsely suggest that supra-individual entities are real, but are also, and more importantly, politically dangerous. The idea that social wholes exist and have needs of their own encourages the further idea that these wholes are greater and more important than individual human beings, and that, therefore, the needs of the whole may require the sacrifice of the life of individuals.

Such criticism arose particularly in the 1940s, after the rise of totalitarian regimes in Germany and the Soviet Union, with, in the latter case, the holistic ideas of Marx being blamed for the totalitarian character of the regime and for the wanton disposal of human life. The methodological individualists' objection to the holistic interpretation of words such as 'class', 'state' and so on are much the same as Weber's; that these terms are actually 'shorthand' expressions which refer to the actions of (typical) individuals, and that failure to keep this fact clearly in mind leads to confusion. Methodological individualists differ from Weber in a way which is indicated by the appendage 'methodological'. They do not necessarily argue, as Weber did, that only individuals are real, but claim, rather, to be making a methodological point, which is that a much fuller and more effective explanation of a collective event is given when it is described in terms of the actions of individuals. To talk of 'the army advancing' without saying anything about how squads of soldiers deployed themselves and what they did is to give a less informative and, therefore, less adequately explanatory account of what went on in a battle than if the latter sorts of consideration are given some detailing. There is, of course, an unavoidable practical limit on the extent to which individual actions can be detailed, but mention of some of these, albeit in the generalised 'typical' form, is more explanatory than talk of the abstraction 'the army'.

Verstehen   Weber accepted Kant's idea that individuals human beings are resident within both the realm of natural causality and the world of values, ideas and beliefs. Against those who argued that this called for a complete separation of the natural sciences from human studies, Weber claimed that it did not, other than to provide a distinctive cast to the human sciences. Social scientists can seek to 'understand' their subject-matter in a way that natural scientists cannot. The natural scientist seeks to determine how the causal interactions between phenomena produce events, and does not have to ask why, for what purpose or with what understandings the phenomena behave as they do. The social scientist, on the other hand, must do this if the explanation is to be adequate. When social actors go about their affairs they are typically pursuing certain ends, and they pursue those ends through the deployment of means which, they conceive, will be effective in delivering the ends they seek. Their choice of means will depend upon their beliefs in many and complex ways and also upon the conceptions they hold of how things happen in the world, of what causes what, and of what should be done to control and manipúlate these causes. Thus, if we want a proper explanation of human courses of action, then it will have to be effective at 'the level of meaning'. That is, if we want to understand the pattern of action of some 'typical individuals', we shall want an explanation which makes appeal to how they see the world, and one which, given that they may not see the world in the way that we do, will none the less make sense to us. For example, we are not Reformation Calvinists, but Weber's attempt to explain how these individuals 'typically' came to act as sober, hard-working businessmen involves laying out the complexities of the Calvinist belief system in a way which allows us to see a logic in the connection between these beliefs and their conduct. It makes sense to us that someone in the situation of the devout Calvinist would indeed be anxious about the fate of their immortal soul and, feeling this way, seek to assuage themselves of the tensions they were experiencing and so on.

Weber's account of the Protestant ethic and its role in the rise of capitalism is an application of his arguments for the *'verstehende'* or 'understanding' sociology we have just outlined. It was intended to complement his analysis of the rise of modern capitalism 'adequate at the level of causality' by an analysis 'adequate at the level of meaning' by attempting to comprehend the sense of the connection between economic activity and the explicit teachings of the Protestant leaders against the sinfulness of possessions. Looking at matters from the standpoint of the devout believer, Weber showed how anxieties about the salvation of the soul could be transmuted into a whole attitude of mind toward conduct in the secular world. He sought to show how the logic of theological doctrines, and the lessons drawn from them, encouraged self-denial and planning in the pursuit of economic gain.

If we were simply told that, as a matter of established fact, Calvinists did engage in sober, systematically disciplined business practice, we might accept that this was a causal contribution to the origin of capitalism. But, and this is Weber's point, we should not feel that we fully understood this causal relationship on the basis of the bare conjunction between religious affiliation and business practice. The nature of the causal relationship only becomes clear to us if we understand the connection from the point of view of those involved in it. If the way in which the Calvinist typically sees the world are described, then the relationship between their religious affiliation and their business practice is clarified for us, so that we can see how those Calvinists were motivated by their beliefs into engaging in their particular kind of business activity.

For Weber, then, the social sciences involved the use of this distinctive *verstehen* method, or, as it is sometimes alternatively called, 'the interpretative' (or hermeneutic) approach. It is the social scientist's task to understand other human beings, often those who have quite different values and beliefs to those of the investigator and engage in very different practices. The investigator is, therefore, working from the assumption that the ways in which different individuals 'interpret' or 'make sense of' the world around them is very different from that with which the researcher is familiar and, typically, takes for granted. So, the aim of research is to understand how those individuals 'interpret' the world around them, and to try to understand how their beliefs and values lead them to act in the ways that they do. It follows that the researcher is, thus, also acting as an 'interpreter' of the beliefs and conduct of other people, seeking to explain them in a way which makes sense to him or herself and those who will read the study, even though those being studied belong to a very different cultural tradition.

The fact that sociological investigations require this 'understanding' or 'interpretative' methodology may distinguish them from the natural sciences, argues Weber, but this does not mean that the methodology of sociology is any less scientific or demanding than that of those natural sciences. The demand for explanation 'at the level of meaning' does not mean that intuition and empathy displace the need for rigorous empirical proof. Achieving explanation 'at the level of meaning' involves the scientifically disciplined examination of evidence about the activities, beliefs, values and so forth of the people being studied, and is no less an empirical venture. Furthermore, providing an explanation which makes sense of a particular connection is by no means the end of the story. It does not dispense with the necessity to establish explanation at the level of objective causality. *The Protestant Ethic and the Spirit of Capitalism* may have succeeded in explaining the connection between the world views of the Reformation sects and capitalist business activity in that one could see how, unintentionally, one led to the other, but the question remains: was this in fact the connection? Did the economic ethic of the Protestant sects engender increased capitalist activity of the requisite sort? Such a question involves much more than just the interpretation of the point of view of the typical Calvinist and the making of an intelligible connection with disciplined business activity. It also requires the examination of the vast multiplicity of circumstances involved in the historical situation of the Western world at the relevant time: the development of its economic base, the organisation of its legal system, the character of its cities, the nature of its political problems and so on, as well as comparative analysis of related situations in other civilisations. This is a task which, as we have seen, took up much of Weber's life.

The antipathy to one-sided explanation   As we have emphasised, Weber's methodological arguments were meant to complement his socio-historical studies. The studies involved both the inspection of the complexities of specific historical 'individuals', such as the civilisations of traditional China and India, and the articulation of a scheme of generalised concepts for sociological analysis. The generalised theory-building of sociology was itself subordinate to historical investigations, for the focus of the latter was upon specific, concrete phenomena and, through this, upon reality.

Reality, in Weber's eyes, consisted in concrete phenomena which could not be directly represented by the abstractions which are, of course, the stuff of sociological schemes. Through these studies Weber worked out an underlying 'image of society' as an arena with which groups of individuals contest, more or less directly, sometimes violently, often by other means, for power over each other and, in doing so, bring about changes in the nature of the society, occasionally transforming its structure entirely.

Weber, however, could not accept the idea of a single pattern or purpose to human history as a whole that can be found in Marx. The history of human societies has not been a unified one, and different civilisations have followed very different courses. The tremendously stable, long-lasting arrangements of traditional China and India are in stark contrast with the dynamic, unstable development centred on Western Europe, for example. The configuration of economic, political and cultural elements makes, in each case, a unique complex, as does the formation of social groups which are the actual bearers of various economic, political and cultural interests. Thus, the way that traditional China's civilisation gave a pivotal role to the administrator, the Mandarin, contrasts with the way the Indian caste system was centred upon the priest/teacher. Both of these contrast with our own world, in which the business entrepreneur is assigned such a significant role.

It is worth inserting here the reminder that Weber's emphasis upon the role of 'culture', particularly of religious belief, does not make him an idealist, in the sense of believing that ideas are the only driving force of history. Such a position involves the kind of outlook that Weber is condemning, namely, the 'single-factor' view of explanation. He rejects, for example, the argument of the Marxists of his day that economic factors uniquely shape the course of history, but not on the grounds that the wrong factor has been identified and that it is culture that is responsible. The prominence which Weber gives to cultural factors is a corrective protest against the preoccupation with economic factors at the expense of cultural ones; a protest which is meant to manifest the importance of cultural factors as well as economic and 'material' ones. Weber's major work is, after all, called *Economy and Society* and it was a routine feature of his investigations to balance the argument that cultural factors shaped economic developments with equally common and persistent reminders that economic developments reciprocally shaped cultural ones.

One purpose of the methodological writings was to remind us of the vast gap between the inevitably and immensely simplified portrayals provided, for example, in *The Religion of India* and *The Religion of China* and the incomprehensibly complex concrete realities that they depict. The portrayals are, as sociological descriptions of social orders go, complex and highly detailed and his elaborate and highly qualified accounts are designed to remind us that the description of the interplay of varied forces involved in real historical configurations are resistant to formulaic representation. Weber's general methodology, however, also reminds us that making these studies even more full and detailed cannot really take us closer to the complete depiction of how reality is, so to speak, 'in itself'. The complexity of the concrete case is such as to defy even the greatest of intellectual powers.

In many ways, the methodology was intended as a corrective to the overestimation of the importance of knowledge. The contrast between our pallid, austere intellectual schemes and rich, teeming actuality is a perpetual reminder of the Kantian assumption that the capacity for knowledge of reality is limited and that, therefore, it cannot be through the advancement of science that confrontation with the great practical problems of human life takes place. Though the development of science may be one of the supreme achievements of 'rationalisation', it needs, in Weber's view, to be recognised and repeatedly recalled that the process of rationalisation itself has non-rational roots and that it is the product of a specific and contingent conjunction of socio-historical circumstances. Like Durkheim, Weber argues that modern Western science is an offshoot of religious developments and motivations. The further development of science may give us much greater practical capacity to achieve our objectives, but it cannot reduce or ease the difficulty of having to choose between objectives. Though science may have the potential to relieve much suffering, it may serve as a vehicle for, and even be a source of, the growth of a deeply unhappy and oppressive society.

The legacy

Weber's impact upon Anglo-American sociology was affected by the manner of his introduction into it. A major step in drawing attention to Weber's theoretical significance was through his inclusion as one of the four major figures (Durkheim was another) in Talcott Parsons' (1902–79) *The Structure of Social Action* (1937). This meant that Weber was understood in terms of Parsons' interpretation of his ideas. As we have mentioned, the translation of Weber's work was a protracted and fragmentary affair, and is still by no means complete. None the less, despite these unfavourable conditions, Weber's work has had a significant impact on many different disciplines. At the present time, for example, there is a rising interest in the implications of his work for the understanding of law (Kronman, 1983; Turner and Factor, forthcoming). In this concluding section we cannot survey the range or the complexity of the issues surrounding Weber's impact and will mention only the sociological implications of Weber's work, and only some of those.

Conflict theory

Parsons was concerned to interpret Weber in relationship to his own theoretical problems which had to do with the conditions for cohesion in complex society, and Weber's emphasis upon the social origin and role of values in society was critical to this campaign. Parsons' own theory rose to prominence in the late 1940s and early 1950s and very shortly thereafter was under criticism from those who identified themselves with a 'Weberian' point of view. The criticism of Parsons' theory – who, it can be argued, was much more interested in a general theory of action and values than in a theory of capitalism – was that it minimised the extent of inequality and injustice in society and thus the extent to which there was antagonism arising from these. Parsons' interpretation of Weber was criticised for minimising the prominence Weber gave to value conflicts and group antagonisms. Even the details of Parsons' translations from Weber were faulted for the same failing, allegedly choosing words which played down the element of 'domination' which Weber saw in social relations.

Weber has sometimes been termed a 'bourgeois Marx', and we have indicated the respects in which he has much in common with Marx, despite certain prominent features of disagreement. One of the crucial points of difference was in respect of the prominence accorded to 'class conflict'. Marx's views provided too close an identification between economic and political power. There might have been a virtual identity of the two in the formative period of capitalism but in the world of developed capitalism the two were separated – Weber had always insisted that economic and political power were distinct elements in stratification. Marx's approach to social conflict was, furthermore, 'reductionist' in that all significant social conflicts were essentially to be understood as class conflict. Conflicts based on such divisions as nationality, ethnicity or religion were to be understood as *superficial* phenomena, even as the distorted expression of the struggle for class domination. Thus, one finds Marxist theorists recanting on the grounds that they have now come to see that, for example, nationalism is a more important and authentic source of social struggle than Marxist theory could allow it to be (Cohen, 1988). Weber's attraction was in emphasising the plurality of sources of social conflict and the diversity of bases on which groups could oppose each other, something which allowed the recognition of the diminishing importance of 'class conflict' within modern industrial societies and took ready account of the rise to prominence of 'status'-based struggles such as those rooted in differences of ethnicity or gender.

Thus, there was an attempt to develop a theoretical alternative, which stood between the 'consensus functionalism' of Parsons and the fixation upon 'class conflict' which was seen to handicap Marxism. Weber was, thus, the inspiration for a 'conflict theory' which would recognise the importance of values in society (as 'consensus functionalism' did) but which would equally recognise the extent to which values were diverse and antagonistic. In addition, this theory would recognise the extent to which social life was a continuing contest for domination, also accommodating the extent to which material and class interests entered into the context (cf. Collins, 1975; Lockwood, 1956; Parkin, 1979; Rex, 1961). This 'conflict' theory was commended as allowing a more flexible interpretation of the forces involved in political struggle and social change than did Marx's more 'formulaic' interpretation in terms of class interests.

The divergence between Marx and Weber on these matters is obviously one which bears upon that focal issue of the analysis of 'stratification', and much contemporary argument in stratification theorising is between the protagonists of these two views. In the 1950s (Lockwood, 1958) it was argued that Weber's account of stratification provided one of the best explanations as to why Marx's predictions about a proletarian revolution had failed. By emphasising the difference between 'class' and 'status', it was argued, one could explain why it was that the rapidly expanding 'black-coated' (later 'white-collar') workers who might, in a crude sense, occupy the same class position as manual workers were more inclined to identify with their employers than with their 'fellow workers'. It was the *status differences* which they perceived between themselves and manual workers which was decisive. Such views did not, of course, settle matters, and whether the position of the 'middle classes' within the current situation is best understood in terms of basically Marxist or basically Weberian terms is still a matter of heated debate (cf. Marshall et al, 1989; Wright, 1985).

The rise of the West

Weber's ideas about domination and conflict have had an impact upon general theorising, particularly insofar as this has been concerned with conceiving social organisation at the level of the whole society and made a formative contribution to the 'third' stream which sought to position itself between consensus functionalism and Marxism.

It would be surprising if Weber's own central preoccupation, which was with the rise of Western society, and which had involved the construction of a comparative sociology, had not, itself, given rise to a significant body of further work. Weber's name is prominently invoked in those arguments which advocate that sociology should be predominantly an historical and comparative discipline, and which has concerned itself with the examination of the general conditions for the rise and change of societies. Again, there was an initial tendency for Weber's conceptions to be adapted into a relatively benign and somewhat ethnocentric view of social development, one inclined to accept that American capitalism, particularly, was exemplary for all other societies. The essential problematic was to understand the conditions for 'nation-building and citizenship' (Bendix, 1977) as a way of assisting in the political and economic development of 'underdeveloped' societies. Such views, however, came into some disrepute: they overstated the benign motivations of the 'advanced' capitalist societies, and they – again – underestimated the extent to which the struggle for domination is a feature of relations within and between societies. There was thus a tendency to take a more neutrally comparative view of social development, one which did not presume that the United States was the yardstick

yardstick by which all other societies must be judged, and one which, furthermore, placed a less exclusive emphasis upon the importance of 'cultural', particularly value, elements in promoting change. This recognised – as, of course, Weber had insisted in doing – the extent to which culture – including values – was embedded in political relations and social struggles and a much more explicit emphasis was given to the role of *power* in these matters (Moore, 1967; Bendix, 1977; Mann, 1986).

Interpretative sociology

Like Marx and Durkheim, Weber's sociology was primarily concerned with the historical analysis of society as a whole. But his 'individualism', and the associated conception of sociology as the study of 'social action', provided potent support for a strand of sociological thought which is often far removed from this concern with society as a whole. The idea that sociology is the study of the actions of individuals provides one pretext for this kind of inquiry. The study of 'society as a whole' in Weber is, as we outlined, a matter of attempting to comprehend the actions of great multitudes of individuals over comparatively long stretches of time, and one is thus dealing with the 'typical' individual, a figure who is reconstructed from historical documents. There is, however, the possibility of studying the actions of actual individuals, for one can observe and examine particular individuals as they go about their affairs, with a view to understanding how they organise their *inter*-actions.

Weber's other emphasis was upon the 'understanding' of conduct, through a grasping of the meanings which the members of society gave to their world and their actions on the basis of their beliefs and purposes. This is much the same emphasis that came to be associated with symbolic interactionism, that is, 'taking the actor's point of view', the 'definition of the situation', but whose origins belong to a different intellectual tradition than the one Weber was writing within.

The extent to which sociologists need to take account of 'the subjective understanding' of the member of society is another matter of perpetually heated dispute in contemporary sociology. Marx and Durkheim are often held up as figures who show that it is not necessary – is indeed undesirable – to take much account of the actor's point of view in explaining his or her actions. Instead, it is necessary to say much more about the situation of the total society, both in terms of its history and overall arrangements, to explain which individuals act in the way they do even if they are acting out their beliefs, ideals and purposes. Against this there are those who seek to give a much more prominent place to 'subjective understanding'. It is not supposed that *everything* can be understood from the actor's point of view, but much about social life will be misunderstood if it is not first understood by being seen through the actor's own eyes.

There is, thus, a great deal of work in sociology which provides something of a counter-tradition to the prevailing concern with, essentially, the power structure of the whole society. This is often termed an 'interpretative' (or 'hermeneutic') tradition because it concerns itself with examining the ways in which people in social relations organise their reciprocal conduct by determining ('defining') the meaning of each other's actions by 'interpreting' each other's behaviour. This is a tradition which emphasises the empirical study of the ways people behave toward each other in actual situations, and treats the understanding of their respective 'points of view' and the ways in which they figure in the interaction as a central investigative issue.

This line of thought was given a powerful initiative by Alfred Schutz (1899–1959 in Germany), who, in 1932, published a book-length study, *The Phenomenology of the Social World*, which re-examined, from the point of view of phenomenological philosophy (which called for the investigation of things in terms of a person's consciousness of them), Weber's ideas about social action. These were not properly worked out and clarified, Schutz maintained, and he undertook what proved to be a lifelong task of articulating what this could mean. Schutz went into exile in the USA in 1939, where he published many papers, which were, however, little noticed at first in the sociological community. In the 1940s Schutz's work had a decisive influence on Harold Garfinkel. Schutz had intended his work to be compatible with the conception of sociology as historical explanation found in Weber. However, Garfinkel directed Schutz's ideas into a radically different conception of what sociology might be, one which took the ideas of studying social action and the 'interpretation' of its meaning to its furthest extreme. Garfinkel created that provocative and still controversial approach 'ethnomethodology'. But it was not until the 1960s that Garfinkel's own work began to draw significant attention and thereby highlight the significance of Schutz's work. Other work done in the 1960s, particularly in Berger and Luckmann's *The Social Construction of Reality* (1967), also ensured that Schutz achieved much wider, if often strongly critical, recognition in sociology than he had during his lifetime.

As indicated earlier, the 1920s and 1930s saw the formation of an indigenous American tradition of 'interpretative' sociology, in the form of symbolic interactionism, drawing upon the philosophical thought of George Herbert Mead (1863–1931) and given explicitly sociological expression by such as Herbert Blumer and Howard Becker. Though not drawing directly from Weber, this approach had certain concerns in common with Schutz and ethnomethodology, and as early as the 1930s Blumer was arguing a dissident point of view within American sociology which raised or prefigured some of the concerns that ethnomethodology would also pursue.

A sociologist of our time?

In this period of (alleged) 'postmodernism' the rival claims of Marx, Weber and Durkheim are still being debated, and Weber has his advocates as 'the sociologist for our time' (Lash and Whimster, 1987; Schroeder, 1992). There are at least three related reasons for putting this case.

First, Weber's scepticism about sociological theory. Weber's nominalism meant that he had modest expectations for sociological theory, and his views on values meant that he did not expect that even the most successful of theories could provide a means for overcoming the conflicts in human life or terminating the struggle for domination. Weber was, therefore, a 'disillusioned' thinker from the start, who could not support either the 'utopian' expectations to which Marxism gave rise, or the 'technocratic' ambitions which those who followed Durkheim might harbour. The incapacity of theory to capture reality led Weber to stress the personal and provisional character of sociological theories, something which also serves to make him attractive in a time in which confidence about and faith in great theories has collapsed and where views are widely 'relativist'.

Second, the lack of faith in science is part of a scepticism about the power of reason as advocated in the 'Enlightenment' tradition. Postmodernism is a strong reaction against the Enlightenment tradition, a reaction to which Weber contributed. The kind of rationalisation to which he referred, of scientific/calculative thought, was the ideal of the Enlightenment tradition. Weber, however, was most insistent that the expansion of 'rationality' throughout the world, throughout more and more societies, and throughout more and more spheres of life, did not result in the *elimination* of irrationality and could not do so. It was his almost paradoxical point that 'rationality' was itself founded in and directed by irrational considerations. Rational actions serve values which cannot themselves be rationally chosen, and the pursuit of rationalisation itself was something undertaken only because it was irrationally valued.

Third, in the 1930s, and subsequently, a group of German scholars known as 'the Frankfurt School' set in motion a train of thought which has had a most potent impact upon social science, and was a decisive contribution to the expansion of the 'critical' element in sociology. The Frankfurt School played a particularly vital role in the revaluation of the idea of 'science', which they construed as 'instrumental reason'. Science, as practised in the capitalist world, was not a neutral, objective form of inquiry, determined to find things out for their own sake, but was, they argued, compromised with the needs of the ruling powers to dominate and render docile and controllable the rest of society. Science sought to provide knowledge which could be used to solve problems in the practical management of the society, accepting the given social order as the framework within which this took place. Since the early days of the Frankfurt School the business of social criticism has become less and less a matter of condemning material inequality and more a matter of criticising the falsifying and controlling role of the culture, in the form of ways of thought, the mass media and so forth, in creating a docile and subordinate population. Weber's notion of 'rationalisation' was a forerunner of this revaluation of the idea of science, insofar as it emphasised the extent to which the expanding power of 'instrumental reason' was to build up the power of capitalist organisations and of administrative bureaucracies. Further, Weber's emphasis throughout was upon the role of 'culture' in the struggle for domination and such views are compatible with many contemporary critical analyses of the postmodern predicament of modern Western society.

Select bibliography and further reading

Useful selections from the full range of Weber's work can be found in Hans Gerth and C. Wright Mills, (eds), *From Max Weber: Essays in sociology* (Routledge, 1948), W.G. Runciman (ed.), *Max Weber: Selections* (Cambridge University Press, 1978) and J.E.T. Eldridge (ed.), *Max Weber: The interpretation of social reality* (Michael Joseph, 1971). Good general, comparatively brief and accessible characterisations of Weber are given by Julien Freund's *The Sociology of Max Weber* (Pantheon, 1968) and Ralph Schroeder's *Max Weber and the Sociology of Culture* (Sage, 1992). Randall Collins' *Max Weber: A skeleton key* (Sage, 1986), Martin Albrow's *Max Weber's Construction of Social Theory* (Macmillan, 1990), Dirk Käsler's *Max Weber: An introduction to his life and work* (Polity, 1988), Wilhelm Hennis' *Max Weber: Essays in reconstruction* (Allen and Unwin, 1988) and Anthony Kronman's *Max Weber* (Edward Arnold, 1983) are all worth consulting. A collection of recent essays considering Weber's contemporary importance is Scott Lash and Sam Whimster (eds), *Max Weber, Rationality and Modernity* (Allen and Unwin, 1987). Friedrich H. Tenbruck, 'Problems of thematic unity in the work of Max Weber' (*British Journal of Sociology*, 31, 1980) addresses the issue of the coherence of Weber's thought. Stephan Turner and Regis Factor's *Max Weber as Legal Scholar* (Routledge, forthcoming) is likely to prove to be an important contribution.

The primary sources for the Protestant ethic thesis are Weber's *The Protestant Ethic and the Spirit of Capitalism* (Allen and Unwin, 1930), 'The Protestant sects and the spirit of capitalism' (in Gerth and Mills, *From Max Weber*, pp. 302–22, in which Weber considers the import of the organisation of the Protestant sects in engendering the spirit of capitalism), 'The anti-critical last word on the spirit of capitalism' (*American Sociological Review*, 83, 1978: 1105–131), in which he seeks to answer some of the criticisms of his thesis, and the *General Economic History* (Allen and Unwin, 1923), in which the thesis is discussed in the context of a more inclusive account of the economic history of the West – with Part 4 focusing specifically on the thesis. Brief sections from this are reprinted in Eldridge's *Max Weber: The interpretation of social reality*. Good discussions of the thesis may be found in Gianfranco Poggi's *Calvinism and the Capitalist Spirit: Max Weber's Protestant ethic* (Macmillan, 1983), Gordon Marshall's *In Search of the Spirit of Capitalism: An Essay on Max Weber's Protestant ethic thesis* (Hutchinson, 1982) and Randall Collins' 'Weber's last theory of capitalism: a systematisation' (*American Sociological*

Review, 45, 1980: 925–42, and reprinted in Collins' *Weberian Social Theory* [Cambridge University Press, 1986]), in which Collins seeks to examine the thesis in relation to the account given in the *General Economic History*. A recent collection on various aspects of the thesis is Hartmut Lehman and Guenther Roth (eds), *Weber's Protestant Ethic: Origins, evidence, context* (Cambridge University Press, 1993) which contains the debate over the MacKinnon thesis. There is also a running debate, precipitated by Luciano Pellicani's paper 'Weber and the myth of Calvinism' (75 [57–85], 78 [71–95] and 81 [63–90] of the 1988–9 volumes of *Telos*). Norbert Wiley (ed.), *The Marx–Weber Debate* (Sage, 1987) contains papers which consider these arguments in relation to Marx's work.

Weber's work on the comparative studies of religion is published in *Ancient Judaism* (Free Press, 1952), *The Religion of China : Confucianism and Taoism* (Free Press, 1957) and *The Religion of India* (Free Press, 1958). His account of the general evolution of religion is given in *The Sociology of Religion* (Methuen, 1965; also published as Chapter 6 in Weber's *Economy and Society* [University of California Press, 1978]). The essay on 'The social psychology of the world religions' (in Gerth and Mills, *From Max Weber*, pp. 267–301) provides an important statement on the role of religion in motivation. Passages outlining the role of two important 'status groups' are reprinted in Gerth and Mills, *From Max Weber*, as 'India: the Brahman and the castes' (pp. 396–410) and 'The Chinese literati' (pp. 416–443). The comparative studies are clearly summarised in Part 2 of Reinhard Bendix's *Max Weber: An intellectual portrait* (Heinemann, 1960), extensively discussed in Wolfgang Schlucter's *The Rise of Western Rationalism: Max Weber's developmental history* (University of California Press, 1981) and in Chapters 2 and 3 of Ralph Schroeder's *Max Weber and the Sociology of Culture* (Sage, 1992). Stephen Kalberg, in *Max Weber's Comparative Historical Sociology* (Polity, 1994), examines the methodological assumptions of Weber's comparative work, connecting this to debates in contemporary sociology.

Weber's writings on power, stratification and domination are exemplified by the essay 'Class, status and party', (in Gerth and Mills' *From Max Weber*, pp. 180–95) and Chapter 3 of Weber's *Economy and Society*, 'The types of legitimate domination' (esp. pp. 212–70). Chapter 9 of *Economy and Society* discusses 'bureaucracy'. Reinhard Bendix's *Max Weber: An intellectual portrait* provides, in Chapter 8, 'Max Weber's image of society' (pp. 265–86) a good brief summary of Weber's conception of society as an arena of conflict, whilst Part 3, 'Domination, organization and legitimacy: Max Weber's political sociology', clearly covers the ground its title identifies. David Beetham's *Max Weber and the Theory of Modern Politics* (Allen and Unwin, 1974), Wolfgang Mommsen's *The Age of Bureaucracy: Perspectives on the political sociology of Max Weber* (Blackwell, 1974) and Anthony Giddens' Politics and Society in Max Weber (Macmillan, 1972) give helpful general formulations of Weber's views on power and on the political condition and fate of contemporary society. Reinhard Bendix's

Nation Building and Citizenship (University of California Press, 1977) is also worth attention, as is Charles Tilly's 'Historical sociology' in McNall and Howe (eds), *Current Perspectives in Social Theory* (JAI Press, 1980) and Barrington-Moore's *Social Origins of Dictatorship and Democracy* (Allen Lane, 1967). Michael Mann's *The Sources of Social Power, Vol. 1* (Cambridge University Press, 1986) is an extensive study of power through the ages. David Lockwood's 'Some remarks on "The Social System"' (*British Journal of Sociology*, 7, 1956) and his *The Blackcoated Worker* (Allen and Unwin, 1958) develop Weberian notions of class and status. Randall Collins' *Conflict Sociology: Toward an explanatory science* (Academic Press, 1975) emphasises the concern with conflict and domination in Weber's work.

Weber's views on these matters and on the responsibility of the scholar in relation to them are given some expression in his essays, 'Politics as a vocation' and 'Science as a vocation' (both in Hans Gerth and C. Wright Mills, *From Max Weber*, pp. 77–128). 'Science as a vocation' is published in a new translation and with accompanying materials in Peter Lassman and Irving Melody (eds), *Max Weber's 'Science as a Vocation'* (Unwin Hyman, 1989).

A selection of Weber's essays on methodological and ethical themes was published as *The Methodology of the Social Sciences* (Free Press, 1949). The crucial methodological comments which define sociology as the study of 'social action' provide the opening sections of the first chapter of Weber's *Economy and Society* (esp. pp. 4–28). A classic source for the discussion of Weber's methodology is Talcott Parsons' *The Structure of Social Action* (Free Press, 1937). More recent discussions include Roger Brubaker's *The Limits of Rationality: An essay on the social and moral thought of Max Weber* (Allen and Unwin, 1984), Thomas Burger's *Max Weber's Theory of Concept Formation* (Duke University Press, 1976) and Guy Oakes' *Weber and Rickert: Concept formation in the cultural sciences* (MIT Press, 1986) Part 3 of Stephan Turner's *The Search for a Methodology of Social Science* (Reidel, 1986), 'Weber on action', provides a sophisticated reflection on Weber's methodology.

Alfred Schutz's *The Phenomenology of the Social World* (Northwestern University Press, 1967 [originally published 1932]), Peter L. Berger and Thomas Luckman's *The Social Construction of Reality* (Allen Lane, 1967) and Harold Garfinkel's *Studies in Ethnomethodology* (Prentice Hall, 1967) are important for seeing how the 'subjectivism' of Weber's approach has been worked out.

4

Émile Durkheim

Émile Durkheim was born on 15 April 1858 in Épinal, the regional capital of the Vosges region of France. Originally destined for the rabbinate, like his father, grandfather and great-grandfather before him, Durkheim abandoned this ambition in his youth and, with his father's agreement, decided to pursue his academic studies. He was finally admitted to the prestigious École Normale Supérieure in Paris, and began his studies along with a number of fellow students who were to become eminent in French intellectual life. It was here that he developed an interest in social reform and national regeneration. However, though exhilarated by the atmosphere of the École, he was critical of its style of education, which he felt insufficiently scientifically robust. After graduation he became a philosophy teacher, and chose the topic of the relations between individualism and socialism for his doctoral thesis. At this time sociology was not highly regarded in France and was normally associated with the followers of August Comte (1798–1857), who had sought to bring the study of society within the orbit of the 'positive' sciences but who had eccentric ideas about creating a new 'religion of humanity'. Apart from Frédéric Le Play's (1806–82) studies of family life, sociology had remained at the level of philosophical generalities. Between the years 1884 and 1886, Durkheim's ideas had begun to coalesce around the problem of the relation between the individual and society, reaching the conclusion that the solution to this problem must come from the relatively new science of sociology. Sociology could identify the processes of social change and the conditions of social order and thus enable the more effective management of both. Like many others in the France of this time, Durkheim was preoccupied with the need to revive the Republic through the establishment of new forms of social membership and the establishment of a new liberal secular civic morality, a concern that never left him. As he saw it, the attempt to reorganise society could only be effective if guided by scientific knowledge and so the first task was to place sociology on a sound scientific footing, with its own distinctive and independent subject-matter dealing with causally operative forces.

In 1887 Durkheim was awarded a post in the Faculty of Letters at Bordeaux and began an immensely productive fifteen years of scholarship. During this period, apart from reviews and incidental articles, he published *The Division of Labour* (published in France 1893), a study of Montesquieu, *The Rules of Sociological Method* (1895) and *Suicide* (1897). In 1902 he founded and edited the *Année Sociologique*. He lectured widely on 'social solidarity', moral education, the family, suicide, legal sociology, political sociology, criminology, religion, the history of socialism and more. He also took an active part in the administration of the University, in the movement for secular education and in educational reform more generally. It was his work on education that gained him an appointment in the Science of Education at the Sorbonne in Paris in 1902.

Despite some resistance to his appointment, Durkheim became a very influential figure. His education courses were the only compulsory ones at the Sorbonne for those students seeking teaching degrees in philosophy, history, literature and languages, and he became a considerable authority within the French education system. At this time, his sociological work began to focus more directly on morality, a preoccupation which is, in various guises, apparent throughout his work, though he was not to finish his intended book on that topic. He always had a great respect for philosophy, though he sought to restate some of philosophy's central epistemological problems in what he regarded as more suitably scientific terms. This work appeared as *Primitive Classification*, in 1903, written with Marcel Mauss. His attempt to turn the philosophical questions about knowledge into those of a sociology of knowledge also figured significantly in another major book which appeared in 1912, *The Elementary Forms of Religious Life*. In 1914, at the outbreak of war, Durkheim devoted all his energies to the national war effort until ill-health intervened in 1916, almost certainly aggravated by the news of the death of his only son on the Bulgarian front. In that year, after one of the innumerable committee meetings he attended, he suffered a stroke and had to rest for several months. He died on 15 November, aged 59, his major work on morality still unfinished.

Unlike Marx, Durkheim became a prominent figure in the intellectual and educational establishments. His work was also to have wide influence among politicians even though he himself exhibited no little disdain for those of his day. However, this did not blunt the critical edge which is visible in much of his work, and it is somewhat ironic that in sociology he is often characterised as a conservative theoretician. Much the same kind of criticism was advanced against his work by the Marxists of his day. Georges Sorel (1847–1922), for example, while acknowledging the rare subtlety of *The Rules of Sociological Method*, also saw it as a treatise supporting 'conservative democracy' which ignored the historical importance of class conflict and was insufficiently materialistic in its analysis. Though certainly no Marxist socialist, Durkheim was intensely concerned to create more justice in economic relations, encouraging national education and moral development and provoking industry to become more scientific in its outlook. Durkheim was liberal in his moral outlook, an anti-clerical and, above all, a moralist whose socialism owed more to the non-Marxist French tradition with its idealism and distaste for party politics. His socialism was reformist rather than revolutionary and focused not on a particular class nor on what were regarded as outdated doctrines of economic materialism, the theory of value and class conflict, but, as he saw it, on a properly scientific analysis of society as a whole. In this respect, in a socialist society the state would perform a major role in conjunction with other centres of influence, subject to the state but strongly constituted so as not to be entirely subordinate to it. However, although Durkheim acknowledged that historically socialism and sociology had had an inter-leaved development, the former was not a scientific enterprise. It was only through the development of a scientific sociology that the malaise to which the rise of socialism bears witness could be properly addressed. Many of Durkheim's followers also espoused this abstract, intellectual, reformist socialism which was inspired by the ideals of co-operation and organisation and was to be buttressed by a fully developed science of society. Thus, whereas Marx saw revolution as the only likely means to cure the ills of society, for Durkheim what was required was an appropriately informed reform of education, of morality, and of social membership to produce the much needed social changes.

However, Durkheim himself felt that it was not the place of an academic to become involved in party politics. Like Weber, he argued that while a citizen had a duty to take a stand on public and political issues, academic authority should not be used for political ends. Such a view did not prevent Durkheim becoming involved in one of the greatest issues in the France of his day, the Dreyfus Affair. Durkheim regarded this as a party political affair, and though he normally had a distaste for these, in this case he regarded the affair as one with serious moral consequences for French society. The trial and imprisonment of Dreyfus, a Jewish army officer accused of espionage, had virtually polarised French society between those who sought to preserve the institutions of the army, the church and the law and those who sought to fight the injustice of Dreyfus' case through an attack on those very institutions which had brought the crisis about. Durkheim supported the Dreyfusards and he became an active member of the Ligue pour la Défense des Droits de l'Homme, becoming the secretary of the Bordeaux branch, which was committed to the view that Dreyfus' conviction was a travesty of Republican justice and a victory for the forces of reaction.

For Durkheim the malaise which afflicted French society derived from a dissolution of the authority and unanimity of moral beliefs. It was these rather than the economic inequalities about which socialism complained that were the true social problem. The task of the sociologist was to discover the ways in which these moral beliefs could be re-established, principally through reform of the educational system and beginning with the educators. At the height of the Dreyfus Affair Durkheim helped to found at Bordeaux an association of university teachers and students known as La Jeunesse Laïque which discussed political and ideological issues. Along with similar associations throughout France, it became increasingly political and moved in a socialist and anti-militarist direction. As far as education was concerned, Durkheim argued that the relation of the science of sociology to education was one of theory to practice and, in this respect, would provide a more rational substitute for traditional religion. Children should be taught to think about society and its moral obligations and, by this means, provide the basis for a more effective and secular morality. It was his appointment to the Sorbonne, in 1902, which enabled him to become a major influence on the formation of a national system of free and secular education which would, it was hoped, secure the moral foundations of French society.

However, although of our three thinkers Durkheim had perhaps the most immediate impact on his society during his life, though both Marx and Weber were politically active, within the discipline of sociology he has worn less well. His main contribution has often been seen as only his study of suicide, to the neglect of the wider range of his work. Nevertheless, it would be wrong to underestimate the contribution he made in identifying some of the key problems of the discipline and the way in which his ideas, often in bowdlerised forms, have become part of the general outlook of sociology. We begin with what is perhaps a surprising topic in view of the contemporary structuralist reading of Durkheim, namely, the theme of social action. It was in addressing this topic that he began his attack on the individualistic presuppositions that had dominated social thought since the Enlightenment.

The study of social action

Durkheim's efforts were devoted to establishing sociology as an academic discipline which could justify its existence as an independent form of inquiry, distinct particularly from psychology. The idea of the 'social' as a topic of study was not, by any means, so well developed in French intellectual life as it was in Germany before and during Weber's time. Durkheim did, however, have some distinguished predecessors. One was Comte, who, as was pointed out in the Introduction, coined the word 'sociology' and founded the doctrine of 'positivism' which proposed that scientific knowledge should become the dominant mode of thought in modern society replacing religious and metaphysical thinking. Another was Montesquieu (1689–1755), whose *Spirit of Laws* (1748) had sought to show that there was a systematic relationship between the laws of society and other aspects of its organisation. Durkheim regarded this as important preparatory work in the definition of sociology's subject-matter.

Durkheim was satisfied that Comte's contribution was to have 'established that the laws of societies are no different from those governing the rest of nature and that the method by which they are discovered is identical with that of other sciences' (quoted in Lukes, 1973: 68). However, although Durkheim's own views on the unity of the scientific method have led him to be frequently termed a 'positivist', he did not regard himself as such. Comte had sought to make positivism the basis of a new 'religion of humanity' and Durkheim was eager to distance himself from such a notion. The positivist aspects of his own thought were the products of his under- lying rationalist convictions. For him scientific reasoning was the only valid form of understanding, and it could be extended to the study of social life to show that social activities were subject to cause and effect in the same way as natural phenomena. An understanding of these cause and effect relations was the only sound basis for planning and the reconstruction of society.

In contemporary sociology it is common to allocate sociologists to one of two supposedly contrasting interests – with 'social action' or with 'social structure'. Weber is typically counted as the leading exemplar of the former type of sociological concern, and Durkheim as the leading exemplar of the other. Such a division is not wholly inappropriate if the basic issue is about whether society consists of anything more than a collection of individuals. Weber denied that it did, holding that collective terms such as 'society', 'class', 'social structure' and so on, were nothing more than shorthand expressions for the actions of large numbers of individuals. Durkheim, however, maintained that social collectivities were more than just aggre- gates of individuals. They were holistic phenomena possessing properties which were not those of separate individuals. The development and working of such wholes is a product of laws which distinctively apply to them, and whose identification was to be the task of the science of sociology. However, although Durkheim thought it necessary for the new science of sociology to press the case forcibly for the independence of the social whole against what he saw as a deeply entrenched prejudice, namely, that social life was to be understood exclusively through the psychology of individuals, his intention was to show that the antithesis between the 'individual' and 'society' was a false one. It was a persistent concern of his work to determine how the elements 'individual' and 'society' were interrelated rather than simply opposed to one to the other.

The highly influential study we have previously mentioned, *The Struc- ture of Social Action* (1937) by Talcott Parsons, sought to trace out a convergence in the ideas of some economists and sociologists writing around the turn of the century who were, in his judgement, breaking out of the frames of reference which had dominated thinking about social life for several centuries. The two most important figures in this 'convergence' were Durkheim and Weber; both scholars who had become dissatisfied with the largely unexamined assumptions built into economic, political and social theory. These assumptions, Parsons argued, were drawn from the utilitarian tradition which could be traced as far back as Thomas Hobbes' *Leviathan* (1651). It was the utilitarianism of the nineteenth-century British sociologist Herbert Spencer (1820–1903) that was the butt of much of Durkheim's attack. Spencer was perhaps the foremost exponent of evolutionary theory in analysing the state and progress of societies; a theory combined with utilitarian individualism. His *Principles of Sociology*, published in 1874, advanced an organic theory of society in which the 'fittest forms' would survive because they were functional for the social system. Social systems, like organisms, adapt to their environment by a process of internal differentiation and integration. In the early days of social evolution a struggle for survival was the main mechanism of adaptation, but in more advanced societies co-operation and altruism would predominate.

Utlitarianism and Durkheim's critique

At its simplest, utilitarianism argues that human behaviour is basically driven by the desire for pleasure and the avoidance of pain. Human thought is, essentially, a form of calculation working out the most efficient ways of obtaining what is desired, so maximising the amount of pleasure the individual gets and, correspondingly, minimising the pain experienced. If we imagine an individual with a variety of wants or desires and a fixed income, then the individual will seek to allocate that income in such a way as to maximise the amount of satisfaction to be gained, and will do so by calculating that combination of wants which will yield the most pleasure for that amount of income. Such assumptions have served economics well. They have enabled the construction of the idealisation 'economic man' upon which an elaborate body of theory could be built. But, however useful such assumptions may have proved to economics, they could not be, so far as Durkheim was concerned, useful in the creation of an emerging sociology.

One of the things to which Durkheim took exception was the utilitarian picture of individual action. Human beings are portrayed as acting on the basis of straightforwardly self-interested calculations. While Durkheim did not want to say that individuals never acted in such a way, he did not think they did so for most of the time. In any event, such a picture was of little use for sociology. Of course, utilitarianism did not claim that people always acted rationally; on the contrary, people could frequently be irrational. However, for Durkheim, this relegated 'irrationality' to the status of a regrettable fact about human behaviour, whereas conduct which lacks the strictly rational character stipulated by utilitarianism is very important to understanding how society works.

Take the example of the universal phenomenon, crime. Although not all societies have laws, courts, police forces and such like, Durkheim insisted that all do, that all must, draw a distinction between activities which are allowed and those which are prohibited; a distinction which the laws, courts and police are prominent in enforcing in societies like our own. The particular mix of the allowed and the prohibited will vary from society to society, but all make this distinction between permitted and proscribed activities, or 'crimes'. In simple terms, utilitarianism argued that crime is forbidden because it is harmful, a cause of pain, and criminal activities are punished to serve as a painful deterrent to potential criminals. Such an analysis was, for Durkheim, seriously flawed. For one thing he notes that the reaction of people to crime is not what would be expected from a rational, instrumental, calculative transaction. People's reactions to crime are deep and strongly felt. From a utilitarian viewpoint, however, such reactions do not make sense. Yet, Durkheim argues, they are the key to a sociological understanding of crime, and a major component in understanding the nature of society itself.

The social significance of expressive action

Our reactions to crime are 'expressive', that is, modes of action which do not have a directly practical or 'instrumental' purpose; they express our feelings, such as an outburst of anger or a show of affection. Durkheim divides our expressive behaviours into two kinds, those through which we express our separation from others, and those through which we express our unity with them. Our reactions to crime cut both ways. Our outrage does not just apply to the *actions* of the criminal, but is also directed toward the *person* who performs the act. We do not just want to stop such actions, we want to make the perpetrator suffer. In the more extreme cases, our reaction is to look on the criminal as a vile and odious person, someone who is completely unlike the rest of us. Thus, in our reactions against the criminal we are setting that person apart; in effect, we are drawing a line between a 'normal' person 'like ourselves' and an 'abnormal' one like the criminal, a line which is sometimes physically represented by the prison in which the criminal is segregated from the rest of society.

However, this setting apart also involves a putting together. As we distance ourselves from the criminal, so we place ourselves with other members of the society who are 'like us'. Our outrage is not just something that we individually happen to feel against the criminal; it is typically something we *share* with others. We do not feel that it is just our own quirky reactions against the criminal that give rise to our outrage. We feel what any 'normal' person would feel, and part of the strength of our feeling is our confidence that a great many other people, the rest of our group so to speak, will feel exactly the same way. In expressing our distance from the criminal we are, at the same time, expressing our closeness to the other members of society. We have a feeling of 'solidarity', of togetherness and unity, with them.

Durkheim suggests, then, that actions which are identified as crimes go against strong and widely held 'sentiments'. Thus, for example, in our society there are some very strong and very common feelings about the sexual inviolability of children. It is because these are both so strong and so widespread that paedophile activities, for example, provoke such an intense response. There are also widespread feelings about people's right to private property and so theft also occasions outrage and punishment, though not such intense reactions as paedophilia involves. Criminals are punished because this assuages the outraged emotions that their offending behaviour has caused: we want to see them suffer and are gratified when they do. Thus, our expressive responses are an important basis for our understanding of crime.

The symbolic character of action

However, for Durkheim, there is also a 'symbolic' aspect involved. The criminal may be punished, deprived of liberty and so forth, but there is another respect in which punishment plays a vital role in the business of crime and that is in symbolising the disapproval of the community. Part of the punishment of being convicted as a criminal is the shame it inflicts due to the disapproval of others. Durkheim wants us to note the very *public* character of the way in which crime is treated, of the way in which the occurrence of crimes and the identification and punishment of criminals is noised about throughout the community, as well as the very public nature of the proceedings through which criminals are handled. For the less hardened, the public trial and conviction for an offence is a humiliating experience. The criminal is meant to feel the disapproval of the whole community. Thus, the treatment of criminals symbolises the community's disapproval and, at the same time, symbolises the contrast between those things that the community will not stand for, namely, those acts the criminal performs, and those things it does stand for. There is, for Durkheim, a very strong connection between our strong positive and negative feelings, on the one hand, and those things which serve to symbolise our society on the other, a connection which acquires great significance in the case of religion, as we shall see.

It is important to realise from the outset that although Durkheim is so thoroughly opposed to 'individualistic' theories of the kind proposed by utilitarianism, both in terms of their intellectual content and their moral and political implications, he is not proposing an opposite but equally extreme view that only society is important. Where, for example, the utilitarians recognise nothing is real save the individual and his or her instrumental purposes, Durkheim is sometimes read as opposing this view by an unrelenting insistence that only society is real. It is to avoid this reading of Durkheim's case that we have begun with a discussion of his conception of individual action. As we shall see in what follows, Durkheim's resolute purpose was to reject the idea that it is a question of the individual versus society. In significant respects, Durkheim's work has a rhetorical point to it. Because initially it might seem that the 'individual' is the obvious, tangible, indubitably real unit and 'society' an intangible and unreal one, arguments to the effect that society is a reality in its own right and the individual a creation of society will seem implausible, especially in a climate dominated by utilitarian assumptions. Accordingly, Durkheim regards his claims, as the position requiring the greater burden of proof, as needing to be made forcefully and overwhelmingly. Thus, his emphasis upon the reality and the consequentiality of society can appear to leave no room for individuals partly because of the intense manner in which he feels it necessary to state his case. We do not deny that the vigour and determination with which he states his case can result in excess. However, we propose that these are overstatements of Durkheim's essential argument, which, as we shall try to show, is much less implausible than it is often made to seem. Durkheim does not seek to deny the reality of the individual but, rather, to understand his or her nature and this, he felt, could only be done through an understanding of society.

Although we have stressed that an important key to understanding Durkheim is through his conception of individual action, the manner in which he attended to this was, as we have indicated, informed by one of his main preoccupations with the way in which such actions contribute to the cohesiveness of society as a whole.

The reality of society

Basically, a society is a bounded unit. However, although societies are often identified with an area of territory, society itself is not an essentially geographical unit. For example, the Australian Aboriginal societies, whose rituals were the central focus of Durkheim's *Elementary Forms of Religious Life*, were societies but were not based upon territory in the ways that ours are. Part of what provoked Durkheim's interest in the Australian Aboriginals was the question of how they maintained themselves as societies despite the fact that they were, for most of the time, dispersed in small groups wandering about the vast Australian landscape. Solving this problem, he felt, could provide insights into the sources of social solidarity of all societies. A society is essentially defined on the basis of membership, that is, on the distinction between those who are within it and those who are outside it; a distinction which, as we have seen, is at the root, according to Durkheim, of the treatment of the criminal. It is a matter of drawing the boundary of society, distinguishing between those who are members of the society and those who fall outside it, who are not a part of its normal life and are, in practice, to be denied the privileges that any normal member of the society may possess. The boundary around the society is, in this case, a *moral* one, and displays, so far as Durkheim is concerned, the fact that society is essentially a moral phenomenon; that is, about the standards of conduct that 'we' as opposed to 'they' subscribe to.

The moral character of society

The conception of society as a moral phenomenon stands in stark contrast to the utilitarian picture in which individuals assess their actions in terms of their efficacy; that is, the extent to which they will lead to pleasure or to the avoidance of pain. Although, no doubt, people often do concern themselves with just such issues, they do not only concern themselves with questions of efficacy. They are also directed in their conduct by considerations of right and wrong; concerned, that is, about the moral character of behaviour. For Durkheim, this fact was so critical to the understanding of social life that he would speak of sociology as the science of moral facts. While we do have 'instrumental' purposes and we do have 'utilitarian' concerns, we do not have purely instrumental and purely utilitarian concerns.

For example, hunger is an unpleasant sensation, a painful one in the utilitarian picture, and is to be avoided. From a strictly instrumental view, one concerned entirely with the alleviation of the discomfort of hunger through the acquisition of nutrients, cooking and eating a baby would serve as effectively as any other to stop the discomfort of hunger. Of course, in real cases, when people are feeling hungry they look in the kitchen, in the refrigerator or the larder for food, not in the baby's bedroom. More to the point, very few of us would even think of eating the baby as a way of assuaging our hunger. Indeed, even the fantasy suggestion of eating the baby is likely to provoke disgust, as it did when Jonathan Swift, in his *A Modest Proposal* (1729), made the satirical suggestion that the Irish famine could be alleviated by such a practice. So, even when we act in a broadly instrumental, utilitarian way we are not just weighing all the possibly efficacious ways of doing things even though, from a practical point of view, they would serve our ends. Eating the baby is not an option because it is, for us, outrageous, immoral and wicked. What is 'rational' conduct for the vast majority of us for the overwhelming proportion of the time is confined within the same space that the fellow members of our society find acceptable. Similarly, our aims in life, and the ways we will seriously consider pursuing them, are likely to be broadly the same as those of everyone else, as the kinds of things that *we and they together* accept are right, allowable, proper – in a word they are *moral*. It seldom, if ever, occurs to us to consider, let alone actually resort to, ways of doing things which, though practically efficacious, are prohibited within our community.

For Durkheim the utilitarian picture was far too narrow in its exclusive emphasis on the 'rational' character of social conduct and, as a result, obscured the importance of the expressive, symbolic and moral aspects of social action and society. However, his objective was not to play up these hitherto neglected aspects of action simply as a corrective to the utilitarian view. He did so because he felt that they were vital in understanding the possibility and nature of society itself. As we mentioned previously, a particular target of Durkheim was Herbert Spencer, who had argued, in a series of substantial works, that society could be understood as though it were a series of transactions between individuals in the market. Like Hobbes and other social contract theorists before him, Spencer argued that society could best be understood as based on a contractual agreement. The fact that society is not out and out conflict between ruthless individuals each pursuing their own interests can be explained by thinking of society's members as having made, and living by, contractual arrangements, albeit implicit ones. Therefore, just as the market operates through individuals making agreements with each other, so society can be thought of in the same way, though on a larger and broader scale. The members of society agree to abide by certain restrictions on their conduct. Durkheim, however, thought otherwise. Indeed, his objection to Spencer's conception, as it was to utilitarian assumptions more generally, was that it put the cart before the horse, as did all arguments which sought to understand society by inferring from assumptions about the nature of individuals. For Durkheim, society was more than the sum of the individuals who comprise it, and this 'something more' is the distinctive domain of study for the science of sociology.

Of course, the science of sociology did not exist as a proper science and the distinctive domain that Durkheim was pointing to had not been hitherto systematically studied. To do so, argued Durkheim, it was necessary to confront some fundamental methodological questions, not least those arising from the inadequacy of utilitarian assumptions.

The domain of sociology

Utilitarianism retained the Enlightenment conception that society is nothing more than the individuals who make it up. 'Society' is simply the name for the interaction of all of these individuals, that is, the name of whatever pattern results from their going about their business on the basis of their instrumental, utilitarian purposes. Understanding 'society' is much the same as understanding 'price' in economics, that is, as an interaction between 'supply' and 'demand', which are themselves the outcomes of the decisions of individuals. 'Demand' is simply the aggregated total of all the decisions individuals make to spend part of their income on a particular good, just as 'supply' is defined simply by adding up all the decisions of individuals to produce and market some good. Thus, understanding how price is determined essentially involves understanding how individuals make economic decisions, and in economics it is broadly utilitarian assumptions that are often drawn upon to shape the model that is proposed. By the same token, then, 'society' is just the name for the aggregate pattern of individual actions and an understanding of how it works calls for a comparable analysis of the ways individuals organise their actions.

It is just such arguments that Durkheim regarded as ruling out the possibility of sociology. If there could be a science of sociology it would have to be because there was a 'level' of reality with which it, and it alone, could deal. If sociology was to be 'the science of society', then society had to be a reality in its own right. 'Society' could not just be the name for the aggregated actions of individuals, for then it would be merely the study of the thought processes and actions of individuals, a domain already belonging to psychology. The project of sociology called for a real phenomenon, society, which was 'more than' just a collection of individuals, and which could provide a genuine subject-matter for a distinct and independent science of sociology. Durkheim was confident that there was such a level of reality. However, establishing this involved, in vital part, destroying what he saw as the hegemony of utilitarian assumptions which misconceived the relationship between the individual, or psychological, level of reality, and the collective, or social, level of reality. Justifying his conviction and making it intelligible involved Durkheim in no little tortuous argument.

The book *The Rules of Sociological Method*, first published in 1895 – which contains the account of crime sketched above – was his initial attempt to establish the consequences of the view that the study of society is a scientific venture, and is most notorious for its injunction to 'treat social facts as things'. For Durkheim, the hallmark of a science is that it deals in facts. Each of the natural sciences studied natural facts. So, for sociology to be a science it, too, must deal in facts, but ones which, though they are no less facts, no less real than those with which the natural sciences deal, must be of a different kind: they must be 'social facts'.

Social facts The injunction to 'consider social facts as things' really consists of two crucial elements: first, the claim that social facts are just as much facts, and just as real, as natural facts, and, second, the claim that in order to construct a science of such facts it is necessary to adopt the same inquiring stance toward them as the natural sciences take to their facts.

Durkheim approaches the issue through the general question of what makes something a fact in the first place. His answer is that natural facts have two principal generic characteristics, namely, they are external and constraining.

The externality of facts. Facts are external to our thoughts and exist independently of whatever we, as human beings, might believe. Facts are things about which it is possible for us to be right or wrong because what those facts *are* does not depend upon the ideas human beings may have about them. It is this independence which gives point to science, namely, investigating things to determine what they are actually like. One of the distinctive features of science is that it investigates matters about which human beings already have preconceptions. But it does so on the assumption that the methodic investigation of things may reveal them to be quite otherwise than they are imagined. What the actual facts about the nature of, say, the movement of the planets proved to be, on methodic investigation, varied significantly from what had previously been believed. Similarly, Durkheim insists, the actual facts about social life will prove, again on methodic investigation, to be otherwise than they have been thought to be.

The constraint of facts. Facts are also 'constraining', that is they are capable of shaping the course of human behaviour, even if we are not always aware of their doing so. Try as we might we can only jump a certain height in the air. The force of gravity limits and counters what it is human beings are capable of achieving in jumping. We readily accept that there are many natural facts which constrain our activities and our behaviour in fundamental ways. What we are perhaps less inclined to do is accept that there might be social facts which similarly constrain us. Yet, argues Durkheim, there are social facts which partake of the character of facts in general in possessing the properties of externality and constraint. What challenged Durkheim was our seeming reluctance to accept this in connection with society as readily as we do in other connections.

Durkheim begins his argument by drawing attention to familiar and recognisable experiences. Human beings do many of the activities they engage in because they want to do them, and for much of the time they are also doing what they are supposed to do. Our motives for taking a particular job, for example, might be because it is just the sort of job that we have always wanted to do. Many small boys want to be soldiers, and if they grow up to be soldiers they will have achieved what they wanted to do. However, those small boys did not invent the job of soldier in order to realise their ambitions. The job already existed and small boys want to do it because they suppose what soldiers do is exciting. The position of soldier is a socially established and standardised one which has particular obligatory activities attached to it. If soldiers do not do as they are told by superior officers, abide by the army's rules and so forth, then they will soon find themselves being treated as military criminals, charged, convicted and possibly even discharged from the force altogether. Others, and it may be that it is their duty to do so, will interfere with the freedom of the individual soldier to do whatever he wants, and will do so in the name of the imposed impersonal obligations covering them both.

Accordingly, while we may not feel that we are 'constrained' in much of our daily lives and that we spontaneously do what we want, such feelings are sometimes illusory. We do not feel constrained insofar as what we do coincides with what we are standardly required to do. So long as we are motivated to carry out the standard responsibilities that attach to the various social positions we occupy then we do not feel constrained. But if our motivations get out of step with those standard requirements we will feel constraint, perhaps of the quite literal physical kind as we are manhandled into a police van, into a cell, into the dock and so forth. Being constrained by both natural and social facts is not a matter necessarily of feeling constrained. We are constrained to breathe, after all, but we are not normally even conscious that we are breathing, let alone possessed of any sense that we are compelled to keep on breathing if we want to live – though we will become aware of the compulsion if we try to hold our breath. The facts of, for example, standard obligations are ones which are the products of our collective life in the sense that we did not invent them. They arise out of the patterns of our individual relations. Moreover, though we encounter these obligations individually, they apply to anyone who occupies the relevant social position – and if we do not feel that they are constraining, we shall become aware that they are if we try to defy them.

The first of the two elements which we identified as constituents of the invitation to 'consider social facts as things' is to be understood as saying 'treat social facts as facts'; that is, as no less real and independent conditions of our individual actions than are natural physical facts even though, as we shall shortly indicate, social facts are not themselves physical ones.

The second element we identified was the requirement that the study of social facts be approached in just the same spirit or attitude as the study of natural facts. Natural scientists have, or so Durkheim holds, appreciated that in undertaking their investigations they start from a position of ignorance. They are proposing to study phenomena which exist in themselves and which may or may not conform to any preconceptions we have about them. Thus, in order to initiate investigations natural scientists have been prepared to set aside their preconceptions and to systematically examine the phenomena to identify their actual and hitherto unknown properties. Similarly, the establishment of sociology requires the adoption of the same spirit in the study of social phenomena. We need to accept that social facts are not transparent to us and that their nature may not conform to the preconceptions that we have about them. Accordingly, it is necessary to set aside any convictions we hold about social phenomena *prior to* the making of systematic investigations into them. Although we are, as individuals, aware of the standard obligations which apply to us in our various social positions, this does not mean, says Durkheim, that we properly and fully know and understand these familiar social facts. We may be aware of what, as members of families, we and others are supposed to do, but that is very far from understanding how the family has grown up as a standard part of social organisation, or what part the family unit plays in the organisation of the society as a whole, or of how the organisation of the family changes over time and, thus, of how the things that we as family members require of each other have come to be as they are, and with what consequences. Without sociological investigation we are ignorant of these matters. Indeed, to the extent that we are ignorant of why the elements of society are the way that they are, there is an important respect in which we are to the same extent ignorant of why we, as individuals, are doing the things we do.

So far Durkheim is not, or does not appear to be, asking us to accept anything that is beyond our own ordinary experience of social life. Most would accept that we behave in the ways that we do because we have been brought up to do so, have learned from others how to behave, but that we have no idea how the social activities we are standardly required to do came to be the way that they are. However, the argument so far has been about the properties of facts and how they should be studied. What has not yet been established is how *social* facts are a level of reality which is the proper domain of sociology.

The emergent nature of social facts   Durkheim's case for social facts is made by way of an argument which, nowadays, is called one of 'emergence'. This argues that the interaction of phenomena can give rise to new phenomena which have characteristics different from the phenomena which constitute them. The simplest example is the interaction of two gases, hydrogen and oxygen, which, combined in the right proportions and under the right conditions, produce a new phenomenon, water. Water has properties which its constituent phenomena do not have. For one, water has 'liquidity', a property which neither oxygen nor hydrogen, being gases, possesses. So, if we can accept the idea that physical phenomena can combine to give rise to emergent phenomena, the idea of individuals interacting to give rise to new social, or collective, phenomena at least becomes a plausible one.

The fact that social phenomena are 'emergent' from the interactions of individual life means that they are likely to require explanation at their own 'level', that is, as a phenomenon relative to other facts of collective life. Just as we suppose that the behaviour of water when spilled, for example, is to be explained in terms of its liquidity and not in terms of the characteristics of gases, so we must expect that the facts of our collective life must also be explained in terms of the laws which govern the behaviour of collectivities and not in terms of those which apply to the behaviour of individuals, which are the business of psychology. In this connection Durkheim makes a strong claim: social life is a natural product of human life 'because it arises from that special process of elaboration which individual consciousnesses undergo through their association with each other and whence evolves a new form of existence' (Durkheim, 1982: 144).

However, if social facts are not natural, physical facts, what kind of reality do they have? In the light of what Durkheim says about the hallmark of a fact being its independence of individual consciousness, what he goes on to say about the nature of social facts may, initially, seem paradoxical; but only because he was struggling to find a way of saying things to which many of us would now give ready acceptance and easy expression. Social facts are not physical but *mental* facts. They are facts of our collective mental life. Society, in essential respects, consists of what Durkheim terms 'collective representations', that is, 'ways of acting, thinking and feeling which possess the remarkable property of existing outside the consciousness of the individual' (ibid.: 51). Among the examples he cites is the case of religious belief and how

> the believer has discovered from birth, ready fashioned, the beliefs and practices of his religious life; if they existed before he did, it follows that they exist outside him. The system of signs that I employ to express my thoughts, the monetary system I use to pay my debts, the credit instruments I utilise in my commercial relationships, the practices I follow in my profession, etc., all function independently of the use I make of them. (ibid.: 54)

The first important point to make in respect of this passage is that it means that these ways of acting, thinking and feeling exist outside the consciousness of the *single* individual. They are things which are common to the various individual consciousnesses and are, effectively, what we would nowadays quite readily talk about as 'shared meanings' or 'common culture' without any danger of being understood as suggesting, as some of his contemporaries inferred, that there is any kind of 'group mind'. Moreover, they are things which are not just incidentally common, such as the fact that we have eyes and arms, but are shared. Thus, the language that any one of us speaks is not the personal possession of that single individual for it is the essence of a language that many individuals speak it in the same way, that they mean the same things by the same words, and so on. They come to share the same language not because of any mysterious process, but because they learn it from one another. The language is, then, part of the consciousness of any individual, but that does not make it the possession of any one of them; it is shared by the members of the linguistic community. So, just as we do not strain at the idea of 'the language' having an existence – as a system whose organisation as a system the linguistic investigator can describe – within the community at large, Durkheim suggests that we need have no difficulty with the idea that practices other than our ways of speaking, our ways of organising our economic trans-actions, of arranging our work activities or of conducting our religious affairs, and more, also have the same existence within the community at large. It is this that makes them 'collective' phenomena.

Durkheim is referring here to shared 'ways of doing things'. What is common to the members of a collectivity is their acceptance of prescriptions for conduct; prescriptions which portray, or represent, how a person should act. The analogy with language is, once again, a useful one here. When we say that a language is shared we mean that its rules prescribing how persons are to order their words, what can be said, when and how, and so on, are commonly held. In the same way, when we say that 'ways of acting' are shared we also mean that the rules for doing various things are common to individuals. Thus, social reality is external to the consciousness of any given individual and consists, in important respects, in the dispersal throughout the consciousnesses of many individuals of standardised under-standings. 'Social facts' are, to that extent, facts of our 'mental life' but this does nothing to diminish their reality. If we want to speak to other human beings we are compelled to use the language they understand. That others hold to this way of talking means that its necessity is imposed also upon us. Similarly, if we wish to use money in payment then we must use the currency that is accepted among the rest of the community; if they put their confidence only in certain kinds of coinage, then, if we are to transact business with them, we are also constrained to employ the appropriate coins. Durkheim's talk about social life as a phenomenon of our 'mental life' points to nothing other than the reality that such things as language and currency have as products of common understandings. But the recognition that they are phenomena of collective mental life does nothing to diminish their reality, for the conventions of the language and the currency effectively *impose* themselves upon the particular individual.

Over the course of Durkheim's career there are detectable changes in the kind of social facts that concerned him, as well as in his conception of the way in which they exercised their constraining power. Durkheim saw society as a composite of both 'material' and 'ideal' elements, if we may use the same terms we used in reference to Marx and Weber. That is, he saw society as made up of what are nowadays called 'structural relations' among parts of society, such as the different groups into which persons are distributed and the necessary arrangements for the conduct of their daily life, and 'cultural aspects', such as religious beliefs, shared systems of meaning, language and so on. In his early work, Durkheim placed a greater emphasis on the 'material aspects' of social organisation, but came to pay the latter much more attention, to the point at which, in *Elementary Forms of the Religious Life*, it was charged that he was giving them too great an importance.

A parallel movement is in respect of the notion of 'constraint'. In his early work, and consistent with his insistence that an essential feature of social facts was their externality, he treated constraint as an external limitation on the individual, stressing the extent to which social rules, particularly, were features of an individual's environment and whose control was supported by sanctions. By the time of *Suicide*, in 1897, he treated constraint as an 'internal' phenomenon, a matter of the individual's own convictions, through social learning, becoming identical with the requirements of social rules. Typically, the individual followed social rules not because of a fear of punishment for deviation, but because of an inner conviction that these were the right ways to behave.

The study of social facts

How are social facts to be studied? Durkheim's short answer is that, first, they should be studied scientifically and objectively; they should be treated not as ideas but as external things. The sociologist must 'emancipate himself from the fallacious ideas that dominate the mind of the layman'; in other words, approach the subject-matter anew, systematically and methodically, rather than from common-sense ideas and beliefs which are a product of confused and fragmentary human experience.

> They are not due to some transcendental insight into reality but result from all sorts of impressions and emotions accumulated according to circumstances, without order and without methodical interpretation. (Durkheim, 1982: 33)

The second step requires the sociologist to define the subject-matter of the research in terms of common external characteristics. Thus, and to use a previous example, certain acts have a common external characteristic in that they evoke a particular reaction from society known as punishment. These are defined as crime and become the object of the science of criminology. We can also observe that within all known societies there are small groups whose special characteristic is that they are preponderantly composed of individuals who are blood-kin and united by legal bonds. These are classified as families. Such categorisations of facts are, of course, only the beginning.

The next task is to explain those social facts, and here Durkheim is at great pains to dispose of the argument that social facts are ultimately explicable in terms of psychology. For him, sociology is not a corollary of psychology. The explanation of social life must be sought in the nature of society itself, and for reasons reviewed earlier. As a methodological rule he sets it out as follows:

> The determining cause of a social fact should be sought among the social facts preceding it and not among the states of individual consciousness. (ibid.: 110)

The only way in which to demonstrate that a given social fact is the cause of another is to compare cases in which they are present or absent, in order to see if the variations they present in these different combinations indicate that one depends on the other. This is, for Durkheim, the comparative method of which the experiment, in which the researcher has control over the production of facts, is a special case. Further, a given effect always follows from a single cause. In other words, and for example, if suicide depends on more than one cause then this is because, in reality, there are several kinds of suicide. Durkheim, in particular, cites the method of 'concomitant variation' as the 'instrument par excellence of sociological research' (ibid.: 132). If two phenomena vary with one another then this is a strong indication that one is in the 'presence of a law' (ibid.: 133). This method is the precursor of what, these days, social research would describe as correlation, though, typically, without the implication that it is a method which discovers laws. Durkheim, however, is in no doubt that the science of sociology should seek to establish the natural laws which connect social facts and, in this respect, is capable of ranking among the more developed of the natural sciences. We shall look at his method more closely when we discuss his work on suicide.

So, Durkheim's argument for his claim that society involves more than the sum of the individuals who comprise it is primarily that this 'more' is the shared patterns of thinking, feeling and ways of acting that, these days, we would describe as a 'common culture'. Thus, a society is a unit comprised of a population of changing individuals among whom are shared certain standard ways of acting, thinking and feeling which distinguish them from other collections of individuals united by different ways of acting, thinking and feeling. Those who are united by shared ways acknowledge what they have in common and hold positive feelings toward one another. Such, at its simplest, is Durkheim's idea of the source of the unity of society.

The unity of society

Durkheim was not just interested in promoting a scientific sociology for its own sake. He also perceived its practical necessity in intervening in a rational way to promote a greater level of social 'health'. The development of a scientific understanding would give us the capacity for greater self-conscious control of our circumstances, just as it has done in the natural sciences, which have greatly enhanced our power to turn nature to our ends. A scientific understanding of the nature of society would, in the same way, enable us to have similarly self-conscious control of our social lives. Since there were, Durkheim was convinced, matters deeply wrong with the organisation of his own society, there was a serious need for a deliberate and informed reconstruction of society. Understanding the manner in which society possessed and sustained unity, that is, the presence of 'cohesion' or 'solidarity', was a principal task for the new science of society and would contribute to an understanding of how the threats to the society's overall integrity could be countered.

One of the more important of these threats in the modern world was that, as Durkheim saw it, people lacked an adequate understanding of their relationship to society. As we mentioned earlier, his arguments about the interrelationship of the individual to society are carried through into the analysis of the unity of society. In his various studies, he analysed the interrelationship between the different 'organs', or institutions, of society, their relationship to the 'conscience collective', or socially shared values and sentiments, and the 'collective representations', or systems of belief, and the way in which these both required and created, or failed to do so, a degree of loyalty to the society, conformity to its rules and reciprocal solidarity among its members. Durkheim sought to determine the optimal level of integration amongst these elements for the well-being of the society, and for its individual members. He was convinced that appropriate levels of social integration were necessary for individuals to flourish, enabling them both to play a constructive part in the life of the society and to develop their own personal capacities to the full.

Earlier we reviewed Durkheim's arguments for his claim that society involved 'something more' than individuals, showing that this 'something more' consists primarily in shared patterns of behaviour or what, in more recent sociology, would be called a 'common culture'. This is not all there is to it, but it is undoubtedly a significant part of it. In the following discussion we will develop another vital theme of Durkheim, namely, the seemingly paradoxical claim that it is only within society that 'the individual' truly exists; that it is only under the 'discipline' of society that an individual is genuinely free.

To speak of 'a society' is to speak of an entity which has both unity and separateness. A society exists in distinction from other societies, and, accordingly, if there are to be societies at all then there must be boundaries which separate each of them off from other groupings and which unite them against others. This is manifestly apparent in the case of war, when a tremendous emphasis is placed on the respective groups within a society to stand firmly together, and to subordinate all their internal differences to the fight against the enemy. Thus, the notions of 'cohesion', 'integration' and 'solidarity' are, in Durkheim's estimation, inseparable from, are indeed constituent of, the very idea of a society. It is not, therefore, surprising that he should think that central to understanding the reality of society is understanding the conditions which provide for its wholeness or unity. For 'a society' to exist as a distinctive entity it is necessary for it to have, first, mechanisms for creating solidarity amongst its membership and, second, ways of showing its unity. And, for Durkheim, the two are related, as has already been suggested by our earlier discussion of Durkheim's comments on crime.

Mechanical and organic solidarity

The earlier discussion of crime was taken from Durkheim's second book, *The Rules of Sociological Method*, in which he intended to elucidate the general rules of sociological inquiry which he had himself sought to implement in his first major book, *The Division of Labour in Society*, first published in 1893. There Durkheim invites us to consider two contrasting types of society. The first type of society comes closest to society as envisaged by Spencer and the utilitarians; that is, a society which is little more than an aggregate of its individual members. It is a small, simple, undifferentiated society in which the basic conditions of its members' lives are homogeneous. They are probably all engaged in subsistence agriculture to provide for their own survival. Each person is virtually independent of each other and, in going about his or her work, places little, if any, reliance on his or her fellows. If any of them decide to break off and leave the group, this would not materially disrupt the lives of those who remain behind. Due to the homogeneity of the circumstances in which they live they will have much in common, have similar experiences, and out of these will grow similar conceptions of what the world is like. The outlook and the thoughts of the members of such a society will be standard, widely shared and strongly held sentiments of the kind that creates a stark distinction between permitted and prohibited behaviour, and which engenders the outraged reaction and the desire to see the criminal suffer that we discussed earlier. Within such a society, Durkheim argues, the overwhelming emphasis will be upon the maintenance of uniformity, and this will be reflected in the kind of law characteristic of such a society. Such law will have an essentially 'repressive' character in that its emphasis will be upon ensuring that conduct which departs from the shared rules, standard conceptions and ways of thinking will be stifled by the punitive suppression of anyone who engages in it. Durkheim, in an analogy deliberately drawn from mechanics, particularly in the way the behaviour of a gas is considered simply as a resultant of the interactions between the molecules composing it, describes such a society as one united through 'mechanical' solidarity. That is, it is held together by the likeness of its members and organised on utilitarian principles simply as an aggregation of individuals.

At this point, it is at this point, worth making a reference backward to Marx's theories, and forward to Durkheim's own later collaboration with Marcel Mauss, as well as to his own work on religion. Prominent in Marx's rejection of the Hegelian tradition had been his insistence that 'social being' determines 'consciousness' and not the reverse. Durkheim is, in *The Division of Labour in Society*, making fundamentally the same point, though he goes on to develop it in a very different way. He is maintaining that the possibility of developing ways of thinking and systems of belief, that is, consciousness, is constrained by the form in which the society, that is, social being, is organised. It is because of the uniform, undifferentiated organisation in this 'mechanical' model of society that a thoroughly uniform outlook is created and sustained among its members. Clearly, by implication, the existence of diverse ways of thinking and a plurality of belief systems is only possible in a society with a heterogeneous and differentiated structure. This emphasis upon the shaping of the very nature of thought by social structure is one which Durkheim's later collaboration with Mauss, published as *Primitive Classification* (1903), and his own *Elementary Forms of Religious Life* would pursue, and intended to demonstrate that even the very basic 'categories' in which we think, such as our notions of space and time, are in fact shaped by the structures of the society in which they appear rather than reflecting any supposedly general features of the human mind.

In *The Division of Labour in Society* Durkheim considers a second type of society, a larger, more complex one which, he argues, is unified by 'organic solidarity'. Such a society is one which has an elaborated 'social division of labour'. Playing a part in the social organisation of society is to play a specialised role; persons tend to do one single task which is their individual contribution to the working of society as a whole. The organisation of work in modern society has been extensively and elaborately organised around such a division of labour, the most famous illustration of this, as we have discussed previously, being provided by the economist Adam Smith (1723–90), who suggested that even in the making of something so simple as a pin, if this was organised as a series of separate and specialised tasks, each performed by a separate person, it would increase the production of pins. Durkheim takes this idea from economics and applies it to society as a whole, and suggests that in a complex modern society economic specialisation is only one aspect of the process of specialisation in all walks of life.

If Adam Smith had characterised an economic division of labour, then Durkheim was concerned to talk about a 'social division of labour', one in which all sorts of activities, not just those of material production, become specialised tasks. For example, the care and education of children has become professionalised, and, furthermore, a task which is shared out among teachers who are trained to deal with children at different ages and levels of educational development and with different kinds of educational problems. The fact that individuals are specialised makes them interdependent. A specialised contribution to the production of some commodity is pointless on its own: it can only exist in interrelation with other specialist activities, as one step in a more elaborate process. Further, those who are specialised in a particular job of work are dependent on others for their needs. If our activities are solely devoted to the carrying out of a single task, then we are unable to provide for our own subsistence through that single task. We can only devote ourselves single-mindedly to our specialist preoccupation if we can count on the other members of the society to be doing other things which complement our activities, busying themselves about the provision of the things we need for our lives but which we cannot ourselves supply.

Of course, a society in which activities are all specialised into a complex structure will be one with a great deal of diversity rather than the homogeneity found in societies of the 'mechanical' type. The activities of individuals will differ from each other, and their lives will therefore differ too, so giving rise to experiences which will vary from individual to individual and, ultimately, engendering divergent outlooks. The kind of strong, shared sentiments which are the basis for the unity and conformity of the mechanically solidary society cannot be found in such a society. Not, of course, that there is no uniformity, for there will, of course, be the standardisation of language, of the currency and more besides. However, the extent of uniformity will be much less and will be interwoven with a vastly greater degree of diversity.

As already indicated, within a society which is thoroughly homogeneous, there will be, correspondingly, a uniform 'conscience collective' which will shape the reaction against crime and deviance. It will be 'repressive'. In a society which is much more differentiated, however, the 'conscience collective' will not be so homogeneous and will not have underpinning it such intensely shared and clearly defined sentiments. Without these widely shared and deeply rooted common sentiments, the reactions which define crime, and sanction the criminal, will be markedly less evident. The law in a modern society is less concerned with the repression of crime than it is with the regulation of commercial, domestic and other relationships. Law has more of a 'restitutive' character, being directed toward repairing the damage done to relations between individuals through breaches of trust or the violation of contract, and toward making matters right again.

'Organic solidarity' draws on an analogy from biology rather than one from mechanics. It refers to the kind of unity found in the organism in which differentiated and specialised parts are combined into a single, functioning whole, with each part's own operations depending upon the whole – the human body being a prime example of this. Though it might be tempting to think that diversity means conflict, this is not necessarily the case. The diversity which is created through a 'social division of labour' means interdependence and mutual indispensability. The loss of a part from a mechanically solidary society has little or no implications for the other parts, but the loss of one part from a whole made up of internally differentiated, functionally interrelated parts can have great consequences for the others. The loss of just one hand, for example, can make much of our life difficult even though our other parts are in good working order.

The two types of society were, Durkheim argued, historically related in that the 'organically solidary' society had evolved out of the 'mechanical' type. In placing the two types of society in this relationship of succession Durkheim was, like Marx, Spencer and many other nineteenth-century thinkers, taking an evolutionary view of society as an entity which developed historically, from 'lower', less complex forms of organisation to 'higher', more complex ones through a sequence of distinct 'stages'. Durkheim would retain such evolutionary views throughout his career, and his last great work on religion was based on the idea that the totemic practices of the Australian Aboriginals could be viewed as representing the earliest stage in the evolutionary development of religion.

However, it is worth pointing out, even if only as an aside, that although they have the word 'evolution' in common with him, the nineteenth-century evolutionists of the social sciences do not otherwise share much with Charles Darwin (1809–82), whose evolutionary theories are the basis of modern biology. The latter's theories are about the emergence of diverse species from common origins, a process which certainly does not take place through the unilinear succession of stages which was the idea common to nineteenth-century theories about society. Nor do Darwinian theories involve the evolution of 'higher' forms out of 'lower' ones.

Though Durkheim's account of the development of organically solidary societies out of mechanically solidary ones is not the same kind of theory as Darwin's biological scheme, none the less the mechanism which Durkheim postulated as instigating such a development was one which Darwin employed within his theories and which he, in his turn, had taken from the political economist Thomas Malthus (1766–1834). This mechanism was the process of competition for survival under the pressure of population growth. Malthus argued that the rate of growth of populations tends to be such that they eventually outstrip the capacity of their environment to support them. This principle led Darwin to the view that the diversity of animal species is a consequence of the pressure of population on environment. Part of his argument is the assumption that a much larger number of organisms can be sustained within a given environment if those organisms are diverse in character, as, for example, belonging to different species. Different species make different demands on the environment and are not necessarily in direct competition with each other. The only way in which life could continue to expand over very long periods without exhausting its environment, Darwin concluded, was to diversify. Durkheim argued similarly. The population which a given environment can support will be much smaller if everyone is doing the same thing than if everyone is doing something different and, accordingly, exploiting diverse aspects of that environment. If, for example, we are all dependent upon subsistence agriculture and all require a certain amount of land to sustain us, substantial population growth will ensure that we will soon run out of land and starvation will threaten. Population expansion would, Durkheim argued, mean that the situation of a mechanically solidary society could not remain stable indefinitely. Eventually the pressure of population expansion would bring about change: either the population would exhaust the potential of its environment to meet its needs, or the society would need to adapt its structure. Since the adaptation would have to sustain a growing population within the same environment, the only way in which this could be achieved would be through the development of diversity within the society.

In drawing upon the 'biological' fact of population expansion in explanation of the mechanism of change from the mechanically to the organically solidary society, many critics have found Durkheim guilty of deviation from one of his own prime rules of method, namely, that one should explain facts by facts of the same kind. In other words, that one should explain one social fact by another social fact. Durkheim, himself, however, was aware of the risk of falling foul of his own rules and, in *The Division of Labour in Society*, tried to argue that it was not population as such which was the cause of the development, but what he called the increasing 'moral density' which was the corollary of population growth. This increasing 'moral density' was, Durkheim insisted, a proper social fact, pertaining to the intensification of interactions amongst the members of society. Critics have, however, often found this manoeuvre unconvincing, as merely a roundabout way of talking about population pressure as the cause of social change and an attempt to conceal the fact that a social fact is being explained by a biological one.

It is in contrasting the two types of society that Durkheim makes one of his more decisive moves in his battle against 'individualist' theories and, in so doing, provides a meaning for the contention we mentioned earlier, namely, that the individual is the creation of society.

The individual and society

We have said that the 'mechanically solidary' society is more like that envisaged by the utilitarians than is the 'organically' based one. The basis of mechanical solidarity is homogeneity: the lives, thoughts and outlooks of the members of society are alike and it is this likeness which is prized. 'Repressive' law regulates activities closely, and in detail, and penalises that which deviates from uniformity. By contrast, 'organically solidary' societies are characterised by diversity, differences in outlook, more complex structures, interdependence and 'restitutive law' which regulates interaction and repairs relationships between individuals that have arisen through breaches of contract and violations of trust.

If we think of 'the individual' as simply the particular, physical human being, then, of course, all societies contain individuals, and one cannot say – and Durkheim does not say – that this kind of individual is possible in only one type of society. However, in the thought of modern Western societies, the idea of 'the individual' is more than this. It is the notion of each separate human being as the locus of an irreducible distinctiveness, as the possessor of a set of unique characteristics, and 'individual' in the sense of special and worthy of respect for this fact alone. Not only are we possessors of such 'individuality' but we are also aware of it: we think of ourselves as quite different from our fellows and pride ourselves on this. It is to this latter conception of 'the individual' that Durkheim's polemics are directed, especially insofar as theorists mistake this distinct, socially and historically specific conception of the 'individual' for a general one characterising human beings in all kinds of societies. Since this conception of the individual is found, and can be realised, only in certain kinds of society, it cannot be the basis for any general sociological theory. The whole point of the 'mechanic'–'organic' contrast is to show that it is not possible for human beings to be 'individuals' in 'mechanically solidary' societies. It is only possible for them to be 'individuals' in a society with requisite characteristics – those of the 'organic' type.

We have already mentioned Durkheim's version of much the same idea as Marx's that 'social being determines consciousness', and his argument about the nature of the 'individual' is an application of this principle. He is maintaining the position that particular ideas can only originate under definite social conditions. Thus, the members of the mechanically solidary type of society simply cannot think of themselves as 'individuals'. After all, if they were to do so, it would be false: they are not such individuals, for the nature of their lives is such that they are like each other. Furthermore, the 'conscience collective', and the 'collective representations' of the society with which they are instilled, are ones which prize uniformity; ones which lead people to value themselves for being alike unto, not different from, their fellows. 'Individuality' can only come with a change in the basis of social solidarity, that is, with the emergence of the interdependence that comes in the context of the complex, organically integrated social system. The variety of lives, activities and experiences which are possible within such a society implies a diversity of possibilities within such a setting so that each person will indeed differ in many important respects from the next. Though there are, of course, elements of 'repressive' law still present, these are less prominent than in the mechanical type of society and are proportionately less significant than the elements of 'restitutive law'. There is less close, and intense, monitoring of individual behaviour and some lack of uniformity in conduct is tolerated, even valued, rather than condemned.

Far from contesting the reality of 'the individual', then, Durkheim is attempting to show what that reality consists in. There is no doubt that in modern organically solidary society we are individuals in this specific sense. In such a society, our 'social being', with its complex social division of labour, means that we are very individualised creatures; the collective consciousness which develops is one which leads us to think of ourselves primarily in terms of our differences from others and to value ourselves, and each other, because of our uniqueness. This is reflected in our social and political thinking, which, in modern societies, tends to be about the extent to which our personal rights and liberties are to be enhanced or constrained, based on our conviction that there is nothing more important or valuable than our individual selves which can have the right to interfere in, or limit, the things we want to do. Durkheim's concern, not to say fear, however, was the development of an excessive individualism; that is, of an individualism so intense that it pathologically exaggerates the extent to which we are distinct from each other, to the neglect of the extent to which, even in modern organically solidary society, the members of society are regulated within a collective life. In thinking about the life of such a society and the problems that it faces, an exclusive emphasis upon individualism may unduly distort the way in which the society is analysed, and the way its problems are consequently identified and tackled. Thus, and we cannot emphasise this strongly enough, Durkheim is neither denying the reality of the individual nor attacking individualism. His target is not individualism as such, but *excessive* individualism, and it is this that he seeks to correct.

Thus, the recognition of the differences that there are between the individuals in modern society should not be at the expense of the things that those individuals share as members of one society. The particular individual is, for Durkheim, a composite of two parts, one which is the product of the distinctive, perhaps unique, experiences of a person, and one which is created through our participation with others in the institutions of the society. So, in the modern individual there is always a tension between the claims of society and those of the independent individual. In his preface to the second edition of *The Rules of Sociological Method*, Durkheim puts the point this way:

> the coercive power that we attribute to the social fact represents so small a part of its totality that it can equally well display the opposite characteristic. For, while institutions bear down upon us, we nevertheless cling to them; they impose obligations on us, and yet we love them; they place constraints upon us, and yet we find satisfaction in the way they function, and in that very constraint. (1982: 47)

However, from a sociological point of view, the individualism of modern society is no herald of a return to utilitarian principles. Though the individual members of modern society are free to contract relationships with one another, this is not the basis on which society is founded.

The institution of contract   Identifying society only with its individuals and seeing those individuals as freely contracting economic and social relationships with each other is to fall into the temptation, as Durkheim accused Spencer of doing, of thinking that it is through their specific relations with each other that individuals are creating society. Thus, in the sphere of business, people will decide with whom they will do business, with whom they will make partners in what they hope will be profitable activities, and will formalise their mutual agreement in a contract which specifies the terms of their future relationship. In social life more generally people likewise make decisions as to with which other person they will share their life and enter into the 'contract' of marriage to create their family unit. Thus, the idea that society can be conceived as the product of contractual agreements between its individual members has some appeal. Social units, like the business firm or the family, *are* set up through contracts among their individual members. It is at this juncture that Durkheim emphasises the point, specifically against Spencer's ideas, of what he calls 'the non-contractual elements in contract'. Although Durkheim's argument is directed against Spencer particularly, it is one which tells against any attempt to see society as originating in a 'contract' among its members and, in so doing, highlights a wider difficulty in thinking about society. The general problem lies in attempting to understand how society could possibly exist and giving an account of this in a way that presupposes the very thing that it is intended to explain. The making of contractual relationships *is* a very prominent and vital feature of a modern society, but the idea that society *is a product* of contractual relations among its members is untenable because the making of contractual relationships is something which *can only take place within* an already established society.

Durkheim is adamant that 'contract' cannot be the basis of society for it is an institution of society. While it is true that in a society of the organically solidary kind the individual members of society are relatively free to make all kinds of contract and to create relationships through contract, they are not free to make any kind of contract whatsoever. There are rules governing the kinds of contracts that can be made. In our society, for example, people cannot sell themselves into slavery. Nor can they contract marriage with someone below a certain age. A particular relationship may be created through a contract, but the practice of making a contract is not created at the same time. Individuals making contracts are taking advantage of the pre-existence of the practice of making contracts, a practice which exists in society-at-large. In making any individual-to-individual contractual agreement persons are depending upon generally circulating prior understandings and rules about what kinds of matters can be legitimately agreed in a contract, as well as understandings about the availability of socially organised ways of enforcing the terms of contracts. The whole point of making a contract between two individuals is that one thereby gains the assurance that should one party default the other will have the support of others, ultimately that of the courts, in enforcing the contract. A properly made contract does not just bind the two parties to it but demands also that the legitimacy of the contract's claims be recognised by other members of the society. In short, and to repeat, 'contract' is a social institution and it is, therefore, circular to explain society in terms of contractual relations between individuals, for that is simply to presuppose the existence of social institutions; that is, the very thing that is purportedly being explained.

The cumulative force of *The Division of Labour in Society* is to argue that far from society being explained in terms of the nature and decisions of individuals, the opposite is the case. Indeed, the nature of the individual and his or her capacity to make individual decisions has to be understood as a product of society. The very 'individualism' of modern society is a result of its social structure. The notion of individualism through which we celebrate our independence and our diversity is itself a socially shared and standardised ideology. It is important to stress that Durkheim does not seek to assert society over the individual, but only to reject a false opposition between 'individual' and 'society', reminding us that our undoubted autonomy from other individuals is concomitant with our mutual dependence with those same individuals in the social division of labour. And nowhere is the attempt to emphasise this balance in the relationship between individual and society more apparent than in Durkheim's most famous, not to say notorious, study, *Suicide* (1893).

Autonomy and constraint

Suicide achieved its notoriety through its promotion as the model for sociology as a scientific discipline, and this, largely, because it features the extensive use of statistics. Though Durkheim drew, for this work, upon a well-established French tradition of the study of suicide statistics, his use of such statistics was pioneering. In seeking to understand the causes of stability and change in the suicide rate, Durkheim recognised the fact that in the study of social life the experimental method, which he felt to be so decisive for the success of the natural sciences, cannot be employed. The experimental method is decisive in the natural sciences in singling out causes, and if sociology is to be a science and therefore, on Durkheim's understanding, to give causal explanations of phenomena, it must contrive some alternative to the experiment. Durkheim thought that one could isolate causes through the manipulation of statistics, and it is in his use of statistics, in an attempt to isolate contributory causes, that his book is pioneering.

We earlier noted that Durkheim's recommendation 'consider social facts as things', involved the claim that the subject-matter of sociology was 'social facts' and that sociologists should adopt the same attitude to those facts that the natural scientist takes to natural facts. This latter claim meant that social facts should be studied with detachment and without preconceptions. However, because the notion of 'science' is, in so many minds, closely wedded to the notion of 'quantification' (more crudely, to the use of numbers) it was Durkheim's extensive use of statistics in his study that became the main feature which established *Suicide*'s claim to exemplary scientific status.

In *The Structure of Social Action* (1937) Parsons noted another common thread in the work of Durkheim and Weber, namely, their claims about the impact of Protestantism on the 'mentalities' of Western European societies. Weber, as we have seen, traced the origin of the capitalist economic organisation which held sway throughout those societies to certain unintended consequences of Protestant, most specifically, Calvinist, teaching;

creating, for example, the motivation for capitalist accumulation. For Weber the pursuit of capitalist accumulation required the kind of determined motivation which would abandon all attachment to traditional social ties and a willingness to overthrow their customs and practices. Thus, Weber's view of the Protestant Reformation was that it had provided a tremendous boost to individualism, and contributed decisively to the idea that individuals should go about their lives guided by the rational calculation of their own interests rather than in accord with the dictates of tradition. Durkheim shared Weber's view that Protestantism was a source of individualism and placed particular emphasis on the way that this led to the separation of the individual from a supportive religious community. Both Weber and Durkheim also claimed that the way in which Protestantism made people individually responsible for their religious salvation placed a considerable burden upon each believer's shoulders, making each feel his or her isolation from his or her fellows in the face of God. While Weber's essay on *The Protestant Ethic and the Spirit of Capitalism* begins from the observation that Protestants are disproportionately represented among successful businessmen, Durkheim notes that they are disproportionately represented among suicides.

The study of suicide

Suicide was intended as a decisive demonstration of Durkheim's case about the reality of the level of social facts and the necessity of using them in sociological explanation. The study would strike a blow against the idea that facts about individuals could be understood *entirely* in terms of other facts about those individuals. There were, rather, some facts about individuals which could *only* be understood in terms of social facts. The case of suicide provided the possibility of such a decisive demonstration not least because committing suicide is normally seen as something strictly personal, to be decided in complete independence of anyone or anything else. However, such a view would have to be reconciled with the observed stability Durkheim's predecessors had found in suicide rates. Without denying that whether or not a particular individual takes his or her own life is a matter for that individual, we have to come to terms with the way that, according to these statistics, the proportion of individuals committing suicide within a given population remains relatively stable over long periods of time and shows, furthermore, a similarity of pattern across different societies. If individuals are making the decision to take their own life, then they are doing so in a way which generates remarkably regular statistical rates. It is essential to remember, then, that Durkheim's purpose in *Suicide* is not to explain why individuals commit suicide but to explain why suicide *rates* exhibit such stability.

   Suicide also continued Durkheim's preoccupation with understanding the relationship between the individual and society. Its primary case can be stated as follows: there is a correct balance between the individual's dependence upon and independence of society, a balance which promotes the individual's well-being. Too little or too much independence from society are both harmful. And what could be a better sign of a lack of individual well-being than that individuals should destroy themselves? Hence, what better setting for an evaluation of the relationship between individual and society than the examination of the patterns of suicide?

The study is also a demonstration of not only the injunction to treat social facts as things but also the method by which this can be done. The statistical rates were not themselves social facts but, rather, indicative of them. The stability of the suicide rates is caused by the 'moral constitution of groups' and these rates thus 'differ from group to group and in each of them remain for long periods practically the same' (1951: 305). The rates are reflections of 'suicidogenic currents' within groups. But by comparing rates with the characteristics of relevant groups within society the social facts could be ascertained and the causal relations identified. Durkheim's method has two components: first, comparing suicide rates between various subgroups and, second, eliminating alternative explanations by comparing suicide rates with the rates of other potentially related factors. For example, he suggests that one explanation of suicide is that it is due to mental illness. He then applies such statistics as can be found relating insanity and suicide. In certain respects there is a connection. Both suicide and insanity are more frequent in urban areas than in rural. Both tend to rise and fall together year by year. However, Durkheim suggests that there are other matters which suggest that there is not a strong connection between insanity and suicide. For example, the number of women in mental institutions is slightly higher than is the number of men, but women in the population as a whole constitute only about 20 per cent of the suicides. Among Jews the insanity rate is above average yet their suicide rate is very low. Catholics exhibit a slightly less than average insanity rate but commit suicide much less often. There is also a discrepancy at the ages in which insanity and suicide tendencies show themselves. The suicide rate increases with age but insanity is highest between the ages of 30 and 45 years. Further, although high insanity rates and high suicide rates are often found together, some countries with low suicide rates have high insanity rates. Nor does close examination of the data available to him show any consistent relationship between alcoholism and suicide. In this fashion, by carefully correlating the statistical rates with other factors, Durkheim felt able to show that suicide is not consistently related to factors such as race, heredity, climate, imitation, and so on, and having disposed of non-social causes to his satisfaction, he feels that he has successfully made the case that variations in the suicide rate are due to social causes.

Durkheim identified four types of suicide, though he gives only passing mention to the fourth, 'fatalistic' type, which he includes 'for completeness sake', because it has 'so little contemporary importance . . . that it seems useless to dwell upon it' (ibid.: 276). However, it is a balancing contrast to 'anomic' suicide in the similar way that 'egoistic' and 'altruistic' suicides contrast with one another. 'Anomic' suicide, as we shall see, arises when the individual is insufficiently regulated by society, and the 'fatalistic' kind is one in which the individual is excessively regulated by social circumstances in which individuals find themselves 'with futures pitilessly blocked and passions violently choked' as, for example, in the suicides of slaves or those subject to despotism.

Durkheim's main attention is reserved for the three other types of suicide. The statistics showed that in societies of roughly comparable character the average number of suicides per million inhabitants was much higher for Protestants than for Catholics. Rejecting the readiest explanation that this difference is due to the intensity of the Catholic prohibition of suicide, Durkheim proposes, instead, as a 'first conclusion' that the 'proclivity of Protestantism for suicide must relate to the spirit of free inquiry which animates this relation' (ibid.: 158). However, this relationship must be understood 'correctly' for it is not that there is some intrinsic desirability to free inquiry. The demand for free inquiry must be understood as 'only the effect of another cause', something which has arisen because it has been made necessary by social change. Durkheim, in fact, reverses what might otherwise be imagined as the causal order. It might be expected that the spirit of free inquiry would have led to the overthrow of traditional beliefs but, he argues, it is because traditional beliefs have been overthrown that the demand for free inquiry has arisen 'to fill the gap which has appeared, but which it has not created'. In a passage which states the essence of the argument that he later developed in *Elementary Forms of Religious Life* (1912), Durkheim asserts,

> If a new system of beliefs were constituted which seemed as indisputable to everyone as the old, no one would think of discussing it any longer. Its discussion would no longer even be permitted; for ideas shared by an entire society draw from this consensus an authority that makes them sacrosanct and raises them above dispute. For them to have become more tolerant, they must first already have become the object of less general and complete assent and been weakened by preliminary controversy. (1951: 159)

We will return to this passage at a later and more appropriate moment, but at this point we can detect a reiteration of the argument in *The Division of Labour in Society* about the transition from the mechanically to the organically solidary society. Where there is a homogeneity of sentiments and beliefs, as in mechanical solidarity, these will be rigorously enforced, and any discussion of the validity of the established beliefs and sentiments would require placing them into question. But even to suggest that established beliefs were questionable would itself be a form of deviation and, therefore, prohibited and punishable. Thus, it can only be in a situation where the 'conscience collective' is less homogeneous, more differentiated, that such questioning becomes possible. There cannot, accordingly, be a uniform acceptance of beliefs if there is to be any possibility of discussing and questioning them. Therefore, the sentiments and beliefs of a group must have less authority than they did previously in order for the idea of 'free inquiry' into them to be even thinkable. Thus, the esteem of free inquiry must be a product of social change, not the source of it.

As far as the religions of Western Europe are concerned, Durkheim considers that the Catholic church produces more of a 'mechanically' solidary grouping than do the Protestant churches. In the former there is still a great deal of homogeneity of belief and sentiment which possesses, therefore, *unquestioned* authority. The Protestant churches' 'concessions' to individual judgements mean that there is no longer any consensus to serve as communal authority. However, the disproportionate inclination of Protestants to suicide is not caused by their commitment to free inquiry, but by their desire for knowledge caused by the 'loss of cohesion of religious society' (ibid.: 169).

Durkheim, then, turns his attention to the organisation of the family and of political society. Looking at the statistical relationships again he finds that in general, though not invariably, married people are less inclined to suicide than are unmarried ones. Considering political society he invokes statistics which show that political crises often reduce, rather than increase, the number of suicides: for example, 'all the revolutions that have occurred in France during this [the nineteenth] century reduced the number of suicides at the moment of their occurrence' (ibid.: 203). Durkheim tries to eliminate all other possible causes which might explain the statistical correlations in order that he may press the conclusion that it is membership in a closely knit social group which 'protects' the individual against the inclination to suicide. It is the fact of membership in a family, of having strong and active social ties with other individuals, which is the essential influence that 'marital status' has on the suicide rate, and it is the capacity of 'great popular wars and great social disturbances' to 'rouse collective sentiment, stimulate partisan spirit and patriotism, political and national faith, alike, and concentrating activity toward a single end, at least temporarily cause a stronger integration' (ibid.: 208) of social groups which explains the way that political disturbances bring down suicide rates.

In all these cases, then, what prevents suicide is the extent to which an individual is part of – 'integrated in', to use Durkheim's own way of putting it – a social group within which there are strong and active ties to other individuals and within which there are strongly shared sentiments and beliefs.

Suicide and social solidarity There are two aspects to this which we should emphasise. One is that within the strongly united group it is the group as such which controls the individual and puts the sacrificing of the individual's life at the group's disposal. The other, and for Durkheim the more important, is the extent to which 'excessive individualism' not only leads to greater tolerance of the idea of suicide, but also itself causes suicide. Although it might be thought that in an individualistic society individual lives might become more fulfilled by people doing what they want to do, Durkheim insists that this is not the case. Some of our greatest satisfactions, those which give most meaning to our lives, are those which are involved in our acting in and for groups. Even in societies characterised by highly developed individualism it does not follow, he argued, that individuals derive their entire and greatest satisfactions from activities which are self-serving. Even in such societies, many of the things we do, and take great satisfaction from, are ones which serve the purpose of the groups that we belong to, such as our family or our country, and which may involve service to others and even self-sacrifice on our part.

Again, we are reiterating Durkheim's deep and abiding point that though the development of individualism is, in many respects, a beneficial development, it must not be conceived as the straightforward antithesis of social regulation. Although that development must be, in certain respects at the expense of social regulation, it should not be invariably at its expense. The well-being of both the society and its individual members necessitates the social regulation of the lives of those members. Durkheim can, perhaps, be understood as saying the same thing, though from a very different perspective, as the founder of psychoanalysis, Sigmund Freud, when he argued that the price of civilised life is the acceptance, on the part of the individual of a measure of constraint and the subordination of purely personal gratifications to other purposes.

'Excessive individualism' leads individuals to become the entire object of their own preoccupations. Without ties to a family, religious or political group, without attachment to a social unit larger and more important than themselves, individuals may truly and powerfully feel their own insignificance and mortality, find themselves living a life that has no true meaning or larger purpose, one which 'is not worth the trouble of being lived', with the result, says Durkheim, that 'everything becomes a pretext to rid ourselves of it' (ibid.: 213). 'Egoistic' suicide gets its name from the nature of its cause, namely, the reduction of a human life to nothing more than the manifestation of the immediate concerns of a socially isolated ego.

'Altruistic suicide' is the opposite of the 'egoistic', and relates to the earlier point about the way in which the strongly solidary social group has the individual's life at its disposal. In the typical case, the group's rules will demand that individuals preserve their life. But there are circumstances under which this will be forfeit. 'Altruistic suicide' is possible only where the individual is very strongly bound into the group, to the extent that the individual's own life seems of less value than the well-being of the group; where the individual's sense of his or her own worth, relative to the values of the group, is so weak that his or her life can be demanded on behalf of that group. Durkheim looks to what were then termed 'lower' societies, because they were held to be less structurally complex in their organisation, and would be typically of the 'mechanically' solidary sort. It was alleged, he says (ibid.: 217), that in such societies suicide was unknown, and it would be a consequence of Durkheim's argument that the intense integration of such a society in terms of shared beliefs and sentiments would mean that suicide would be forbidden. Hence, 'egoistic suicide' is not to be found in such societies. However, he cites cases in which suicide was commended as a matter of honour and suggests suicides in such societies fall into three categories: those in which the old or the sick are required to die, those in which widowed are required to do so, and those in which those who have lost their leader must follow him into death. In such cases the suicide is not a matter of individual motivation but of what is required: it is, in a phrase, a matter of duty.

Put simply, Durkheim's point here is that the individual's entire being is tied up with his or her socially defined position, the loss of which will render him or her entirely without worth in the group. Thus, old age or sickness deprives a man of his position as a competent warrior; the position of wife defines the woman for the society and widowhood takes away this vital position; one's attachment to a leader's band provides one's position and the death of the leader destroys it. Without a position to make one's life valid then one is required to remove oneself from the society. Such 'altruistic' suicides are not commonly found in our society, save in those groups which, like certain sectors of the military, are tightly solidary. The name of 'altruism' then attaches by virtue of the individuals putting the group before themselves. Of course, important to Durkheim's development of this point is that 'altruistic' suicides occur in groups which are so strongly integrated that the individual has no very strong sense of having a separate, individual existence; conceptions of self are so strongly wedded into social positions, and into membership of the group, that there is little sense of personal independence from the group.

The 'egoistic suicide', the contrary to 'altruistic suicide', is the result of insufficient integration into the social group so that it cannot provide the individual with the meaningfulness of life that comes from the feeling of being part of something greater than oneself. The fourth type, 'anomic suicide', is the opposite of the 'fatalistic' type mentioned earlier. This latter type involves the stifling of the individual's hopes and objectives by the oppressiveness of social circumstances, as the slave's imposed position may render his or her life hopeless. The 'anomic' type, therefore, results from the absence of society's control over the individual's hopes and aspirations, and is of considerable importance to Durkheim.

A life in which desires were disproportionate to the means available to satisfy them would be unbearable. Imagine an insatiable thirst: the desire for drink would be an acute torture with no prospect of alleviation. Of course, in human life we rarely have wants which are so unrealistically related to the possibility of their satisfaction. Like other animals, there are natural limits to our wants. Our thirst is not endlessly demanding and a modest amount of drinking will satisfy it. However, unlike other animals our wants are not exhausted by our material needs. We have many other desires, such as those for well-being, comfort and luxury, for example, and there is no natural, biological limit to these. Accordingly, in Durkheim's view, such appetites are inherently infinite. Normally, desires are regulated by our conscience, our inner sense of what is right and wrong, of what is appropriate and inappropriate. But why should the strength of conscience be capable of containing potentially insatiable needs? Because the limitation which is set is recognised to be a just one, that is, as a limitation which has authority deriving from a source which individuals recognise as greater than and superior to themselves. In Durkheim's scheme of things there is only one source which has the requisite greatness and superiority to provoke the respect which is given to the morality which regulates social life: society itself. Hence, a crucial part of our individual mentalities is made up by the moral rules of the society.

The internalisation of the moral order   In more contemporary terms, this making over of aspects of the society's rules into features of our individual personalities is called 'internalisation' and involves the making of society's 'external' requirements a part of the individual's own 'internal' personality. This, of course, explains why it is that though social facts are external and constraining they are not necessarily experienced directly as such. The notion which is nowadays complementary to that of 'internalisation' is that of 'socialisation', the process whereby the new member of society is trained in, learns and identifies with the ways of the group he or she is entering. Through this learning the new members come to share, that is, internalise, the ways, beliefs and the sentiments of the group. In the typical case, then, individuals rightly feel that their actions are spontaneous, springing from their own desires, not being done because of the imposition of any external requirement. The individual is indeed acting spontaneously, but the psychic make-up from which the action originates is one which itself consists of a moral sensibility which has been derived from society. Through internalisation the society's requirements have become the individual's own feelings, attitudes, convictions and responses, so what the individual wants to do and what society requires are one and the same thing. Thus, it is through this emphasis upon what we now call 'internalisation' and 'socialisation' that Durkheim seeks to bridge the gap that others find between the 'freely acting' individual and the 'constraining' society.

It is society, then, that defines a particular individual's wants. By this Durkheim did not mean to nominate society as some supernatural agency, only that the organisation of society will typically consist of arrangements in which standards of individual want and aspiration will be made compatible with their satisfaction, and that these standards will be 'internalised' by the individual. Not surprisingly, given the logic of his argument, one of the primary ways in which such standards will be set is through the stratification arrangements of a society. It is important, Durkheim maintains, that our wants should be proportionate to the resources that we have to satisfy them, but, of course, the resources that people have access to are unevenly distributed. This uneven distribution of resources is a stratification arrangement, and it is, therefore, the next logical step to argue that standards should specify a properly proportionate relationship between wants and resources for different strata. What is a realistic aspiration for someone in a higher stratum would be unrealistic for someone in a lower one. Thus, individuals who have internalised the standards of their social class would have a realistic relationship between their expectations and the likelihood of their satisfaction, and though life may be, as a result, in varying ways pleasant and unpleasant depending on one's place within the stratification order, it is not the perpetual torture alluded to above. Durkheim argues that in the typical case the standards associated with the class system will be such as to make individuals feel that inequities in the distribution of resources and the conditions of life are *legitimate* ones such that those who have more resources and better conditions are regarded as deserving of them. Such legitimacy is not automatic for there can surely be cases in which people doubt their justice, as in the modern societies of Durkheim's time when 'aristocratic prejudices begin to lose their old ascendancy' (ibid.: 251). But in such cases the arrangements are unstable and 'appetites superficially restrained are ready to revolt'.

Earlier we offered Durkheim's view that the individual could only truly flourish under the 'discipline' of a society, and his account of the way in which institutionalised standards of life discipline what would otherwise be unrealistic and insatiable appetites is one of the best examples of what is meant by this. If individuals were left entirely to themselves they would be ruled by completely uncontrollable desires and would, on Durkheim's argument, be constantly tortured by frustrated aspirations. It is because people live within a framework which sets realistic limits to what they want that they can have the satisfaction that comes from fulfilling, at least temporarily, those desires.

Accordingly, and to return to the discussion of 'anomic suicide', while fatalistic suicide is one which results from society's excessive limitation of individual aspirations, 'anomic suicide' results from society's insufficient regulation of them. Since individuals are brought up within their society's stratification arrangements, there will typically be a regulation of individual's wants in a way that will 'adjust' them to what is realistically appropriate for someone in that social position. Thus, the situation of anomie will develop when the discipline of desires established through internalisation breaks down, when the standards which have become part of the individual's conscience are rendered inappropriate to external circumstance. Such situations can occur when there are rapid socio-economic changes, when people's social positions are rapidly readjusted, more rapidly than will allow the adjustment of their expectations to their new situations: situations when individuals move rapidly down *and up* the socio-economic scale. Times of social crisis or economic boom and bust are ones which will produce the tendency to anomic suicide. The internalised standards which regulate appetites are rendered inapplicable by the change in the individual's social and economic circumstances, which means that the limitations upon appetites are lifted, and the experience of uncontrolled, unsatisfied desires is such that life would be unbearable. Furthermore, during times of such rapid, drastic change the whole order of society is perturbed and other features of social life which could serve to constrain and calm the individual are also inoperative, the end result being suicide. 'Anomic suicide' is, then, to a large extent the product of periodic disruption of the social order. But within industrial society there is also a constant source of such suicide, namely, economic activity. Durkheim thought that the economic sphere had become too independent of other areas of social life, so much so that it was able to go its own way, without regard for the consequences of its activity for the rest of society, with both religious and political powers losing their capacity to regulate it. Industry, instead of being still regarded as a means to an end, has taken on a life of its own and has become the supreme end of individuals and societies alike (ibid.: 255). Together with the tremendous success of economic activity, this loss of regulation has made the possibilities of economic activity seem unlimited, with the (otherwise) pointless pursuit of novelty and with the whole frenzied atmosphere of economic expansion bordering upon fantasy. In such a context, inevitable economic setbacks will be more shocking and shattering than they might otherwise be to individuals who have invested their whole life in such frenetic activity.

While Durkheim distinguishes four types of suicide, 'fatalistic', 'egoistic', 'altruistic' and 'anomic', each distinguished by its causal characteristics, he does recognise that more than one of these types may be involved in any actual instance of suicide, as when anomie and altruism combine. An example of this could be when someone is bankrupted and thus placed in an anomic relationship to his or her environment, but commits suicide for the altruistic reasons of sparing the rest of the family the social disgrace thereby incurred.

As noted earlier, the various things that we might ordinarily consider as motivations for suicide, such as depression, financial setbacks, divorce, poverty and so forth, are all considered by Durkheim in the course of his study. Typically, they are considered with the purpose of showing that they are not invariantly associated with suicide and cannot, therefore, be its true cause. It is only under certain external, and, for Durkheim, therefore social, conditions that these factors are associated with suicide. The suicide rate is not determined by features of individuals at all but is, in fact, set by the properties of the organisation of the collective life. It is because the organisation of the collective life remains stable over long periods that suicide rates show their remarkable stability. The properties of that organisation create varying types of situation and these act upon individuals. But they act upon individuals differentially – some individuals are more prone to desperation in a desperate situation etc. – and the operation of forces at work throughout a community will, therefore, impact upon individuals who are more predisposed to respond to the situation by taking their own life. Durkheim talks of 'suicidogenic currents' which can sometimes sweep through society, and can, in their effect, be analogous to the wind shaking leaves off a tree. It is the strength of the wind, and not the characteristics of the leaves, which is the cause of their fall, though, of course, the wind will most easily remove those leaves which are less strongly attached to the tree and, thus, poorly protected from the wind's strength. Once again, one of Durkheim's very strange- and implausible-sounding contentions – that society 'demands' a given rate of suicide – is not quite so nonsensical as it might sound, but is making the point that only if the social conditions which cause suicide are stable, then so too will be the rate that they cause.

However, even though arguing this, Durkheim is at the same time wary of having his arguments about the relationship between the individual and the society taken too 'deterministically' as though he were implying that the individual is only some puppet of supra-individual social forces. As a corrective to such an impression he argues that we lead a double existence, one which is based on the fact that our personalities are partially formed by the internalisation of shared rules, beliefs and sentiments and another shaped by our own, distinct, individual experience and, therefore, not always in accordance with socially standardised obligations. This means, says Durkheim, that we are drawn in two directions at once. As socialised members of a collectivity we are drawn to fulfil its requirements but, insofar as we have distinct individual personalities, we also rebel against the collectivity's constraints. Even as we, as individuals, kick against the constraints imposed upon us, we expect others to respect their obligations to us. However, although mutual pressure is important for containing individual impulses to rebel, this is much less important for Durkheim than the way in which society imposes its moral authority on us. In other words, we obey the rules of society because we regard them as having the right to our compliance.

Toward the end of *Suicide* Durkheim, resolutely and consistently opposing any effort to seek the origin of social institutions in the characteristics of individuals, makes a preliminary statement of the theme of his last major book, *The Elementary Forms of Religious Life*. He says:

> Usually the origin of religion is ascribed to feelings of fear or reverence inspired in conscious persons by mysterious and dreaded beings; from this point of view , religion seems merely like the development of individual states of mind and private feelings. But this over-simple explanation has no relation to facts. . . . The individual would never have risen to the conception of forces which so immeasurably surpass him and all his surroundings had he known nothing but himself and the physical universe. . . . The power thus imposed on his respect and become the object of his adoration is society, of which the gods were only the hypostatic form. Religion is in a word the system of symbols by means of which society becomes conscious of itself; it is the characteristic way of thinking of collective existence. (ibid.: 312)

The immediately relevant point is the way in which society is encountered by individuals as something which 'immeasurably' surpasses their own capacities, as something which is commanding of respect to the point of becoming the object of the greatest adoration, something which is surely capable of gaining the individual's acceptance of its moral authority.

The solidarity of society

Although Durkheim's attentions after his work on suicide transferred to religion, his sociological preoccupations remained constant. *The Elementary Forms of Religious Life* represents an investigation into the way in which religion serves as a source of society's moral authority and also provides, through its rituals, a mechanism for the creation of social solidarity. Durkheim also weaves into the book an argument that he was to develop later, namely, that even the constructs by which we think, are given to us by society. The whole book elaborates the remarks in *Suicide* about the gods being the hypostatic form of society's power and religion being 'the system of symbols by means of which society becomes conscious of itself'.

The study of religion

Durkheim starts from the assumption that religion is not to be explained in its own terms, that is, as a response to the presence of supernatural powers in the world. There are no superhuman powers, except those of society. In this respect, Durkheim's views are comparable to those of Feuerbach, so significant an influence on Marx, who held that to think of God as creating humankind is to get matters the wrong way around. God is a human creation. However, while it may be that there is no God, Durkheim does not want to dismiss religion as simple error or complete delusion, but, like Marx, argues that to understand the hold that religion has upon people one must investigate its social role. The very fact that religion is such a widespread phenomenon testifies, for Durkheim, that there must be something to it. The problem is, therefore, to determine what truth religion represents. In this connection, Durkheim takes a very different direction to that of Marx. The latter supposes that religion is the ideological expression of the inadequate capacity of existing social conditions to realise the full human potential of people, whilst for Durkheim religion expresses some profound truths about the relationship between society and its members. There are two directions in which his search could have gone, one of which we have already seen that Durkheim does not favour, namely, seeing religion as the 'development of individual states of mind and private feelings'. The other is, of course, to examine religion as the product of collective life.

For this purpose a general account of religion is required, and the first step is the identification of the range of phenomena to be covered by it. Not all things we should want to call religious phenomena necessarily involve notions of the supernatural, and the very capacity to make a distinction between a 'natural' order of things and a 'supernatural' one is found only in certain kinds of societies. Nor do religions necessarily involve any divinities: the Buddha is a focus of worship but is not himself a divine being. Religions typically involve two main parts, beliefs and rites. Religious beliefs separate the things of the world into two kinds, those which are 'profane' and those which are 'sacred'. The sacred is identified by being set apart within our lives, segregated from profane matters, and is the recipient of a special attitude of exceptional respect: we look upon the sacred with awe. Rites are activities which have a sacred aspect and which perform the actions that relate us to sacred things. This distinction between the sacred and the profane Durkheim alleges to be universal. The heart of religion, then, is a set of beliefs about the sacred and a set of rites which relate us to the sacred. However, these beliefs and practices make up a unified system and are, further, associated with a social group, what Durkheim terms 'a church', that is, a group of people, whatever organisational form it might take, who hold in common the relevant set of beliefs and rites.

The second task becomes that of understanding the nature of the beliefs and rites involved in religion. For the purpose of this investigation Durkheim chose to focus upon the religion of the Australian Aborigines, on the grounds that the very small and simple structures of their society meant that the religion found there must be the underlying form of religion to be found in *all* societies, including much more complex ones. We earlier mentioned that Durkheim held characteristically nineteenth-century views about the evolutionary development of complex societies out of simpler ones, views which are no longer generally accepted, and certainly no one accepts that any existing society, like that of the Aborigines, can be thought of as representing any primitive evolutionary precursor of other, structurally more complex societies. It was, however, his evolutionary ideas which allowed Durkheim to suppose that the religion found in the smallest, simplest societies must contain the essentials of religion – must possess its 'elementary forms' – out of which all religion could develop. Hence, through the re-examination of the anthropological studies of the Aborigines Durkheim thought he was examining the early beginnings of society and religion.

The religion of the Aborigines was a 'totemic' one. The society was divided into groups, each of which was associated with a 'totem', that is, with some natural object which was the recipient of special attitudes and treatments. These natural phenomena were quite ordinary, such things as a place, for example, a particular rock or lake, or some species of animal, such as a parrot or a wallaby. The group would identify itself by the name of the totem. In fact, these totemic practices served the purpose of Durkheim's argument well. He could make the crucial point that the totemic objects themselves were hardly awe-inspiring things. They were very ordinary and utterly profane in all respects save that in which they were approached by the totemic group. There was nothing *intrinsic* to the totems which made them deserving of the respect that they received. Their role had, rather, to be a symbolic one: they were treated with respect because what they stood for deserved respect.

The nature of the totemic practices readily enabled Durkheim to make a further vital argument. The totem was associated with a group, and the role of the totem was in many ways comparable to that which the flag plays in our society, as an object 'standing for' the group. Thus, Durkheim makes the connection between religious symbolism and the collective life: the totem symbolises the group with which it is associated. Since it is not the totemic item itself which is capable of evoking the awe and the respect which is directed toward it, and if there is no genuine level of supernatural phenomena for it to symbolise, then, since the totem symbolises the social group, it must be this which is capable of giving rise to the responses which are associated with the totem, and with the sacred more generally.

In the passage cited above Durkheim speaks of the gods as 'only the hypostatic' form of society, that is, as standing for that which is in fact the true object of religious adoration. However, even if it is conceded that society is the sort of entity capable of generating the responses that are associated with the sacred, the question remains as to why the 'worship of society', if we may provisionally put it that way, takes 'hypostatised' form; that is, why is it done in this oblique symbolic way, with 'the gods' or 'totems' being the ostensible focus of religious observance? Durkheim's answer is that the conceptions involved are not really 'digestible' by the human intellect, save in a symbolic form. The human mind cannot directly comprehend the fact of its relation of dependence upon and subordination to society. In its most basic terms, his case is that systems of religious beliefs do represent a reality; the fact that they are so ubiquitous throughout human history and human societies signifies that they cannot be entirely illusion. Were it so, then presumably that illusion would be exposed for what it is, and could not persist so extensively in the face of the facts which patently negated it. However, religion is extensively persistent and it cannot, therefore, be viewed as being opposed to the facts but must – or so Durkheim argued – be seen to be compatible with them. Since there is no 'supernatural' reality to conform to, religious beliefs must therefore be conforming to that which exists only naturally. Insofar as religious belief appears to postulate something which is different from the natural world, then it cannot truly be so doing, since there is nothing of that kind.

Underlying these arguments is Durkheim's assumption that the major creations of the human mind cannot be products of pure imagination: ideas cannot just come from nowhere. Ideas must, for Durkheim, be inspired by some external model. Hence, if we are to explain where religious ideas – such as those of superhuman, immortal and impersonal forces – come from, then we will have to look for something in the world external to the human mind from which those ideas can be derived, upon which they can be modelled. Religious belief, therefore, must be modelled upon natural realities, even though it represents them in forms which do not naturally occur. Accordingly, religious representations must capture a reality which naturally exists but expresses this in indirect symbolic form. Inanimate nature has often been offered as a candidate reality which religion seeks to apprehend, inspiring thoughts of greater-than-human forces in us by its powers and glories, but Durkheim rejected this possibility. However inspirational natural phenomena may be, there is nothing about them to suggest the idea of a higher, indeed exalted, level of reality, and it is, of course, the conception of just such a higher, sacred level that is one of the essentials of religious belief. If we cannot look to the world of inanimate natural phenomena, then there is only one place within the world of natural phenomena which remains as a possibility. It is to social reality that we must look – to society itself – for there we can find something which could give rise in the human mind to the idea of something greater and more exalted than our individual selves.

The notion of impersonal forces which control individual behaviour is one which is very prominent in our scientific thinking. That our behaviour is governed by the inexorable laws of physics is one which is nowadays readily acceptable. Durkheim alleged that science has taken over this notion of impersonal forces from religion and, thus, the comprehension of nature in terms of scientific laws means their comprehension in terms of an idea which is modelled in religion and, therefore, as we shall see, on society. Totemism may focus upon particular totemic objects but the object of worship is an anonymous and impersonal force which is independent of individuals, which is not itself mortal in the way that they are, but which is capable of entering into those individuals: both the totemic object and the members of the totemic group partake of this force, and individuals are affected by it, made to feel exalted and exceptionally powerful. The force is, then, abstract and intangible, one which can only be made manifest in the form of some visible object, 'the material form in which the imagination represents this immaterial substance' (Durkheim, 1976: 189). The capacity to form an idea of an abstract and universal force is itself something that can only be achieved under appropriate social conditions, and those of the Australian Aboriginal groups are not so appropriate. Their society is divided into sub-groups which, organised on a totemic basis, lead them to think of themselves as groups which are essentially distinct from each other. Their identification with their respective totems makes them different kinds of beings and they cannot, therefore, think of themselves as embodiments of the same principle. The capacity to develop the idea of a universal and impersonal social force requires the emergence of forms of organisations which can subsume divergent groups under a wider unity.

As we have said, Durkheim is developing his argument about religion on the supposition that the human imagination cannot create something from nothing; that is, it cannot create ideas which are purely its own products, which envisage things that are utterly imaginary. Durkheim sees the imagination, rather, as a faculty for the recombination of extant ideas, and this is dependent upon there being things to model them after. Thus, religious ideas are modelled on social arrangements and so the religious ideas that are possible in a society will be limited to those for which there are exemplary instances of social organisation. It is not the 'primitiveness' or 'simplicity' of intelligence or imagination of the individual Aborigines which confines them to producing certain kinds of representations and disables them from making the representations available in our society. It is, rather, the relative simplicity of the Aboriginal social organisation which ensures this. We will return to the topic of how ideas are generated shortly.

Since they inhabit society, no matter how simple or how basic its form, the Aborigines do experience society and so experience its superiority to, and its transcendence over, their individual selves. They experience society as something that is independent of their individual existence, greater and more powerful than their individual selves and which prevails, impersonally, over them all, which can alter their feelings about themselves and make them feel more powerful than mere individuals. These characteristics of immortality, of transcendence, of superior power, of the capacity to control individual lives and to bring us to exaltation, are all ones which are characteristic of the sacred. Though they experience these features of society, the Aborigines lack the conceptual apparatus to conceive of the influence of society as abstract and universal, and must therefore comprehend society in terms of the concepts that are available. Expressing the idea of society in a concrete way must, then, involve the employment of something tangible, something from the material world; hence, the totem.

For Durkheim, then, it is society that is symbolised in religious ideas. The fact that society is something greater than and dominant over individuals and upon which they are dependent is drawn upon to make the case. However, the assertion that society is capable of creating exaltation in individuals, of lifting them to a new level of being, is something that may be more puzzling. It is here that we need to examine Durkheim's analysis of rites.

Rites Society can affect our feelings, can make us feel more powerful than each of us might as an isolated individual. It is common and familiar enough that we feel more powerful when we have the collaboration and support of a group. If society can make us feel more potent, then it can also lift us to levels of exaltation, and it is in this connection that Durkheim invokes the Aborigines' rites. The life of an Aboriginal group is divided into two phases, one in which the group is scattered across the landscape sustaining its livelihood, and another when the group reassembles and engages in rituals. The period of assembly is one in which people are altogether more excitable and what Durkheim calls a 'collective effervescence' is created among the individuals through their association and interaction with each other. It is the kind of excitement which is visible in crowds, at parties and on other group occasions, but which people tend not exhibit when they are alone. Among the Aborigines, this excitement is created by their joint ceremonials.

Thus, argues Durkheim, our participation in collective activity can engender exaltation which, in the course of rites, can reach such intensity that we feel we are altogether lifted out of ourselves, made over into some new being, as in the way masks and decorations are used in ritual to enable participants to represent figures other than themselves. The rites give rise to exceptional and intense emotions which are often experienced as coming to us from the outside. And since the rite is focused upon the sacred object it is natural to attribute the effects produced by 'collective effervescence' to the powers that the sacred object possesses and focuses. Thus, again, in an indirectly symbolic way true reality is apprehended. The celebrants' ecstasy is generated by 'collective effervescence', by social relations, and it is focused upon and attributed to the sacred object. That object, of course, symbolises society, and in treating the object as the source of their elevated feelings the celebrants are, in Durkheim's terms, symbolically acknowledging that it is society which creates these feelings.

The association of the totem with the group expresses the common membership that this involves and that which is common to, and unifying of, the group. Thus, the totem plays a pivotal part in structuring the organisation of Aboriginal society and uniting the group. It is the recipient of awe and respect, as is signified by the special treatment which it is given relative to everything else. Since the totem signifies the society, the society is given awe and respect, but responses to the sacred are things reserved for special occasions. If we now recall that society is for Durkheim very much a matter of the authority of its moral rules we can appreciate that the attitude toward the sacred consists in exhibiting respect for society's rules. Respect for moral rules is, of course, something that exists only if those rules are complied with in everyday, profane, conduct. Our religious beliefs and rites involve, then, the symbolisation of our relationship to society, but they do not merely display the facts of our social life, of our dependence upon the collectivity and so on; they commend the rightness of that relationship, and *reinforce* the commitment which people have to those moral rules. In Durkheim's view, our attachment to society's rules is subject to attenuation: the practicalities of life, the demands and tensions this brings and the difficulties of relations with our fellows are all likely to put a severe strain on our moral feelings. In which case, over a protracted period of time our sense of loyalty to the rules of the society and of solidarity with its other members will progressively weaken. If morality is to continue to be enforced the attachment of individuals to it cannot continuously attenuate but must be reawakened, and it is in this necessity that Durkheim finds the explanation for the periodic character of rites. They play the role of renewing the individual's attachment to other members of his or her group and to the moral order of the society of which they are all a part.

Religion in the modern world The account in *The Elementary Forms of the Religious Life* is most closely and directly linked to the totemic practices of the Australian Aborigines but, as its title indicates, it is about the fundamentals of religious life in general. Durkheim was, of course, aware of the weakening hold of organised religion in the societies of Western Europe, but did not regard his arguments about the necessity in all societies of a division between the sacred and the profane as being invalidated by the fact that societies like ours are less explicitly, and since Durkheim's day far less explicitly, religious. Though the sacred, as symbolised by God, was increasingly less influential in modern societies he felt that there was still an inclination to develop a new form of the sacred, one which elevated to that level the very idea of 'the individual', a point which is, of course, very much in line with the argument of *The Division of Labour in Society*. In modern societies it is the rights and freedoms of the individual that must be treated with greatest respect. The retraction of explicit, organised religion is one of the things which Durkheim saw as an inevitable consequence of the progression of science.

However, Durkheim's version of this particular development is not one which involves the *opposition* of science and religion, one which sees religion as 'retreating' because science has revealed it to be illusory nonsense. Note that Durkheim's book was meant to be the first genuine and successful scientific treatment of religion and presents the argument that religion is not essentially in error. His account of religion's 'retirement' in the face of the rise of science is that 'scientific thought is only the more perfect form of religious thought' (1976: 429), operating on the same basic principles of thought as religion does, albeit applying them, in the case of science, in a less dogmatic and more methodologically disciplined way. Religious speculation provided a form of inquiry into the subjects of human thought, nature, man and society:

> Religion sets itself to translate those realities into an intelligible language which does not differ in nature from that employed in science; the attempt is made by both to connect things with each other, to establish internal relations between them, to classify them and to systematise them. We have even seen that the essential ideas of scientific logic are of religious origin. It is true that in order to utilise them, science gives them a new elaboration; it purges them of all accidental elements; in a general way, it brings in a spirit of criticism into all its doings, which religion ignores; it surrounds itself with precautions to 'escape precipitation and bias', and to hold aside the passions, prejudices and all subjective influences. But these perfectionings of method are not enough to differentiate it from religion. In this regard, both pursue the same end; scientific form is only a more perfect form of religious thought. (ibid.: 429)

Indeed, the very growth of science is partially a product of Christian belief, for it is through viewing matter as profane that it has been able to give over the business of finding out about that profane reality to the work of profane inquiry.

Thought and society

Durkheim's arguments invert views about the origin of religion and also, perhaps, turn upside-down conceptions about our whole ways of thinking, not least about our science. He set out specifically to refute views which supposed that religious thought had been built by trying to model itself on natural phenomena, and wanted to argue, instead, that it was to be understood in terms of its social origins. He then argues that the basic elements of scientific thought are the same as those of religious thought. But religious thought is itself derived from and modelled upon society. Therefore the way in which we think about the natural world, our most basic categories and procedures of scientific thought, are themselves modelled upon, derived from, the structure of society. Our classification of nature, Durkheim says, is itself derived from society. The ways in which we conceive the most basic categories of all experience, such as 'time' and 'space', are themselves constructed on the model of social organisation.

Earlier we mentioned Durkheim's view that the imagination is not truly creative, but involves only the reorganisation of given elements. This implies that the apparatus of thought, the ideas or concepts with which we think, must have been produced on the basis of experienced realities, such that for people to conceive of something abstract and impersonal they must have experienced something abstract and impersonal and have a model to represent that experience. The Aborigines experienced society's abstract, impersonal reality but they could not represent it because their social organisation did not provide them with any form upon which to model their experience. Not unreasonably, Durkheim is supposing that the development of our equipment for thinking, our conceptual apparatus, is an historical development and that it has an orderly character. We do not start human history with the complete stock of ideas inbuilt in each individual, but have to build up that stock over time. Nor has our conceptual apparatus accumulated in a random fashion. It has been built up under conditions which would have constrained the course of its development. Furthermore, the generality of our ideas or concepts is a consequence of their being used in communication between human beings, and so they must have the same meaning for each of us if we are to communicate. This apparatus of communication is not the work of any single individual but an evolving product of a great many different hands and constrained by the needs for communication among them. Even so, reasonable as such suppositions might sound, it still sounds odd to say that logic, time and space were built up in, by and on the model of society. In this respect, Durkheim opposes the view of such as Kant who argued that the basic categories of space and time were built into our minds. But though it may not be ultimately correct, the argument is not altogether as implausible as it might first seem.

Durkheim does not deny that it is, indeed, an innate feature of our human endowment that we experience things in space and time. We find ourselves placed in a world of things and in relation to them; for example, we experience things as being nearer to and further away from us, above us or below, and so on. We also experience things as happening one after another. It is held that it is these and other facts about our basically animal experience which enable us to develop the concepts of time and space, and it is the latter suggestion that Durkheim is especially concerned to discount, and, in so doing, enter a fundamental objection to another important philosophical theory, and direct rival to Kant's idealism, namely, the empiricist account of knowledge. This holds that our knowledge of the external world comes to us exclusively through our sensory contact with it, and involves no contribution of 'the mind'. Against such a view, Durkheim argues that the concepts of space and time that we have are complex ones, too complex simply to be found in our animal, sensory, experience.

Our experience of space is a personal one, but our *concept* of space is impersonal. We experience space each from our own singular vantage point, but we do not think of it as organised around that singular vantage point as though it were something that radiated out from where we individually are. Though we are each at the centre of our experience of space we do not think of space itself as something with a centre. Rather, we think of space as a 'totality' which encompasses everything, including each and every one of our individual viewpoints. We cannot, however, directly experience the totality that we conceive space to be, so we cannot from our personal experience of space have derived the concept that we have of it. As Durkheim says,

> the space which I know by my senses, of which I am the centre, could not be space in general, which contains all extensions, and where these are co-ordinated by personal guide-lines which are common to everybody. (ibid.: p.441)

He is reminding us that although our personal space is individuated, the concept of space and our location within it is one which is common to all of us. Since that concept cannot be extracted from the experience of our senses, and it is from experience that Durkheim thinks our concepts must ultimately be drawn, there is no reason why each one of us should individually have developed a common concept of it, and so the concept will only be the same if it is derived from a common source. Since this cannot be experience of space itself there is, in Durkheim's scheme of things, only one genuine possibility: a whole from which the idea of 'totality' can be derived, namely, society.

Earlier we talked about the way in which our ideas are 'modelled' upon social organisation, but this is not entirely accurate as a characterisation of Durkheim's views about the origins of logic and the categories of our thought. The arguments in the latter part of *The Elementary Forms of Religious Life* were prefigured in an essay that Durkheim co-authored with Marcel Mauss, *Primitive Classification* (1903). Durkheim affirmed (1976: 432) that 'logical thought is made up of concepts' and so to demonstrate that logic has a social origin is the same thing as showing that our collection of concepts, our system of classifications, has a social origin. *Primitive*

Classification is, as the title indicates, about the schemes of classification of societies that were, in Durkheim's day, considered to be simpler than our own: the Australian Aborigines again, Native American peoples such as the Sioux and so on. Its purpose was to argue not that the first logical categories were modelled on social phenomena, but that they were social categories themselves, created out of the necessities of organising social life. Things can only be put into what we think of as logical relations insofar as they are clearly distinguishable from one another, insofar as they can be counted together as members of an ensemble (in the language of logic, 'a class'), and as being capable of mutual combination or separation, and, finally, as capable of being ranked in hierarchical relations of inclusion. For example, two classes of things such as 'bedroom' and 'living-room' furniture are contrastive, with items that are included in one class being excluded from the other. But of course both 'bedroom' and 'living-room' furniture can be counted together within the higher, and more inclusive, class of 'household furnishings'. Natural as these aspects of thought may seem to us they are not, according to Durkheim, invariant to all human thought, and the idea of the logical hierarchy, of the clearly demarcated class, of the unification and decomposition of classes, must all have had an origin – even though this is very far back in human history. Since these ideas originate from quite basic features of social organisation, such ideas must have relatively early origins.

As we have already indicated, the setting together and keeping apart of individuals, their inclusion and exclusion, is constitutive of Durkheim's whole idea of society and it can, therefore, hardly be surprising that he goes on to argue that it is in the production of such relationships that logical ideas are formed; that is, through the production of groups whose memberships are sharply distinguished and mutually exclusive. There is, thus, created the idea of the clearly demarcated ensemble of individuals which can then be generalised as the logical notion of 'the class'. The ways in which individuals are collected together and set apart is, of course, variable, with individuals who are at one point in time included within counter-posed groupings being at another point unified as co-members of a larger, and more inclusive, unit. Mancunians who support one of the city's two teams, United or City, will be in footballing matters intensely opposed to each other, but in other contexts they will show local solidarity as Mancunians opposed to, say, Liverpudlians or 'Southerners'. And, of course, Liverpudlians and even 'Southerners' may feel themselves unified with Mancunians as 'English' against 'foreigners'. The idea of the logical hierarchy, of inclusion of a lower class in a higher one, is created in and by a process which makes logical hierarchy an aspect of social hierarchy.

Further, in *Primitive Classification*, Durkheim argues that the way in which the natural world is divided up is related to the ways in which social groupings are divided up. The totemic organisation of the Australian Aborigines again provides key examples. For if 'totemism is, in one aspect, the grouping of men into clans according to natural objects (the associated totemic species), it is also, inversely, a grouping of natural objects in accordance with social groups' (Durkheim and Mauss, 1963: 18). Effectively, social groups, at least those of the kind involved in totemism, project the form of their organisation onto the natural world. Thus, if certain groups divide themselves into two parts then this division applies equally to nature. 'All nature is divided into class names and said to be male and female. The sun and moon and stars are said to be men and women, and to belong to classes just as the blacks themselves' (ibid.: 12). In another case, a tribe divided itself into two groups, 'Youngaroo' and 'Wootaroo', and all else in nature, animate and inanimate, was divided between the two, with alligators and the sun being Youngaroo, kangaroos and the moon being Wootaroo, and so on for all the constellations, trees and plants. Durkheim and Mauss report the anthropologist Fison as saying that 'Everything in nature, according to them, is divided between the two classes. The wind belongs to one, and the rain to the other. . . . If a star is pointed out they will tell you to which division it belongs' (ibid.). The situation is much the same vis-à-vis the notions of how time and space are structured, for societies will project the forms of their own social organisation onto the universe at large. Thus, in *The Elementary Forms of Religious Life*, Durkheim argued that it is out of the needs of groups to distribute their organisation across territory and to co-ordinate the scheduling of their activities that the notions of space and time are created. The forms which these notions take naturally, therefore, conform to the structure of spatial and temporal relations which they are developed to organise, with, for example, a group's notion of space as, say, a circular thing being a generalisation of the group's circular organisation of its residential arrangements.

Once again, Durkheim's arguments are dependent upon much the same distinction as that between 'mechanical' and 'organic' solidarity. The case developed about the nature of thought depends very much upon assuming that the totemic and classificatory schemes of the Australian Aborigines and comparable societies represent the most basic, literally the elementary, forms of the phenomena of religion and thought, with religion being a most elementary vehicle for thought about the nature of things in general. The Aboriginal, and comparable societies represent the most simple form of social organisation, out of which all other, and more complex, forms of society have subsequently evolved. Such a picture of these societies as 'simple' and the associated idea of an evolution would not, nowadays, be accepted. But, taking Durkheim's argument on its own terms, it was these views which meant that though the study of Aboriginal totemism and classificatory schemes taught us something about the essentials of religion and thought, the lessons drawn could not be extrapolated straightforwardly from those 'mechanic' type societies to more 'organic' ones like our own. Both the length of evolutionary history leading to the latter type of societies and the complexities of their structure would need to be taken into account.

Thus, it was not Durkheim's supposition that our concepts of 'time', 'space' and the rest would show the kind of straightforward projection of intergroup divisions onto time and space. The transformation from 'mechanical' to 'organic' solidarity means that the social control of thought and sentiment on the part of the community is decreasingly intense and direct, so that the elaboration of categories and thought schemes can become, at least relatively, independent of the community's group structure, and directed more by its own cognitive purposes than by the requirements for structuring the organisation of group life. In this respect, we have already noted how the development of science involves an increasing autonomy from religion, which also involves an increasing autonomy for the concern to understand how things work; cognitive concerns which were present in religion but were embedded in, and subordinated to, religion's role in the symbolic representation of social reality.

The diagnosis of society

So far we have been dealing with Durkheim as a sociological analyst, but he was, like the other two figures described in this book, also dedicated to the idea of providing a scholarly basis for the reform of society. While it was part of his intention to analyse society, he also wanted to diagnose and prescribe for it. The contrast between, broadly, the 'mechanical' and 'organic' types of society has run through our discussion as it ran through Durkheim's own, and a prominent purpose of that contrast was to highlight the characteristics of the more 'organic' type, that is, societies like our own, with a view to evaluating the extent to which these were 'pathological' and in need of adjustment. In *The Rules of Sociological Method* Durkheim specified the utility, indeed the necessity, of a contrast between 'normal' and 'pathological' states of society, a distinction which he presumed could be adapted to society from medical science and which would, in comparable fashion, require grounding in scientific knowledge of the character and requirements of the society, just as medical knowledge of the nature and conditions of the healthy organism themselves need to be grounded in scientific knowledge of organisms.

The account of 'crime' given in *The Rules* was meant to illustrate the point that preconceptions about what is good and bad for society, about what is normal and pathological in it, should not be allowed to stand without scientific re-examination. After all, what could be more readily and universally agreed to be harmful to society than crime? However, Durkheim's argument about crime is precisely that it is a 'normal' and *not* a pathological feature of society – so long, at least, as the amount of it remains within a certain level. Durkheim does not mean that individuals should now change their attitude toward crime and regard it as something harmless and acceptable, for crime may indeed be harmful to individuals and can be deeply offensive to them. Recall that Durkheim's very definition of crime was of activity which was offensive to strong and shared sentiments, which means, of course, that crime necessarily involves offence and outrage to individuals. Durkheim is talking as if he were an anatomist of society, as if society were the equivalent of the organism, and is therefore talking about crime as a 'normal' phenomenon relative to the state of society as a whole. Crime is 'normal' in the sense that *every* society has a crime rate, and something which is common to every instance of an organism cannot be called 'abnormal' or 'pathological'. Further, not all crime is necessarily harmful to society. On the contrary, it can be beneficial, providing a crucial contribution to the society's very existence, a mechanism for the reinforcement of social boundaries and of social solidarity within them. Of course, features of an organism which are normal to it can develop into pathological forms, and so it is with crime, and with the division of labour. Thus, though the healthy society requires enough solidarity to create crime, and thus requires that enough crime occur to provoke the reactions that renew and reinforce the sense of moral unity amongst individuals, there must obviously be a specifiable limit to the amount of crime which could go on without it beginning to damage the society.

The development of the division of labour is likewise a normal feature of the development of a society, but, as already pointed out, pathological phenomena can arise out of normal ones, and Durkheim's view of the development of organic solidarity gave rise to abnormal forms of the division of labour. In *The Division of Labour in Society* he identified three of these. Naturally, given the disposition of his argument, these forms were pathological in that they threatened the unity of the society by introducing elements of disorganisation, incoherence and friction into its life.

The anomic form of the division of labour

The 'anomic' form of the division of labour resulted from the very essence of the social division of labour, namely, specialisation. The word 'anomic' here means, as it does with respect to the similarly named type of suicide, normlessness in the sense of inadequate regulation by rules. The division of labour produces specialisation and as part of its development it can create solidarity among individual parts of the specialised process through the awareness that individuals have of their interdependence with each other. But the development of specialisation may create situations in which individuals are effectively enclosed and isolated in their specialism to the extent that they are unaware of the unity of common purpose and inter-dependence that they have with other specialist individuals. Durkheim uses the case of the sciences as an instance of this. Scientists can become so immersed in their own work and specialist discipline that there is no overall coherence or unity to the sciences. The extent to which the appropriate sense of solidarity will be created depends upon the interaction between individuals: if individuals make specialised contributions to society in a fashion which brings them into close and constant contact with other, and complementary, specialists, then they will be aware and, typically, appreciative of mutual interdependence. But if they conduct that specialised activity in a solitary fashion, requiring little direct interaction with others to carry out that task, then this awareness of the necessity of others' contributions will be attenuated. The development of an intense and complex social division of labour is itself a complex process and it cannot be assured that the specialisation will automatically produce mechanisms which will contribute to the sense of solidarity. So, from the point of view of society, the growth in the division of labour will give rise to the necessity of a specialist co-ordinating function as a part of social organisation, a function which has, as its primary role, the regulation of the interrelation of the society's varied parts. This specialist function is performed by a specialist organisation, the state. However, while the state may have the task of regulating the social division of labour it is not infallible and, in Durkheim's view, it had not established the right kind or sufficient amount of co-ordination within the economic sphere to prevent pathological conditions. Thus, in economic life there were economic and commercial crises which testified to the absence of co-ordination within the economic domain.

The forced division of labour

This second type of abnormality of the division of labour results from the possibility, with the increasing autonomy of individuals from a uniform 'conscience collective', of a discrepancy between the individual's social position and his or her wants and aspirations. Under a strong, uniform 'conscience collective', individuals may experience frustrations, disappointments and injustices, but so dependent are they upon the group, and so intensely is their life bound to it, that such dissatisfactions do not turn them against the group. With the development of the division of labour the uniformity of beliefs and sentiments is considerably attenuated and, as noted, not only does the individual become more autonomous relative to the society as a whole, but there are also conditions under which individuals become less than aware of the extent to which their lives are intertwined with, and dependent upon, the society. The result may be that such dissatisfactions may well be turned upon the society, perhaps taking the form, if the dissatisfactions are widespread enough, of class-based opposition to the social order. Thus, if a society with a developed division of labour is to be thoroughly integrated the allocation of individuals to their roles within it will have to be such that the distribution of positions is perceivedly legitimate. Individuals must feel that their positions are not 'forced' upon them, against the grain of their inclinations and abilities, or as a consequence of essentially irrelevant contingencies and inequities of life. It is this mismatch between position and desserts that leads Durkheim to call this abnormal form 'the forced division of labour'.

Lack of co-ordination

The third 'abnormal' form that Durkheim identifies is the case when the functional contribution of each worker is hampered by a lack of co-ordination which, in turn, causes a breakdown in solidarity and, instead, creates incoherence and disorder. For Durkheim, a 'normal' system of production would make sure that useless work is avoided and that each individual is sufficiently occupied, so increasing functional activity. As functions become more specialised, in order to maintain adequate levels of solidarity, their mutual and co-ordinated interdependencies must also be increased, in much the same way that in human beings compared with frogs (the example Durkheim uses), the suppression of breathing very quickly induces the failure of other bodily functions. In other words, in human beings and, by analogy, complex divisions of labour, functions need to be more 'continuous', more active, in order to ensure a sufficient level of social solidarity. If co-ordination and effort is not adequate then this gives rise to an 'abnormal' form of the division of labour.

Beyond socialism

It is the necessity to achieve the overall legitimacy of the allocation of positions within the division of labour that accounts for the intense preoccupation with equality and justice in societies like ours. The treatment of workers in industry as though they were just human forms of machines without appreciation of their need to be fully rounded beings would ensure the intensification of resentments. Socialism, or so Durkheim argued in his study called *Socialism* (originally called *Socialism and Saint-Simon*, 1926), was a pre-scientific expression of the awareness of the economic anarchy and injustice of the economic sphere in modern societies. Its rise would encourage the full development of individualism, eliminating arbitrary inequities, co-ordinating the operation of economic enterprises, regulating and making more equitable contractual relations and generally mitigating the arbitrariness and harshness of the social environment upon the individual.

Mechanical solidarity, with its strong and uniform 'conscience collective', expresses its unity through its religion, but the growing division of labour changes the basis for such expression from a religious to a political one. The rise of the state is associated with and necessitated by the growth of the division of labour, with the state having the role of overseeing the unity of the society and thus having to be, for those within the society, the representation and expression of its overall unity. However, the complexity of modern society, particularly in the organisation of its economic activities, is such that it cannot possibly be overseen in sufficient detail by the state to ensure the adequate regulation of activities in a way that will integrate them and prevent extensive anomie. The capacity of the state to achieve assent to its regulation is, of course, due to the moral authority it carries by virtue of being the representative of society. So if the activity of the state is to be supplemented by some other form of organisation to undertake the more local and close regulation of activities, then that form will only be able to promulgate effective rules if it, too, is a bearer of authority.

In the 'Preface to the second edition' (1902) of *The Division of Labour*, Durkheim held that since it is within the economic sphere where much disorganisation reigns, and since the economic sphere is the one within which the most competitive and self-interested conduct is legitimated, then it is necessary to develop some form which can bring solidarity among those who are otherwise in competition and which will possess the authority to legitimate its regulation of economic life. Durkheim suggested that the occupational grouping, the profession, could provide such a basis. The professional group has a sense of unity and it typically possesses a set of ethics which regulate the work behaviour of its members. The introduction of organisations in the form of the profession within the economic sphere would therefore provide the basis for the requisite moral authority. It would, furthermore, provide a group with which the individual could immediately identify and which could also mediate that individual's relationship with the society-as-a-whole in the form of the state.

Part of the development of the social division of labour is the development of specialised agencies for child-rearing and, particularly, for their education. In a simple and undifferentiated society the child learns primarily within the family, but within a society like ours learning is mainly acquired through the educational system. From the point of view of society, a most important part of what is learned by the growing child is the society's morality, and not just practical skills and information. Thus, the school is an important agent in moral education, and it was the school's role in imparting the common morality of society (and doing so in a way which squared with the moral, cultural and practical diversity of the varied groups making up society) which attracted Durkheim's attention in the latter days of his career. Within a secularised society, where reason is highly valued, it is important that morality be legitimated on a reasoned basis, rather than, say, on that of religious revelation. Durkheim thought that sociology's rational and scientific understanding of the importance of morality in society, and therefore to the life of the individual, would contribute to such legitimation and a claim that sociology itself could play a part in 'moral education'. Further, Durkheim had notions about how teaching should be organised, on the way in which, for example, punishment and rewards should be administered. The weight of rewards was too heavily on scholarly attainments and insufficiently on the individual's moral development, and thus, he argued, there was a need to restructure evaluation within education, the better more explicitly to recognise the proportionate importance of the moral element.

The aftermath

The reputations of Marx, Weber and Durkheim have had variable careers within sociology. Durkheim's standing is probably the weakest of the three in contemporary sociology, for the affections which were hitherto bestowed upon Marx can be more easily transferred to Weber than they can to Durkheim. In the climate of post-1960s sociology, Durkheim stands accused of a number of sins, briefly those of positivism, structuralism, functionalism, reification and conservatism.

Positivism

Positivism is, most simply, the view that science is characterised by a shared method whatever the subject-matter being investigated. Thus, the social sciences should follow the same basic method as the natural sciences. This is the view that Durkheim accepted. However, as mentioned, Durkheim did not like to think of himself as a 'positivist' but more as a 'rationalist'. More recently, 'positivism' has come to be associated with a belief that the progress of sociology involves the adoption not only of the scientific method but also of quantitative methods. By these standards, there are prominent positivist aspects to Durkheim's work. His study of suicide, particularly, is considered as a classic in some sociological quarters because of the way in which it uses statistical manipulation to uncover relationships as a means of illuminating theoretical problems. However, although quantitative methods have come a long way since Durkheim's pioneering effort, his own achievement has proved difficult to match, let alone surpass. *Suicide* was, and remains, the classic example of this kind of social research, and although there have been numerous further studies of suicide after the fashion of Durkheim, as well as endless statistical studies of numerous other social phenomena, it would be difficult to cite any which approach its stature. Nevertheless, such a status erects Durkheim as the arch-enemy of those sociologists more sceptical of the aspiration to make sociology into a quantitative science, and he has become the focal point of the campaign against 'positivism' in sociology. However, it is also fair to say that within empirical social research this tradition is alive and well, although it now owes, perhaps, less to Durkheim than to others such as Paul Lazarsfeld and his colleagues who developed much of the current research apparatus of modern social inquiry. It has, however, lost the strong theoretical purpose which Durkheim invested in his own inquiries. For although Durkheim was strongly committed to the idea of sociology becoming a science, and although the most famous of his empirical inquiries, *Suicide*, made use of statistics, it would be misleading to treat Durkheim as arguing that scientific status could simply be achieved by the use of quantification and statistics. This would be to take little cognisance of his other work, which, as we have already suggested, shows a much more rationalistic bent than it does a simple-minded equating of science with quantification.

Structuralism, functionalism, reification and conservatism

The complaint of reification, that is, the treatment of things which are really the creation of human actions as though they were realities in their own right, arises from one of the prominent themes in Durkheim's sociological thought, namely, his idea that society is more than just an aggregate of individuals and represents an independent reality. Much of his work can be seen as an effort to work through just what this 'more' was. However, such an effort perhaps involves the 'reification' of society, that is, treating something which is entirely the product of the actions of human beings as though it had an existence and life of its own. The strongest form of resistance to reification is manifest in the 'methodological individualism' we discussed in Max Weber's thought. This insists that there are only individuals, and that notions of 'society', 'the state' and 'social classes' do not refer to anything which exists in its own right. They are simply abstract expressions referring to the actions of individuals. Although the term 'structuralist' in sociology has different uses, one of them is to identify those sociologists who, like Durkheim (but without necessarily sharing his specific views on this matter), want to say that society is a structure, or an arrangement, which is 'something more' than a product of the actions of individuals, so endowing the structure with the capacity to control or determine the lives of individuals. There has been continuous debate between the 'structuralist' and 'individualist' strands within the discipline but, despite this, it is not always clear just what the differences are and whether or not they are significant. Durkheim is a good example of the confusion here. Although he campaigned vigorously, sometimes eloquently, sometimes none too clearly, for the idea of society as 'something more than the sum of its parts', and though he sometimes might have expressed himself in ways that made it sound to his contemporaries that he was proposing the existence of a 'group mind', and though he has often been taken by some subsequent sociologists as if he were advancing a thoroughly reified conception of society, we have suggested in the foregoing exposition that these interpretations of his work are by no means entirely fair.

Related to this question is Durkheim's functionalism, a structuralist theory in the above sense and, worse, allegedly conservative in its political inclinations. Functionalism is a mode of analysis which is reificatory in seeking to understand society as though it were a single, unified entity in the way that the human body is an integrated assemblage of organic parts. Briefly, and somewhat simply put, functionalism portrays the parts of society, its institutions, its groups, its processes, as contributing to the survival of the whole and, in doing so, runs the risk of suggesting that society works in the way that it does in order to fulfil this function. It invites, as some critics of functionalism claim, the idea that given social arrangements of society do not need change since the way they are contributes to the harmony and continuity of society. More basically, functionalist doctrines are charged with implying that the harmony and unity of society is the over-riding objective, regardless of the inequity and injustice current arrangements might involve. In this respect, Durkheim's account of crime as seeking to show that the occurrence of crime was necessary to keeping society together, and his analysis of the contribution of religion to solidarity, both exemplify such a functionalist stance. Indeed, these studies became models for functionalist analysis in sociology and anthropology, particularly in the hands of Talcott Parsons, who became the most influential sociological theorist in American sociology in the 1940s and 1950s and who promoted 'structural-functional' analysis. However, as should be clear from our exposition, Durkheim's functionalism did not prevent him from criticising the social order nor from identifying its injustices and inequities.

As indicated, functionalism seeks to identify the conditions under which a society remains stable and unchanging, and it develops a methodology which focuses upon the way in which 'parts' of society, institutions and practices, contribute to holding the society together and keep it going. Such a conception, it is often argued, is inherently conservative in its denial of obvious facts about societies, particularly the endemic conflicts and struggles generated by major inequalities in society, inequalities of opportunities, of rewards, of gender, of ethnicity, of power and more. Functionalism is, it is claimed, a social theory which supports the status quo and is, thus, essentially ideological rather than scientific. It puts forward a picture of society as a united harmonious whole and an argument that it is neither necessary nor desirable to change society. Thus, functionalism is really only a distraction from the fact that many aspects of society are negative and disruptive, overestimating the extent to which society is unified, let alone harmonious, and preventing people from looking into the ways in which institutions and practices may be counterproductive and need changing.

It is commonly Durkheim's functionalism rather than his explicit political views, which were liberal and inclining toward socialism, which gives rise to the charge that he was conservative. Such a criticism is neither very discriminating nor, by and large, very accurate. Without denying that there are conservative elements in Durkheim's thought, and he was certainly opposed to revolutionary change, there are radical elements in his thought which emphasise his sympathy for socialism, as well as the importance he attached to the cause of reform in, for example, education and industrial policy. Indeed, his whole conception of sociology as a diagnostic tool was predicated on a conception that much in the society of his day needed changing. However, this could be achieved not by returning to some putative Golden Age, as conservative social theorists often tended to argue, but by a serious scientific inquiry into the working of the complex social order of industrial society to lay the basis for a rational reform of society.

However, it would be quite wrong to dismiss Durkheim as merely a target for sociological criticism, or a minor figure among the classic contributors to sociological thought. He has been widely influential and upon approaches which have been, in recent years, of some vogue in the discipline. We will mention three of these.

Some contributions: Goffman, labelling theory and the structure of human thought

Durkheim's concern with the drawing of social boundaries, his emphasis upon the importance of inclusion and exclusion in the conduct of social life, has been pervasively influential, even upon sociologists who might otherwise consider themselves far removed from any 'Durkheimian' influence. The first of our three examples is from work in the 'interactionist' tradition of sociology, one which is normally considered to be antithetical to the 'structuralist' aspects of Durkheimian work. Broadly, the 'interactionist' approach, as its name implies, insists that social life consists in the interaction between individuals, and develops such an insistence against the threat of the reification of 'society' and 'social structures'. However, in two leading examples of the interactionist tradition, the work of Erving Goffman (1922–82) and the 'labelling theory of deviance', the Durkheimian influence is strongly manifest.

Goffman's almost exclusive preoccupation was with 'public order', namely the organisation of interaction between individuals who are 'copresent', that is, who are in face-to-face contact with each other. Central to his analysis, and directly derived from Durkheim, was a concern with the conditions under which the face-to-face encounter could be sustained as a coherent transaction without disruption, itself a markedly Durkheimian notion, and with the part 'rituals of interaction' played in preserving that solidarity. Another Durkheimian theme in Goffman's concerns was his use of Durkheim's view that, in modern society, religion is increasingly becoming the worship of 'the individual', that our individual inviolability is the thing that is most sacred to us. Applying this idea, together with the point that rituals are a mode of relationship to the sacred, Goffman emphasised the degree to which the 'interaction rituals' through which individuals relate to one another were ones which were directed toward the individual self, toward preserving our individual sense of our own worth.

Also from within the 'interactionist tradition' is the 'labelling theory of deviance', an approach which is concerned with the way in which people are 'identified', or 'labelled', as 'deviants'. Once again, the motivation of many of these studies was to attack the 'structuralist' conception of crime and other forms of misbehaviour. The idea that the structural conditions of society make people commit crimes was anathema to sociologists in the interactionist tradition, and their account of the almost incidental way in which people enter into criminal or other 'deviant' activities and, indeed, into a 'life of crime' was meant to counterpose such conceptions. However, in their account of the ways in which people in society are singled out as 'criminals', or other deviants, they followed very closely upon Durkheim's example, first, by confirming his observations about the importance and consequences of the essentially public nature of the process of identifying people, and, second, in recognising the way in which such identification – or 'labelling' – was tied up with the moral boundaries of society. The classic in the labelling genre is almost certainly Howard Becker's (1963) book *Outsiders*, which carries, in its very title, the recognition of Durkheim's work, for it signifies that it involves the study of those who have been set 'outside' of conventional moral boundaries. Third, such studies give great emphasis to the extent to which the process of 'labelling' is a dramatic one, involving rituals, through which a person is transported (effectively degraded) from one status to another, lesser one, continuing Durkheim's emphasis on the public nature of the treatment of crime and criminals.

Although it is treated as, perhaps, the lesser and more insignificant part of his work, Durkheim's arguments in *The Elementary Form of Religious Life* concerning the social origins of our categories of thought has been one of the most influential aspects of his work. His arguments about the social origins of classification was, of course, an extension of his interest in 'exclusion' and 'inclusion' and the way in which systems of classification involve the inclusion of items in one category and their exclusion from another, as well as the way in which the classification of both natural and social things is essential to the conduct of human social life. Durkheim's bold suggestion that systems of classification are socially organised has been tremendously important in respect of two bodies of work of a power comparable with Durkheim's own. The first is a body of writings generated by Claude Lévi-Strauss (b. 1908) on the analysis of the fundamental structure of human thought through the investigation of the narrative structures of myth.

There are important differences between Lévi-Strauss and Durkheim, not least in that the former's view is that the basic forms of thought are determined not by society but by the structure of the brain, but the 'structuralist' mode of analysis which Lévi-Strauss developed is built upon the inclusion and exclusion properties of classification. It is not just that Lévi-Strauss' work is itself of a powerful quality, sufficient to earn him the status of a classic theorist, but that it has also been potently formative on contemporary thought not only in sociology but in other disciplines, too. His work played a vital role in shifting the direction of social thought and sociocultural analysis more generally. Lévi-Strauss' 'structuralism' is not to be confused with the kind of 'structuralism' discussed earlier, although connections have been made. His concern was with identifying the underlying principles of human thought. These principles would express our common humanity and the means by which our cultural artefacts and institutions come to express meaning in systematically structured ways. Our forms of religion, our myths, our cuisine, our kinship systems, are not simply the contingencies of history but are part of the collective consciousness of humankind. In his analysis of myths, what Lévi-Strauss is trying to draw attention to is the common logical structure which the different myths display. It was not long before it was recognised that his methodology could be applied not only to myth but also to the thought and culture of society more generally. Soon a 'structuralist' approach developed drawing very much on French and European thought. Although it has lately ceded ground to 'post-structuralism', the fact remains that it was Lévi-Strauss' Durkheimian influenced work which was a significant impulse behind this tradition of social thought and that many of the issues considered to be central to modern sociological thought derive from this strain of French social thought.

A second major school which exploits Durkheim's work on the social origins of human thought is the programme of work in the social studies of science, known as the Strong Programme, a tradition which originated within British sociology but which has assumed a more international presence. Durkheim's insistence that the categories used to classify 'natural' phenomena should be understood as having social origins provided the inspiration for the attempt to resuscitate the more or less moribund sociology of knowledge. While the sociology of knowledge, it was argued, had allowed that our ways of thinking about society were themselves shaped in and through our experience of social organisation, it had typically exempted science from such a claim. Science was independent of social determination. However, for the Strong Programme, such an exemption was, scientifically speaking, scandalous. The first requirement of scientific investigation is that it treat similar phenomena in the same way and, thus, there is no reason for subscribing to the view that our ways of thinking about the natural world are distinct from the ways in which we think and study the social world. Both are susceptible to sociological analysis. Thus, the content of the natural sciences, their theories and their findings should be subject to sociological explanation. Our conceptions of nature are shown not to depend on 'how nature itself is', but upon how the social structures and the cultures in which we live require us to think. The work of Durkheim and Mauss on 'primitive classification' is invoked as a leading model for the policies of the 'new' sociology of science.

As we have already suggested, Durkheim has received less charitable treatment than either Marx or Weber. In many ways he has been treated as the epitome of many of the wrong ways of doing sociology; guilty, that is, of the 'sins' we identified at the beginning of this section. Although Durkheim did, on a number of occasions, overstate his arguments, a concentration on his alleged sociological misdemeanours hardly does his thought justice. Indeed, such a concentration, as we have pointed out, obscures, to the point of concealment, the manifold influences that his thought has had in a number of very different sociological fields and approaches ranging from structuralist thought and its wide-ranging influence on the study of language and discourse as well as social structure, to the more interactionist focus of Erving Goffman and labelling theory. Far from being simply the scholar who tried to develop a quantitative method of social research, Durkheim's more theoretical ideas about the nature of society and social life, about the sources of social solidarity, about the social origins of the structure of our thought are all themes which have become important issues in contemporary sociology.

Select bibliography and further reading

Steven Lukes' *Emile Durkheim: His life and work, a historical and critical study* (Harmondsworth, Penguin, 1973) provides a very comprehensive and detailed discussion of all Durkheim's writings. Peter Hamilton's *Emile Durkheim: Critical assessments* (4 vols, Routledge, 1990) provides an immense collection of articles on all aspects of Durkheim's work. Short and accessible general introductions to Durkheim's work are provided by H. Alpert's *Emile Durkheim and his Sociology* (Columbia University Press, 1939), which remains, despite the date of publication, a lucid and helpful introduction; R.A. Jones' *Emile Durkheim: An introduction to four major works* (Sage, 1986); Kenneth Thompson's *Emile Durkheim* (Ellis Horwood, 1982) and Anthony Giddens' *Durkheim* (Fontana, 1978). Giddens has also edited *Emile Durkheim: Selected writings* (Cambridge University Press, 1972) and *Emile Durkheim on Politics and the State* (Polity, 1982).

Durkheim's main views are presented in the central books: *The Rules of Sociological Method*, which, in the new 1982 translation, published by Macmillan, contains additional selections on method; *The Division of Labour in Society* (new translation, Macmillan, 1984); *Suicide: A study in sociology* (Routledge, 1951) and *The Elementary Forms of Religious Life* (Allen and Unwin, 1976). Also important is *Primitive Classification* (co-authored with Marcel Mauss; Cohen and West, 1963), which is concerned with the social organisation of the categories of thought. *Moral Education* (Free Press, 1961), *Professional Ethics and Civic Morals* (Routledge, 1957) and *Socialism* (Collier, 1962) involve the application of Durkheim's approach to the moral and political problems of society. The Giddens selection *Emile Durkheim on Politics and the State* covers some of this ground.

The view that Durkheim has often been misrepresented as a conservative thinker – as he is by Robert A. Nisbet *The Sociological Tradition* (Basic Books, 1966), for example, and in Lewis Coser's 'Durkheim's conversatism and its implications for his sociological theory' (in Kurt Wolff [ed.], *Emile Durkheim: Essays on sociology and philosophy*, Ohio State University Press, 1960) – is indicated by the titles of two recent books, *The Radical Durkheim* (by Frank Pearce, Unwin Hyman, 1989), and *The Radical Sociology of Durkheim and Mauss* (edited by Mike Gane and Keith Tribe, Routledge, 1992).

There are very many sources which provide discussion of Durkheim. Talcott Parsons' *The Structure of Social Action* (Free Press, 1937) provided very influential interpretations of the work of both Durkheim and Weber, and of the potential similarities between their thought. Parsons' interpretation has been contested, as, for example, by Whitney Pope in 'Durkheim as a functionalist' (*Sociological Quarterly*, 16, 1975: 361–79) and 'Parsons on Durkheim, revisited' (*American Sociological Review*, 40, 1975: 111–15). Whitney Pope has also written a book on *Durkheim's Suicide: A classic analyzed* (University of Chicago Press, 1976). Mike Gane has written *On Durkheim's Rules of Sociological Method* (Routledge, 1988) and W.S.F. Pickering *Durkheim's Sociology of Religion* (Routledge, 1984). Stephen Lukes and Andrew Scull have collected scattered writings into *Durkheim and the Law* (St Martin's Press, 1983). Stephen P. Turner provides a thoughtful discussion of 'Durkheim as a methodologist', as Part 3 of his *The Search for a Methodology of Social Science* (Reidel, 1986) and has edited *Emile Durkheim as Moralist and Critic* (Routledge, 1993), a collection of essays on current views of Durkheim. Steve Fenton's *Durkheim and Modern Sociology* (Cambridge University Press, 1984), assembles essays which relate Durkheim's ideas to strands in contemporary social thought.

The Presentation of Self in Everyday Life (Doubleday Anchor, 1959) is a good start for Erving Goffman's work referred to in the discussion. Howard Becker's *Outsiders: Studies in the sociology of deviance* (Free Press, 1963) is a good example of the 'labelling perspective'. Claude Lévi-Strauss' *The Savage Mind* (University of Chicago Press, 1966) and *Structural Anthropology* (Penguin, 1968) are sources for the structuralist developments deriving from Durkheim's writings on the social origins of thought. The work of the Strong Programme is extensive but see David Bloor's *Knowledge and Social Imagery* (Routledge, 1976) and Barry Barnes' *Scientific Knowledge and Sociological Theory* (Routledge, 1974) and *Interests and the Growth of Knowledge* (Routledge, 1977).

5

Conclusion

What we have tried to do in the previous chapters is present as clear an exposition as we can of the sociological ideas of Marx, Weber and Durkheim. A large part of our objective in doing so has been to emphasise the tradition of sociology to which they made major contributions. Although it would be too extravagant a claim that all contemporary sociology is owed to these three thinkers, none the less the discipline continues to make use of an intellectual apparatus which derives in considerable part from them; not always directly and not always with acknowledgement, but still to an enormous extent. This is not to say that the apparatus, the analytic frame, is a settled one. It is still very much a framework which is evolving, which consists of questions and problems rather than settled principles. Despite this, we would want to stress the continuities of the discipline rather than, as postmodernist thought would have it, the break with Enlightenment ideas. This is not to present sociology as some sterile discipline incapable of moving beyond the ideas of three nineteenth-century figures and their predecessors. Rather, it is a testament to the considerable difficulties there are in formulating an agreed upon framework for the study and the investigation of the social. Although sociology can often seem to be an almost endless generation of new approaches, new perspectives – we would suggest that much of this is a recycling of ideas – there is, none the less, a continuity of problems and questions which serve to characterise the discipline's tradition. By trying to see how contemporary approaches still draw upon a discourse which was substantially though not exclusively formed by Marx, Weber and Durkheim we can, perhaps, appreciate not only how crucial these scholars were, but also how difficult are the problems they were writing about.

As we suggested in the Introduction, if anything the influence of Marx, Weber and Durkheim is stronger than ever, often reaching beyond sociology and the social sciences to pervade the humanities. So much so that in some fields the traditional boundaries between disciplines, for example between sociology and literary criticism, have been significantly eroded. As we mentioned in the exposition of Marx's theory of ideology and its subsequent adaptations by, in particular, Gramsci and the Frankfurt School, this has been important in shaping the assumptions of contemporary approaches in cultural and media studies. Similarly, Durkheim's thought was a decisive influence on the conception of language developed by one of the founders of modern linguistics, Ferdinand de Saussure (1857–1913); a conception which was, ironically, to transform much of anthropology, literary criticism and philosophy half a century later in the hands of Claude Lévi-Strauss. His 'structuralism' precipitated a sequence of developments from 'structuralism' to 'post-structuralism', playing a major part in the work of the Marxist scholar Louis Althusser (1918–90), and stimulating the work of two dominant figures of the moment, Michel Foucault (1926–93) and Jacques Derrida (b. 1930). Weber, in his turn, had a considerable effect upon the work of Theodor W. Adorno, a founding figure of the 'Frankfurt School' of social analysis and criticism which has itself played a major part in shaping the intellectual agenda of cultural studies, and upon Jürgen Habermas (b. 1929), the leading theorist in Germany today. Not all that indirectly, our three 'classical' scholars are at the heart of contemporary intellectual life.

Our concern has, however, been a more modest one than trying to trace through in detail all the ways in which Marx, Durkheim and Weber have influenced contemporary social and cultural thought. As we have indicated elsewhere, much of this influence has been in forming what might be described as a sociological mentality in addition to the more direct contributions that we have pointed to. Our concern has been primarily with the sociological aspects of their work and the import of their ideas and we cannot emphasise strongly enough the degree to which their theories prefigure the continuing preoccupations of sociological thought.

In the Introduction we mentioned the charge, made by 'postmodernists' such as Jean-François Lyotard, that the kind of theorising which we have been describing has become an irrelevance to the contemporary world. The world has changed in ways beyond the imaginings of these theorists and has passed beyond the resources of analysis which they sought to create. The whole tradition of thought which they, or at least Marx and Durkheim, sought to carry forward, the so-called 'Enlightenment tradition', has broken down and been exposed as a fake. The Enlightenment idea was the emancipation of humankind through the application of rational, scientific knowledge, but this has singularly failed to deliver its promise. The Enlightenment tradition itself has been re-examined and shown to be, it is argued, an essentially oppressive rather than a liberating mentality. The feminist case, for example, has been that such a tradition sought, at best, only to emancipate *man*kind, in that it embodied and perpetuated what was basically an apparatus of patriarchal assumptions which contributed to the continued oppression and exploitation of women.

It is not, of course, our purpose to defend Marx, Weber and Durkheim against all criticism or to suggest that they were unfailing in their analyses of the conditions, problems and prospects of the Western societies on which their attentions were mainly focused. Our emphasis has been upon the theoretical aspect of their work rather than upon their most substantive investigations, for it is from these that we see the continuing salience of their work. We would, for example, readily concede that Marx and Weber's predictions, such as they were, about the future of industrial societies – as involving proletarian revolution or evolving into an utterly oppressive bureaucratic nightmare – have not been fulfilled. We would also readily grant that much of Weber's work on the 'world religions', dependent as it was on the historical scholarship then available, has been invalidated in many of its historical specifics. However, we do not accept that this detracts from the interest and value of his ideas which guided the accounts of Western societies or the world religions.

Of course, the world has change in significant respects since all three theorists wrote, though there are many respects in which the changes which took place in the first half of the twentieth century continued to be in terms of those aspects of society to which Marx, Weber and Durkheim had given such emphasis. The expansion of the industrial economies of the major states of Western Europe and the United States continued, and they became even more dominated by industrial manufacturing, while their economies became ever more global in their reach. The division of labour on which these theorists placed such stress reached its apogee in the development of mass-production, exemplified by the conveyor-belt methods so paradigmatically employed in the motor industry. It was this which earned the period of industrial organisation dominated by the conveyor-belt approach, and which extended into the third quarter of the century, the characterisation of 'Fordism'. Under this system, the organisation of work was centralised and disciplined. Work tasks were decomposed into their smallest constituents, and the main requirements of those employed in such a system were to be obedient and disciplined, so that they could function as adjuncts to the machines. A great many sociologists felt that this kind of society, dominated by mass-production and with a large industrial working class, was one to which the analytical tools developed by one or another, or some combination, of our three theorists could still be applied, for in important ways there was a continuity between it and those of nineteenth-century industrial capitalism.

However, in recent years there have been considerable changes in industrial societies. The economic significance of industrial manufacturing has greatly diminished within the last decade or so, certainly relative to service work and employment which has been expanding in the post-war period. 'Fordism', as a system of production, has been exported to other parts of the world. The symbol is no longer the conveyor-belt, but the computer; no longer the production line, but the electronic office; no longer material goods, but information. The emphasis is less and less on the worker as an adjunct to the machine and more on him or her as an educated, highly skilled, autonomous decision-maker. Such changes in the economy are also seen as ramifying throughout other areas of society and, as Marx might well have argued, are manifesting themselves in its culture.

Naturally enough, changes such as those just alluded to have their impact on sociology. Indeed, sociological thinking has played a major part in identifying and presenting various analyses of such changes. A particular example is the way in which research into class is now having to come to terms with the diminishing significance of the 'working class' in Western societies. With the coming of 'post-Fordism', as indicated earlier, traditional industrial work is being increasingly eliminated or transported to the 'Third World'. We do not doubt that these economic and social changes are taking place, but would argue that it is not the emphasis on industrial organisation and the role of 'class struggle' in Western societies in the work of these three theorists that is their most influential impact. Rather, this lies in their contribution to a mentality and to a mode of analysis. For example, the decline in the size and the importance of the working class in Western societies might mean that the problem of how the working class are dominated and incorporated in the capitalist system ceases to be of importance. However, this does not mean that the problem of domination itself thereby evaporates. On the contrary, sociologists – and all kinds of other social and cultural analysts – are just as preoccupied, perhaps more than ever, with the identification and analysis of oppression. If class is decreasingly significant to sociology – and there are disputes about this – the purposes for which the notion was intended to serve in Marx and Weber as part of the analysis of social change, of conflict, of domination, have not been displaced and remain among the more predominant concerns of contemporary sociology. The determination to demonstrate that various aspects of society are oppressive is as resolute as it ever was, and it is from this that, for example, Foucault derives his present far-reaching influence. Although there are other elements in the mix, Foucault's own thought is, in important ways, the working out of variations on Durkheimian and Weberian themes.

Foucault follows through Durkheim's and Weber's joint insistence upon the way in which systems of thought and modes of classification are shaped by social organisation. This connects with a Weberian emphasis on the importance of rationalisation in the modern world. Foucault has developed these themes to present a picture in which direct political domination of one group by another has been displaced by much more indirectly oppressive arrangements. Rationalised systems of thought and administrative procedures provide a diffuse but pervasive web of regulation and social control. The extent of Foucault's influence serves to ensure that the notion of domination is as prominent in social thought as it has ever been and, in some respects, can be seen as an elaborate expansion of Weber's idea of the modern world as an 'iron cage' for the soul of the modern individual.

From the point of view of sociology perhaps the most profound implication that has been drawn from the economic and social changes alluded to above is that they represent a break with the modern epoch and the beginning of another, the 'postmodern' era; a break which is not only a discontinuity in the nature of society itself, but a transformation in expectations of what knowledge (including sociology) can be and can achieve. Lyotard, one of the more formative of the exponents of this idea, subtitles his book *The Postmodern Condition* (1984), 'a report on knowledge'. The 'modern' and the 'postmodern' are distinctively different outlooks. The modern outlook, to use the metaphor of the conveyor-belt, embodies a centralised and integrated system, an arrangement which is set up and directed from the managerial centre which arranges things through a master plan. Thus, understanding society is about gaining knowledge of society as a whole, that is, providing a single unified framework, a 'master plan'. The acquisition of sociological knowledge, on the modernist view, requires the creation of an over-arching scheme of thought – a 'grand narrative' – within which the whole of history and the contemporary world could be comprehended. It is the rejection of the 'grand narrative' which is the hallmark of the postmodernist view of the condition of knowledge; a rejection, too, of the kind of ambitions represented by Marx and Durkheim, though less so by Weber. The attempt to provide general sociological theories and over-arching conceptions of the world, it is said, are doomed to failure.

For our part, the idea that the movement of social thought has carried the social sciences and the humanities away from these nineteenth-century 'founders' we regard as a misleading one due, we suspect, to the problem to which this book is a small, and partial, corrective, namely, the lack of awareness of the history and tradition of the social sciences. Ideas which are often considered distinctly contemporary are, in fact, ones which have been elaborated before. Indeed, the irony is that some of the most decisive contributors to the underlying structure of postmodern thought, as they were to modernist thought before this, are the three figures we have been discussing. The merits of the arguments about the nature and the differences between modern and postmodern thought do not concern us here, but a major purpose is to insist that the postmodernists are not so far from their nineteenth- and early twentieth-century predecessors as they might encourage us to imagine. Let us just mention some of the important respects in which the postmodern critique is directly derivative from these nineteenth-century sources.

Although the intellectual aspirations of such as Marx, Weber and Durkheim might be seen to have failed – though such judgements have been fickle enough in the past – the irony is that the methods of analysis which they developed are now being turned against them since the 'postmodernist' critique itself makes use of them. The postmodern analysis of society shares the objective of analysing the condition of contemporary, principally Western, society and seeks to show that the dissolution of the 'grand narratives' is the result of the decomposition of the central institutions and structures of modern industrial society to which Marx, Weber and Durkheim attended, and the transformation of the role of conflict within these societies. Marxist-influenced notions of 'disorganised capitalism' might, however, be employed to draw attention to many of the selfsame social, economic and political developments which have dispersed industrial production on a global scale away from the older industrial societies, eradicated class conflict as a central feature of these societies and encouraged the rise to prominence of conflicts among what are, in

Weberian terms, status groups and parties. Thus, much of the emphasis in contemporary sociology is upon gender and ethnicity as the bases of oppression and conflict, and upon the role of 'new social movements', such as those now forming around ecological issues, as vehicles of opposition.

Indeed, drawing the distinction between 'modern' and 'postmodern' societies in terms of their economic structure, and suggesting that such changes in the organisation of production and work give rise to changes in the wider society and in its cultural outlook, has a distinctly Marxian cast to it. The postmodernists might reject Marx's aim of providing a unified story about the rise and the course of the modern world, but they are as much dependent on his mode of analysis in the formation of their own theses as he was. Furthermore, the critique of the 'grand narratives' is itself one which is influenced, in varying degrees, by each of the three theorists we have been discussing. Each of them, for example, made important contributions to the idea that thought is a function of social position and needs to be understood in terms of the role it plays within social organisation. Marx and Weber particularly emphasised the way in which theories are to be examined for the often close connection they have with domination. Marx and Weber were, as we have pointed out, two of the decisive figures in shaping notions of stratification into tools of social analysis as well as emphasising the extent to which social relations involve domination.

They also railed against parochial conceptions which sought to base social analyses on the assumptions obtaining in the society of their times. Though not exempt from charges of Eurocentrism, Marx, Weber and Durkheim were among its pioneering critics. It is a clichéd but unavoidable comment on the history of sociology that it originated in the industrialising societies of Western Europe, notably France and Germany. It developed very much as a response to the emergence of the capitalist industrial system and the tensions and social changes associated with it. The Eurocentrism of Marx, Weber and Durkheim was partially dependent upon the assumption that the newly industrial civilisation was a 'world historical' one and would have an impact not only on those who were living within it, but also on those others who came within its sway. And, given the inherent expansionist, even 'globalising', tendencies of such a society, this could mean the whole planet. For these theorists, the 'Western world' was a special phenomenon, though this is not to say that it is an admirable one. The emergence of the industrial system and its forms of social and economic organisation were unprecendently dynamic with a capacity to disrupt and restructure social relations on an immense and continuing scale. All three of the thinkers had as their primary objective the understanding of developments in their own societies even though they did have, to varying degrees, comparative and historical interests to pursue.

In the postmodernist conception it is the Enlightenment which is the source of current problems in the Western intellectual tradition, in particular its advocacy of the systematic application of reason to all areas of human experience. Reason was envisaged as instrumental in the reconstruction of the social order, the 'master plan', for it was reason which created the possibility of control. If it could be understood how something operated, then these operations could be controlled. The rational understanding of society created the prospect of a rational reorganisation. All three of these classic thinkers, like many of their predecessors as well as their contemporaries, were confident that without the application of reason to society and social change human life would continue in its miseries. Both Marx and Durkheim were confident children of the Enlightenment and had an immense faith in the prospects for the development of science and its application to human social affairs, though the scale of Marx's ambitions for a comprehensive emancipation of humankind was much greater than Durkheim's design for institutional reform. Weber had a much more ambiguous relationship to the Enlightenment legacy, and one which places him closer to the spirit at least of the postmodernists. He regarded the pursuit of scientific knowledge as a valuable objective and one which promised the prospect of enhanced control. He also recognised that there were limits to the powers of reason and that the capacity of science to bring about improvement was dependent upon the purposes with which it was applied. It could serve as an instrument of oppression just as much as it could serve as one of human freedom. All three thinkers, then, were united in seeking to develop a sociological understanding in order to contribute to the solution of the emerging problems of the modern world, including those not only of conflict and deprivation but also of spiritual desolation.

We are not, of course, claiming that these classic thinkers fully anticipated the ideas of the postmodernists. We do suggest, however, and as said earlier, that current social analysis is extensively influenced by them and that many of the current controversies are often but the more recent manifestations of their central concerns. The deeper understandings of what postmodern theorists are about, and the terms in which the controversies over their work are framed, require an awareness of the strong and still vital connections they have with the work of Marx, Weber and Durkheim.

In stressing the persistent influence of Marx, Weber and Durkheim, we are not suggesting that their work is intellectually stifling and that nothing has happened since they wrote. On the contrary, what we are emphasising is the vitality of their thought as well as the extent to which it initiated engagement with issues arising from the development of industrial society which are still at the centre of public and intellectual attention. We have also suggested that one of their strengths is the nature of their broad method of approach rather than that their specific ideas necessarily stand in light of changed ways of thinking and changed circumstances. What these thinkers bequeathed were broad conceptions of what it means to take a sociological approach. There is, of course, a great deal of room to manoeuvre within these and they have proved fertile sources for the working out of radical variants upon, and sometimes outright rejections of, the schemes. A great deal has happened in rethinking the ideas of 'classical theory', and although we have emphasised the continuities of many of the ideas of the present from the past, this has been in order to draw attention to just such continuities. It does not mean that we underestimate the extent to which many of the recent developments in theoretical sociology are remote from these ancestors. Structuralist theories, to pick one example, have their source in Durkheim, but the shape their work has assumed in recent years has been formed by a great deal of linguistic theorising which has a character and a sophistication that Durkheim could not have imagined.

Our account of the ideas of the three theorists has also been a positive one, but this does not mean that we regard them as infallible. Indeed, we have been at pains to draw out the differences, often profound ones, between them. The bibliography of criticisms of them would be an extensive one, indeed. However, it is a misfortune of sociology that critique is often confused with the kind of criticism that can be described as 'shoot first and ask questions later'. In our discussion of Durkheim, for example, we mentioned that he persistently tried to dissociate himself from the equally persistent complaint that he postulated some kind of 'group mind'. Many of the current debates over the Weber thesis still reveal critics who attribute to Weber positions from which he dissociated himself in his 'Anti-clerical last word' on the topic published in 1920. Indeed, and as MacKinnon (1994) suggests, the longevity of the debate owes much to the persistent misrepresentation of Weber's thesis. Similarly, the resurgence of Marxist scholarship in the 1960s and afterwards, and prior to its recent decline, frequently involved giving reinterpretations of Marx's theories in reaction to the 'vulgar' versions which had received wide circulation.

It is in light of this tendency to over-hasty and undiscriminating criticism that we have sought to be charitable in our account of the theorists' ideas, trying to provide reasonable, even plausible, interpretations of some of their stranger assertions and, certainly, in such a way as to evade some of the more popular caricatures and crude criticisms. We do not want to deny that Marx, Weber and Durkheim might often, and importantly, be found in error. We do want to defend them against the implication that they are makers of naïve mistakes.

The influence of these theorists has run in many directions and been incorporated into many different combinations of outlooks and frameworks. Their ideas are endlessly enmeshed in the topics contemporary sociologists address and an awareness of their ideas will help understand better what it is the contemporaries are saying. Marx, Weber and Durkheim were not the founders of sociology in any strict sense. In important respects their work was derivative from and dependent upon the work of others. They had numerous predecessors and contemporaries and there are many important innovations which fall outside the range of their considerations as well as conceptions of the sociological enterprise which are very different from theirs. These three are, we might say, the founders of dominant traditions within modern sociology with their schemes of thought exercising a decisive and marked influence on current thinking. It is for this reason that we have singled them out for it is through understanding their basic ideas that we can begin to get a genuine grasp on the underlying logic of the discourse of much of current sociology.

References

Abercrombie, Nicholas and Urry, John (1983) *Capital, Labour and the Middle Classes*, London, Allen and Unwin.

Abercrombie, N., Hill, S. and Turner, B.S. (1980) *The Dominant Ideology Thesis*, London, Allen and Unwin.

Adorno, Theodor W. and Horkheimer, M. (1979) *Dialectic of Enlightenment*, London, Allen Lane.

Althusser, Louis (1969) *For Marx*, London, Allen Lane.

Althusser, Louis (1971) 'Ideology and ideological state apparatuses', in his *Lenin and Philosophy and Other Essays*, London, New Left Books, pp. 121–73.

Baran, Paul and Sweezy, Paul (1968) *Monopoly Capital*, Harmondsworth, Penguin.

Bendix, Reinhard (1977) *Nation Building and Citizenship: Studies of our changing social order*, Berkeley, California University Press.

Berle, Adolf and Means, Gardiner C. (1991) *The Modern Corporation and Private Property*, New York, Harcourt, Brace and World.

Bottomore, Thomas and Brym, Robert J. (eds) (1989) *The Capitalist Class: An international study*, Hemel Hempstead, Harvester Wheatsheaf.

Bowles, Samuel and Gintis, Herbert (1976) *Schooling in Capitalist America: Educational reform and the contradictions of economic life*, London, Routledge.

Bradley, Dick (1992) *Understanding Rock 'n' Roll: Popular music in Britain, 1955–64*, Milton Keynes, Open University Press.

Braudel, Ferdinand (1984) *Civilization and Capitalism, 15th–18th Century* (3 Volumes), London, Collins.

Braverman, Harry (1974) *Labour and Monopoly Capitalism*, New York, Monthly Review Press.

Burnham, James (1941) *The Managerial Revolution*, New York, Doubleday.

Carver, Terrell (1982) *Marx's Social Theory*, Oxford, Oxford University Press.

Carver, Terrell (1983) *Marx and Engels: The intellectual relationship*, Brighton, Harvester Press.

Cohen, G.A. (1978) *Karl Marx's Theory of History: A defence*, Oxford, Oxford University Press.

Cohen, G.A. (1988) 'Reconsidering historical materialism: themes from Marx', in his *History, Labour and Freedom*, Oxford, Oxford University Press, pp. 132–54.

Collins, Randall (1975) *Conflict Sociology: Toward an explanatory science*, New York, Academic Press.

Collins, Randall (1985) *Three Sociological Traditions*, New York, Oxford University Press.

Collins, Randall (1986) *Weberian Social Theory*, Cambridge, Cambridge University Press.

Dahrendorf, Ralf (1959) *Class and Class Conflict in an Industrial Society*, London, Routledge.

Dallmayr, Fred R. (1993) *G.W.F. Hegel: Modernity and Politics*, London, Sage.

Dulman, Richard von (1988–9) 'Weber's thesis in the light of recent social history', *Telos*, 78: pp. 71–80.

Durkheim, Émile (1951) *Suicide: A study in sociology*, London, Routledge.

Durkheim, Émile (1976) *Elementary Forms of Religious Life*, London, Allen and Unwin.

Durkheim, Émile (1982) *The Rules of Sociological Method*, London, Macmillan.

Durkheim, Émile and Mauss, Marcel (1963) *Primitive Classification*, London, Cohen and West.

Eagleton, Terry (1991) *Ideology*, London, Verso.

Engels, Friedrich (1844) 'Outlines of a critique of political economy' reprinted in Karl Marx (1959) *Economic and Philosophical Manuscripts of 1844* ('The Paris Manuscripts'), Moscow, Progress Publishers, pp. 161–91.

Engels, Friedrich (1878) *Anti-Duhring*, Peking, Foreign Languages Press (1976).

Engels, Friedrich (1884) *The Origin of the Family, Private Property, and the State*, Peking, Foreign Languages Press (1978).

Friedman, Milton (1962) *Capitalism and Freedom*, Chicago, University of Chicago Press.

Galbraith, John K. (1967) *The New Industrial State*, London, Hamish Hamilton.

Glasgow University Media Group (1980) *More Bad News*, London, Routledge.

Godelier, Maurice (1978) 'System, structure and contradiction in *Capital*', in D. McQuarie (ed.), *Marx: Sociology, Social Change, Capitalism*, London, Quartet Books.

Hall, Stuart and Jefferson, Tony (eds) (1976) *Resistance Through Rituals: Youth subcultures in post-war Britain*, London, Hutchinson.

Hayek, Friedrich (1949) *Individualism and Economic Order*, London, Routledge.

Hegel, George Wilhelm Friedrich (1991) *Elements of the Philosophy of Right*, Cambridge, Cambridge University Press.

Hennis, Wilhelm (1988) *Max Weber: Essays in reconstruction*, London, Allen and Unwin (trans. Keith Tribe).

Hunley, J.D. (1991) *The Life and Thought of Friedrich Engels: A reinterpretation*, New Haven, Yale University Press.

Kasler, Dirk (1988) *Max Weber: An introduction to his life and work*, Cambridge, Polity Press.

Kolakowski, Leszek (1978) *Main Currents of Marxism: Vol. 1, the founders*, Oxford, Oxford University Press.

Kronman, Anthony T. (1983) *Max Weber*, London, Edward Arnold.

Langford, Paul (1989) *A Polite and Commercial People: England 1727–83*, Oxford, Oxford University Press.

Lash, Scott and Whimster, Sam (eds) (1987) *Max Weber: Rationality and modernity*, London, Allen and Unwin.

Lockwood, David (1956) 'Some remarks on "The Social System"', *British Journal of Sociology*, 7: 134–46.

Lockwood, David (1958) *The Blackcoated Worker*, London, Allen and Unwin.

Lukes, Stephen (1973) *Émile Durkheim, his Life and Work: A historical and critical study*, Harmondsworth, Penguin.

Lyotard, Jean-François (1984) *The Postmodern Condition: A report on knowledge*, Manchester, Manchester University Press.

Macfarlane, Alan (1978) *The Origins of English Individualism: The family, property and social transition*, Oxford, Blackwell.

Macfarlane, Alan (1986) *Marriage and Love in England: Modes of reproduction, 1300–1840*, Oxford, Blackwell.

MacKinnon, Malcolm H. (1994) 'The longevity of the thesis: A critique of the critics', in Hartmut Lehman and Guenther Roth (eds), *Weber's Protestant Ethic: Origins, evidence, contexts*, Cambridge, Cambridge University Press, pp. 211–43.

McLellan, David (ed.) (1976) *Karl Marx: His life and thought*, Oxford, Oxford University Press.

McLellan, David (ed.) (1977) *Karl Marx: Selected writings*, St Albans, Paladin.

McLellan, David (1980) *The Thought of Karl Marx: An introduction*, London, Macmillan.

McLemore, Lelan (1984) 'Max Weber's defense of historical inquiry', *History and Theory*, 23: 277–95.

Mandel, Ernest (1983) 'Economics', in David McLellan (ed.), *Marx: The first hundred years*, London, Fontana.

Mann, Michael (1986) *The Sources of Social Power, Vol 1*, Cambridge, Cambridge University Press.

Marshall, Gordon, Rose, David and Newby, Howard (1989) *Social Class in Modern Britain*, London, Unwin Hyman.

Marx, Karl (1843a) 'On the Jewish Question', in David McLellan (ed.), *Karl Marx: Selected writings*, Oxford, Oxford University Press (1977) pp. 39–57.

Marx, Karl (1843b) 'Critique of Hegel's Philosophy of Right', in David McLellan (ed.), *Karl Marx: Selected writings*, Oxford, Oxford University Press (1977) pp. 26–35.

Marx, Karl (1844a) 'Towards a critique of Hegel's Philosophy of Right: Introduction', in David McLellan (ed.), *Karl Marx: Selected writings*, Oxford, Oxford University Press (1977) pp. 63–74.

Marx, Karl (1844b) *Economic and Philosophical Manuscripts of 1844*, Moscow, Progress Publishers (1959).

Marx, Karl (1845) 'Theses on Feuerbach', in David McLellan (ed.), *Karl Marx: Selected writings*, Oxford, Oxford University Press (1977).

Marx, Karl, (1847) *The Poverty of Philosophy*, Moscow, Progress Publishers (1955).

Marx, Karl (1852) 'The Eighteenth Brumaire of Louis Bonaparte' in David McLellan (ed.), *Karl Marx: Selected writings*, Oxford, Oxford University Press (1977) pp. 300–25.

Marx, Karl (1859) Preface and Introduction to 'A contribution to the critique of political economy', in David McLellan (ed.), Karl Marx: Selected writings, Oxford, Oxford University Press (1977).

Marx, Karl (1909) *Capital, Vol 3: Capitalist production as a whole*, Chicago, Charles H. Kerr and Co. (first published 1984).

Marx, Karl (1954) *Capital, Vol 1: A critical analysis of capitalist production*, London, Lawrence and Wishart (first published 1867).

Marx, Karl (1973) *Grundrisse: Foundations of the critique of political economy*, Harmondsworth, Penguin (originally written 1857–8).

Marx, Karl and Engels, Friedrich (1948) *The Communist Manifesto*, in David McLellan (ed.), *Karl Marx: Selected writings*, Oxford, Oxford University Press (1977) pp. 221–47.

Marx, Karl and Engels, Friedrich (1974) *The German Ideology*, London, Lawrence and Wishart (written 1846–7).

Merquior, J.G. (1986) *Western Marxism*, London, Paladin.

Miliband, Ralph (1969) *The State and Capitalist Society*, London, Weidenfeld and Nicolson.

Mills, C. Wright (1956) *The Power Elite*, New York, Oxford University Press.

Moore, Barrington (1967) *Social Origins of Dictatorship and Democracy: Lord and peasant in the making of the modern world*, London, Allen Lane.

Nelson, Cary and Grossberg, Lawrence (eds) (1988) *Marxism and the Interpretation of Culture*, London, Macmillan.

Oakes, Guy (1988–9) 'Farewell to the Protestant Ethic?', *Telos*, 78: 81–94.

Parkin, Frank (1979) *Marxism and Class Theory*, London, Tavistock Publications.

Parkin, Frank (1992) *Durkheim*, Oxford, Oxford University Press.

Parsons, Talcott (1937) *The Structure of Social Action*, New York, McGraw-Hill.

Pellicani, Luciano (1988) 'Weber and the myth of Calvinism', *Telos*, 75: 57–85.

Poggi, Giafranco (1972) *Images of Society*, Stanford, Stanford University Press.

Poulantzas, Nicos (1973) *Political Power and Social Classes*, London, New Left Books.

Rattansi, Ali (1982) *Marx and the Division of Labour*, London, Macmillan.

Rex, John (1961) *Key Problems of Sociological Theory*, London, Routledge.

Rigby, S.H. (1992) *Engels and the Formation of Marxism*, Manchester, Manchester University Press.

Sayer, Derek (1991) *Capitalism and Modernity: An excursus on Marx and Weber*, London, Routledge.

Schroeder, Ralph (1992) *Max Weber and the Sociology of Culture*, London, Sage.

Scott, John (1991) *Who Rules Britain?*, London, Polity Press.

Tenbruck, Friedrich H. (1980) 'Problems of thematic unity in the work of Max Weber', *British Journal of Sociology*, 31: 313–51.

Thomas, P. (1991) 'Critical reception: Marx then and now', in Terrell Carver (ed.), *The Cambridge Companion to Marx*, Cambridge, Cambridge University Press, pp. 23–54.

Thompson, E.P. (1978) *The Poverty of Theory*, London, Merlin Press.

Turner, Stephan P. and Factor, Regis A. (forthcoming) *Max Weber as Legal Scholar*, London, Routledge.

Weber, Max (1930) *The Protestant Ethic and the Spirit of Capitalism*, London, Allen and Unwin (trans. Talcott Parsons).

Wright, Olin (1985) *Classes*, London, Verso Books.

Zaret, David (1994) 'The use and abuse of textual data', in Hartmut Lehman and Guenther Roth (eds), *Weber's Protestant Ethic: Origins, evidence, contexts*, Cambridge, Cambridge University Press, pp. 245–72.

Index